Always at Sea

Always at Sea

Mary Wardle

Whittles Publishing

Typeset by
Whittles Publishing Services

Published by
Whittles Publishing,
Roseleigh House,
Latheronwheel,
Caithness, KW5 6DW,
Scotland, UK

ISBN 1-870325-74-5

Printed by J.W.Arrowsmith Ltd., Bristol

Contents

To Fiona, Dave, Matthew and Robert
and all Merchant Mariners, past and present

Preface

When my father died a manuscript six inches thick, 1521 pages, became mine. It was consigned to the back of a cupboard and almost forgotten, but not quite. I read it once, enjoyed it then returned it to its resting place. When we moved it moved with us, six times in all.

Through the years my husband tried to persuade me to 'do something about it' but I always found some excuse. In the end I could find no valid reason why I should not attempt to turn it into a book; perhaps the grandsons would like to know about their great-grandfather.

I discovered that I had taken on a monumental task. I read and reread the manuscript and each time found it more fascinating. From the time he became an officer my father wrote very detailed accounts of every ship in which he sailed; he personally inspected every inch of them, almost down to the last rivet. The only exception was the engine-room which was strictly the province of the chief engineer. A meticulous man he left nothing to chance, as something overlooked could cost a life.

In writing this book I found a father I had never known. He was, I thought, a quiet man, with the occasional flash of temper, who listened more than he spoke. He claimed to be tone deaf, but I found he had a love of opera and visited various opera houses around the world. He had an impish sense of humour and found great delight in the characters he met. A born sailor, he never wanted to be anything else from his earliest childhood. He knew what he wanted to achieve and nothing would stop him.

He was also something of an artist, mostly with pen, ink and crayons and the sketches in this book are all his work. He also took up photography, but as his workload increased he found little time to indulge, and his camera and photographic equipment were unceremoniously dumped overboard.

The very first page of his manuscript starts, 'I have read somewhere that if one could write down an account of actual day to day happenings, just as they occur, it would turn out to be a story of absorbing interest. I will endeavour to do just that, not day-to-day, but as memory can recall. It will be something to pass the time; remembering people, places, ships and incidents which have faded into the mists of time.' You are about to find out if this is true.

With such a wealth of material it was obvious a great deal would have to be left out. This was the most difficult part and I hope I have been successful. If any mistakes have been made in the interpretation of nautical matters they will be my errors. I had hoped to include maps but over the years these change, as do place names, Some locations could no longer be found so the idea was discarded. What were then small ports became large ones or disappeared altogether, but it would still be possible for the interested reader to search out maps and plot the various voyages.

It may occur to you to wonder why, when drunkenness was commonplace, my father never succumbed to it himself He enjoyed his beer but rarely drank spirits, the more he drank the more sober he became, and he considered it a waste of money if it had no effect. He did, however, indulge in a pipe and was a heavy cigarette smoker.

The times that have been written about in this book are long past and the world has moved on. At the beginning of the last century sailing ships had almost died out, by the end of the century we had container ships and enormous tankers. I wonder what he would have thought of it all?

Mary Wardle

The currency mentioned in the book is pounds, shillings and pence (£ s d). It may be of interest to readers to know the rough equivalent values today. For example, £1 in 1912 would now be approximately £61.50p, and £1 in 1940 would now be £39!

Acknowledgements

I would like to thank Gordon Ponting for teaching me how to use a computer, Elizabeth Cuthill for suggesting a Scottish publisher and Bob Maslen-Jones for invaluable support. To my husband I owe everything; without him this would never have been written.

Chapter 1

The model maker

*W*hen I was born, my father held me in the palm of his hand and asked 'What's this?' I was very small with brown eyes and reddish brown hair, and I gave trouble from the start. My sister Jenny was father's favourite but I was the favourite of no one.

I have no memories of the place where I was born, Colombo, Ceylon. Father had arrived there with the Argyll and Sutherland Highlanders with the rank of quartermaster sergeant, and was the obvious choice to be seconded to form the Ceylon Volunteers; he was good at everything and a born soldier. It was here he met and married in 1895, Jane Bain, from Clynelish in Sutherland, who was then working as a lady's maid. My sister Jane (Jenny) was born in November 1895 in Kandy, and I, William, on the 4th July 1897.

My father's 21 years' service terminated in 1900. The Volunteers wanted him to stay but my mother insisted on going home to Scotland, so we arrived back in the middle of 1899 when I was two years old. He took his discharge late in 1900 but it was some time in 1901 before he arrived back home in Aberdeen.

It had been arranged that we would stay with my grandparents at Den Farm, Kildrummy, in Aberdeenshire until my father came home. It was unfortunate that my mother and her mother-in-law didn't get along together, I suppose that is traditional. Whether Granny Donald was fond of my sister Jenny I couldn't say, but she didn't like me at all. I was an impertinent little brat and she was forever telling my mother that she was unable to control me.

My first memories of playing with things that float were of pieces of wood in rainwater puddles in the farmyard. My mother and grandparents thought this to be a very odd way of amusing myself. Later mother found that by putting an inch of water in a baking tin with some used matchsticks I could be kept quiet for hours. Thus was born my desire to have a piece of wood that could move itself or, in other words, sail. Who it was that first stuck a matchstick through a piece of paper and

1

then into a small piece of wood, I don't know, but it was most probably my mother. Perhaps being the granddaughter of a sailor she had inherited an instinct for boats. Maybe I too had inherited something.

The final break between my mother and grandmother came one evening brought about, of course, by me. I have always been very fond of cheese and this was the cause. I knew where the cheese was kept, in a large cupboard in the downstairs bedroom. I got in there one evening without being noticed, dragged a chair over to the cupboard, climbed up and opened the door. I don't know how I managed but I got the heavy dish down on to the floor and was happily eating when in came Granny.

'You little rascal,' she screamed. She flew at me, got me across her knees and began administering a beating with her slipper. I howled, which brought my mother rushing in. She snatched me away, and one thing led to another, with the result that we left the farm the next day and went to Aberdeen.

My mother took a flat in Williamson Street in the district of Rosemount. Living opposite were a Mr and Mrs Morgan who, I think, were some kind of relations as we were told to call them Auntie Nellie and Uncle Jonathan.

The short, steep street where we lived led down to a park with a small circular pond about a foot deep. I now possessed a small sailing boat, a gift from Uncle Jonathan. Seeing how I could be kept quiet he had made me a boat about six inches long and being a joiner by trade he made a real job of it, but instead of keeping me quiet this caused more trouble. Now I wanted plenty of water in which to sail my boat. The bath didn't satisfy me for long, so the upshot was I had to be taken down the park every day, where I could walk round the edge of the pond pulling the boat along by a length of string.

Always being one who preferred to do things for myself it was natural for me to want to make my own boats. From Uncle Jonathan's boat I got the hull design, sharp one end blunt the other. (All this at four years old!) The next thing, after finding a piece of wood, was to obtain a tool to work with, and the time my mother found me at work with a table knife I well remember. The cutlery was kept locked up after that episode. I was concerned that when the wind caught the sails (pieces of paper) of my home-made boats they immediately turned upside down, but Uncle Jonathan's boat did not. I was puzzled. My tiny boats were very roughly the same shape, and the sails not large for the size, but they would not remain upright once they began to move. I asked Uncle Jonathan about this and he explained that the boat he made had a keel, mine had not; the keel made the bottom of the boat heavier than the top which had the weight and pressure of the sail. He demonstrated this by inserting a nail in the bottom of the boat I had made, then the boat sailed upright. I had been given my first lesson in ships' stability. Looking back I find it strange that a child of only four years old could grasp the reason governing this, but I did. It must have been inherited knowledge or, as the saying is *born with it*, I just seemed to know.

Time passed, and my interest in boats grew. The day I won the battle to possess a pocketknife marked a considerable advance in my shipbuilding activities. I would be, I suppose, about seven years old by then. I should not by rights have been allowed to have one at that age, but I had developed the technique of wearing down my parents to the point where they would say, 'let him have it for God's sake, if he cuts himself it will teach him a lesson.'

The boats I carved out with my pocketknife were usually small and shallow; they had to be, as they were usually sailed in rainwater puddles. They were from an inch to two inches in length and a quarter inch in depth. This required a fine adjustment in weight of keel otherwise the deck would be under water, or the boat would capsize when the wind caught the sail. A larger size could be used in the bath but, as the bathroom also contained the lavatory, sailing was continually interrupted. Another problem, when using the bath, was the lack of wind. To overcome this the fire bellows could be used but mother couldn't be convinced of the necessity for this, so it had to be done when she was out of the house. Life seemed to be beset with problems.

When father arrived back home we didn't stay long in Aberdeen but travelled around visiting his friends. I asked my mother why we were moving around so much; she said father was looking for somewhere to settle down and had not yet found anywhere suitable.

Father had an uncle, John Copland, a builder and joiner by trade, who had been urging him to settle in Uddingston. The Coplands lived in Dunnolly Cottage and we went to stay with them for a while, then moved to a house of our own in Garvald Place. Father had decided to invest his money in the business. John Copland then put him in charge of all his buildings as a House Factor, and in time he became known and obtained other properties to manage. In the spring of 1906 John Copland died and after the funeral the storm broke – John Copland hadn't a penny. He had been on the verge of bankruptcy when father came to Uddingston and it was only his money that had staved off the creditors, until now. My father, not being a partner and his money only on loan, was one of the creditors, but that meant nothing – all our money had gone. The effect on us was immediate, food was cut down and there was no money to spend on unnecessary things. Of course father had his pension and, with care, it was sufficient. By selling his shares in the Eastern Telegraph Company he had enough money to buy an insurance book which happened to be for sale, and with this, his house factorage and pension we managed well enough.

As father now had to depend on his insurance agency and house factoring business it was necessary to move into the main street where people could easily reach him. So we left Garvald Place late in 1906, after the birth of my youngest brother James (Alexander having been born in 1904) and took up residence at 143 Woodview Terrace. At street level were shops and the two storey dwelling above was approached through a close at the back. We lived in this house until 1925 when the Co-op bought the whole building.

The shop below our house was that of the Neil Brothers whose business was cabinet making and upholstery. The store and workshop were in the basement and opened into the back yard. I had the free run of the place and was taught by them to use the tools of their trade. Next door was a painter's shop and they taught me to use paintbrushes properly and mix paint – before the days of ready mixed paint. I was also allowed to go with them on jobs during the school holidays and was a competent painter long before I went to sea. On the corner of the next block was a grocer's shop owned by a Mr Latta. They had two sons, the youngest Matt and I became close friends and remained so all our lives.

In the road opposite our back yard there was a depression between two trees. Whenever it had been raining this filled up and the water took a long time to drain away. I suppose I must have started the idea of racing tiny boats and, in suitable weather, it attracted boys and girls from all around. The number of designs made and discarded were legion and a good racing design was as carefully guarded as a present day racehorse.

As I grew older I came up against another problem. All my boats were solid with their decks level with the water and any ripple washed over them. I knew the deck had to be some distance above the water; the boats had to have buoyancy, a word I had not yet heard. This could only be obtained by hollowing out the hull and my attempts to do this usually met with failure. Mother found me one day trying to hollow out a piece of wood with the kitchen poker, heated red hot in the fire, and accused me of trying to set fire to the house. If I heated the poker again I would be handed over to father to be dealt with.

For my birthday I now demanded a carpenter's tool set for my present. Giving me this was considered by my parents to be very dangerous indeed. After anxious consultation it was agreed I could have one but, at the slightest sign of any damage to the furniture, the tools would be taken away.

Now I could make progress. Shaping the hulls was easy enough although I never got both sides exactly the same. The hollowing out was the trouble. If both sides were not the same thickness the boat leaned over. The difficulty in hollowing out resulted in my vessels being flat bottomed with only a turn of the bilge like a modern vessel, although I had never seen any modern vessel; at that age I had seen only pictures of ships. In the end the bow and stern were left solid and the sides cut down square with the bottom. In this way there were no curves to worry about. Of course the boat did not float as high as she would if fully hollowed out, but that did not worry me, all I wanted was to make my boats sail. This detailed process is recounted to show how a young but determined boy, with no one to give him any advice, gradually worked out by trial and error the principles of ship design, including trim and stability. These thing became permanently fixed in my mind and, when studying for examinations, remembering the boats I tried to construct gave me a clear picture of all the problems involved, and made it easy for me to learn the solutions.

When I obtained my set of carpenter's tools I turned part of the coal cellar into a workshop by shovelling all the coal to one side and fitting up a rough shelf and bench. Pottering about in the carpenter's workshop I found a length of wood and I asked Peter Neil if I could have it. He said I could, but wanted to know what I proposed to make. I told him a sailing ship.

He laughed. 'That wood won't float.' I didn't believe him but tried it in the bath and he was right. I had undertaken quite a job. My own tools were not much use for that kind of work but I was allowed to borrow the chisels used in cabinet making as long as I didn't damage them. Eventually, after a lot a hard work, the hull was completed, hollowed out, decked over and sandpapered smooth. I had by then quite a collection of sailing ship pictures and, poring over these, eventually worked out a rigging and sail plan using different lengths and thickness of string tied on to nails and tacks. I didn't know the name of a single sail or rope, but copied what I saw in the pictures. Having no money, and only the materials I could lay my hands on, that model was a weird sight. I raided my mother's workbox for beads to make blocks. When she saw the model and recognised her beads the fat was in the fire, but I eventually got away with it. The sails were the trouble. I asked Jenny to make them out of my handkerchiefs, but she refused, and asking mother was out of the question. The less said about the fit of those sails the better.

Finding a stretch of water to put the vessel through her trials was another problem. I dared not ask to be taken to one of the Glasgow ponds, and the pit ponds were covered with scum which effectively prevented any sailing, except in very strong winds. That left the Clyde but that was forbidden territory. I had just got over an illness caused by falling into that river, so I had to be careful. The stretch between the railway bridge and the Red Bridge was deep, quiet and fairly straight. On the near bank was Kyle Park with gardens down to the edge of the river, but on the other side were open fields where contact could be kept, with a long string, while walking close to the water. The danger was the swift current which, on that stretch, was not apparent owing to deep water. The first three attempts to sail were successful; for all its weird appearance that craft could sail and fast too, once the ballast was properly placed. My friend Court Robertson was with me one cold afternoon and the vessel, pulling hard on the string, took some holding. How it happened I do not recall but the string went sliding away along the ground towards the edge of the bank. I tried to get my foot on it but was not quick enough. Released, and with all sails set, away she went with a strong wind and the current behind her. We ran down to the Red Bridge and then to the sandy turn where the East Calder came in from the opposite bank and the river took a big sweep round to the left. There was a small sandy beach on the bend, and we hoped she would come in to this beach, but the trailing string acted as a drag and prevented her making leeway. When abreast of the Calder the inflow of that stream pushed her round. Now she had the wind on the other side and went round the bend as if steered by hand. We could go no further, as the land beyond was enclosed, so we had to give up and face the long walk home. All I got out of the episode was experience.

When the unemployment insurance commenced father obtained the position of local agent for Uddingston. The downstairs bedroom, which he now used as an office, became the local Labour Exchange, but soon grew to such an extent that he had to find another office and an assistant became necessary. He rented shop premises at the Cross, just inside the Bellshill Road, and that was the Uddingston Labour Exchange.

I was now approaching my 14th birthday and my future had to be considered. I was adamant that I was going to sea, if not as an apprentice, then as an ordinary sailor. Father's business had expanded considerably and he wanted me in his office. But, as he always said, he would not stand in anyone's way, everyone was entitled to their chance. He started making enquiries with shipping firms and found out that no boy under 15 was acceptable as an indentured apprentice. I wanted to go to sea in a sailing ship, so he somehow got in touch with a firm called the Inver Line, of Aberdeen, who ran a fleet of barque rigged vessels, but they required a £100 premium. Father didn't like that arrangement at all. As he said to mother 'I am not going to spend £100, plus fitting him out, to find he can't stand life in a sailing ship.' So that, thought father, was that and he arranged a course of shorthand and bookkeeping to prepare me for his business. *But to sea I was going*, and as father made no further effort I had to go to work on my own behalf.

My mother was very friendly with an old lady, a Mrs Cluny, who lived in Kyle Park. Near them lived the commodore master of the Anchor Line, a Captain John Black. I prevailed on my mother to talk with Captain Black, through Mrs Cluny, which she eventually managed. Captain Black had said that, in his opinion, sailing ships were dying out, and there was no sense in being trained to drive a horse and cab when your life would be spent running a taxi. He would see what he could do but I would have to be at least 15 years old. So there the matter rested. Neither my mother nor I told father what we had been doing as nothing definite had come up as yet.

One morning at the beginning of March 1912, Father received a letter from the Anchor Line offices in Glasgow asking him to bring his son for an interview, with a view to his being taken on as an apprentice, if found suitable. He was considerably taken aback, he thought this *going to sea* business had died a natural death. He said nothing except that he would take me in to the Anchor Line on the appointed day and that was the start of my seafaring career.

We were shown into a room and introduced to Mr Hendry, who dealt with apprentice affairs. He told my father the firm did not, as a rule, carry apprentices, except the sons of people connected with the company. However, as Captain Black had recommended me, they were prepared to take me provided I passed a medical and produced a good school report.

'Well,' he said 'we have two vacancies around the end of the month and, as he will only be three months short of 15, we will let it go at that. He is small but will grow soon enough.' He went on to explain details of the premium, wages, uniform allowance and we were given a list of clothing requirements. I would receive 10*s* per month for the first year, rising to £2 per month in the fourth year. The Anchor Line would provide a new uniform each year or £2 10*s* in lieu.

The Anchor Line carried native crews on their Eastern trade route, and apprentices joined on an officer basis from the start, so the list of requirements was considerable, amounting to around £100. Father had been in Ceylon and knew all about the cost of white suits and light underwear out there. He said he would give me money to buy them in Calcutta, the trade route I would be on. Mother then took me to Paisleys, the Naval and Merchant Service outfitters in Jamaica Street, to be fitted for a uniform and other necessary clothing. I was to join the *Algeria* when she arrived in Glasgow in about a week's time.

I passed the medical examination, and the school report was favourable, so we were asked to call again to sign indentures.

When I handed in my books at school everyone in Uddingston seemed to know I was going to sea, and I was amazed at the presents I received. These included a Bible which, although I never opened it, became a sort of talisman. I had the conviction that, as long as I had it, everything would come out right.

INDENTURE 4 YEARS' SERVICE.

THIS Indenture made this *27th* day of *March*
19 1 2 between ANCHOR LINE (Henderson Brothers) LTD.,
Glasgow, hereinafter called the First Parties, and

NAME OF MIDSHIPMAN APPRENTICE, *William Donald Junr*
Age *14 9/12* Place of birth *Colombo Ceylon*
(hereinafter referred to as the Midshipman Apprentice), with
the consent and special advice of his * *father*

* Parent or Guardian.

NAME, *William Donald Sen.*

ADDRESS, *143 Main Street, Uddingston, Lanarkshire*

OCCUPATION, *House Factor*

hereinafter called the Second Parties, WITNESSETH that the
First Parties have agreed, at the request of the Second
Parties, to take the said *William Donald*
into their service as a Midshipman Apprentice upon the following terms and conditions :—

First.—The said *William Donald* with the advice and
consent aforesaid, hereby binds himself to sail in the Steamers of THE ANCHOR
LINE (HENDERSON BROTHERS) LIMITED, when and where as required by the
Managers of the Company, remaining continuously by the Ships as may be
required, except when granted leave of absence, for the term of FOUR years
from the date of this Indenture.

Second.—The said *William Donald.* with the advice and
consent aforesaid, hereby binds and obliges himself that during such term he will
faithfully serve the Party of the First Part, and any shipmaster with whom they
may appoint him to sail from time to time, and obey their and his lawful commands,
and keep their and his secrets, and will, when required, give to them and him true
accounts of their and his goods and money which may be committed to the charge
of, or come into the hands of, the said Midshipman Apprentice, and that the said
Midshipman Apprentice will not during the said term do any damage to the First
Parties or their property, nor will he consent to any such damage being done by
others, but will, if possible, prevent the same and give warning thereof; and will
not embezzle or waste the goods of the First Parties, nor give nor lend the same
to others without their license; nor absent himself from their service without
leave; nor frequent taverns or alehouses, nor play at unlawful games.

Third.—In consideration of the premises, the First Parties hereby bind and
oblige themselves to use all proper means to cause the said Midshipman Apprentice
to be taught the business of a Seaman, and the duties of a Navigating Officer, and
to provide him with sufficient meat, lodging, medicine, and medical and surgical
assistance, and pay him salaries at the rates following, viz.: For and during the
first year of service at the rate of 10s. per month; for and during the second year
of service, £1 per month; for and during the third year of service, £1 10s. per
month; and for and during the fourth year of service, £2 per month. Also, the
said Midshipman Apprentice shall be provided by the First Parties with bedding,
and £10 towards cost of uniform, distributed over the period of agreement. The
said Midshipman Apprentice shall provide for himself all wearing apparel and
necessaries (except as hereinbefore agreed to be provided by the First Parties).

Fourth.—In the event of the said Midshipman Apprentice being unable to
fulfil the conditions of this Indenture through ill health, it will be at the option
of the First Parties to cancel this Indenture, and should such illness necessitate
the said Midshipman Apprentice being discharged at any Port outside the United

Chapter 2

Learning the ropes

*F*ather had been told to take me on board when the ship berthed at Stobcross Quay, and ask for Mr Fraser, the chief officer. This would give me time to get familiar with the ship before we sailed. We eventually found him and father introduced himself. Mr Fraser stared and me, and I stared at him; it was instant dislike on both sides.

'So you are one of the new apprentices,' he said, in a tone which suggested I was just another nuisance. 'Go and find your berth, you will have to learn your own way round.' I found it in the port alleyway on the deck below. Two young men in shore-going suits were packing up, and a boy of my own age was sitting on the settee. We introduced ourselves. Robert MacPherson was the son of the shore steward and didn't want to go to sea.

As Mr Fraser did not require me around – did not require me period – father and I left soon afterwards and went home. All he said to me was 'you are now embarked on what you have always wanted to do, so it's entirely up to you whether you sink or swim.'

Next morning I took the 8.10 a.m. train with my trunk and sea bag, then a cab (horse drawn in those days) at the Central Station to Stobcross Quay and reported aboard.

When an Anchor Line ship was in Glasgow no food was served on board for officers or engineers, neither were they allowed to sleep on board as all bed linen, crockery, silver, in fact everything, was put ashore on arrival and only returned when the vessel was ready to leave. An allowance was made for victualling and I received 1*s* 6*d* per day, as things were then it went a long way. I found a restaurant which gave a three course dinner for ·1*s*, and 3*d* on the tram took me home in the evening. I had tea and breakfast at home.

As everyone, with the exception of the native crew, lived in or near Glasgow the sea going complement did not take any interest in anything except getting home,

S.S.Algeria. Anchor Line of Glasgow.

when they thought the superintendents were out of the way, so we were totally ignored.

I had been onboard for several days when we left for Liverpool. On leaving the berth we were put on watch, four hours on and four hours off. I found myself that first night on the middle watch, midnight to 4 a.m, with the second mate, Mr Booth, whose family had been acquainted with father in Ceylon. I had to walk up and down on one side of the bridge, while he did the same on the other, and report any lights I saw on ships or shore. I was so small, only five feet and a half-inch, that I couldn't see over the weather cloth, and it had to be lowered on my side. It was a cold, clear night and, being the first time I had to stay awake during the night, I could hardly keep my eyes open. I spent most of the time watching the wheel house clock certain it had stopped.

The first thing I learned was the apprentice on watch had to keep the scrap log which was entered every two hours. In a notebook I wrote down what the watch officer told me, times of passing lights, lighthouses, log, barometer and thermometer readings, weather and so on. After this had been looked over and passed it was entered up in the scrap log. I was so tired at the end of my four hours I was glad to go below. When I came on watch again we were passing the Isle of Man and by noon had the pilot on board for Liverpool. In the late afternoon we berthed at Vittoria Wharf, East Float Dock, Birkenhead, across the river from Liverpool, to load general cargo.

By the time we left there I was beginning to know who was who and what the various duties were. Apart from the British section, captain, first (chief officer), second and third mates, carpenter, two apprentices, five engineers and the chief steward/purser, there was a large Lascar crew. The quartermasters, deckhands, greasers and firemen were Lascars, a term applied to all the seafaring people of India. The deckhands, *kalassies*, and ordinary seamen and boys, *chocras*, were run by the bosun, *serang*, assisted by the first bosun's mate, *burra tindal*, and the second bosun's mate, *chota tindal*. The storekeeper/lamptrimmer, *cassub*, came under the control of the chief officer, and he was responsible for all deck stores and did the paint mixing. Then came the *topaz*, man of no caste, whose job it was to sweep the decks and do all the dirty work. The four quartermasters, *secunnies*, were under the direct control of the officers. The engine-room department were under the same arrangement. In the galley there were three cooks and a butcher, pantrymen and stewards and they answered to the chief steward. There were also the boys who looked after the captain, officers and engineers.

As we passed Cape Finisterre and headed towards Gibraltar the weather gradually got warmer and the sea quieter. It began to appear that we apprentices were to be bridge trained as it was called, never out of uniform, and four on and four off watches at sea. When on watch I was given two cards, one with the points and quarter points of the compass and the other with the Morse code signs on one side and semaphore on the other. These had to be learnt by heart and repeated to the officer of the watch until they became permanently fixed in my mind. Then we were occasionally allowed to take turns at steering. In the evening, if there was no traffic about, I was given practice in reading and sending Morse, and by the time we got into the Mediterranean I was signalling passing ships during Mr Fraser's watch. He also made a practice of pointing out and naming the various headlands and lighthouses and, if I could not repeat them afterwards, I got told off. It seemed to please him no end to catch me out.

One evening, a couple of days before we reached Port Said, a ship bound west called us up and, after the usual exchanges of names and destinations, went on to give us a long signal. I was reading out the letters and Mr Fraser was writing them down. When the message was completed he got very excited and said to the third mate, Mr Laurie, 'the boy must have got this wrong, call them up and ask for a repeat.'

He did but the message was the same. '*Titanic* collided with iceberg and sank with heavy loss of life'. The name meant nothing to me at the time but caused a sensation on board.

We bunkered at Port Said, then came the long tedious business of getting through the canal. It was completely different to what I had imagined, just a long ditch. Tying up, as it was called, hauling in to the bank to let pass ships bound the other way, made it a lengthy business and everyone was pleased when we were through. A searchlight was taken on board, with two attendants, to light up the buoys and banks at night and was landed when we reached Suez Bay.

11

The Red Sea was like an oven and this brought out all the insect life. Being an old ship, and fumigation still unknown, she was alive everywhere. The cockroaches were all sizes, the largest as much as two and a half inches in length – I measured one! All we could do was seal everything edible that happened to be in the room. Then the rats emerged but, for some reason, they were ignored by the ship's cats.

Now we began to have more time steering in open sea and I was taken in hand to be taught navigation. Mr Booth put me in the chartroom to study when I was on watch with him. I had to use a large tome, about four inches thick, called Nories Epitome. The first half was the textbook and the other half comprised tables. I began with logarithms then went on to meridian altitudes (latitude), chronometer and azimuth (longitude). I was taught how to take the altitude with a sextant, take bearings of the sun and work out compass errors. On a coast there was no studying but I was shown how to take bearings of lights and landmarks and lay them off on the chart. By the time we arrived in Calcutta I could take the sun, work out latitude and longitude, and found myself working out Mr Fraser's sight on morning watch. I was certainly getting a good grounding as a navigator.

On this ship there lived an old cannon, and when in port I had to drag it to the head of the gangway and set it up facing outboard. I asked what it was for and was told it was an old minute gun, fired as a distress signal before rockets came into use, and also to announce a ship's arrival into port.

We had passengers aboard amongst whom were an elderly couple and a young man in his early twenties. The young man, unused to sleeping in the afternoons spent them racing round the decks on roller skates, and talking to anyone who would listen. One afternoon, while crossing the Arabian Sea, I asked the Mr Booth for something to do.

'Alright,' he said, 'go to the cassub and get some Brunswick black, Venetian red and varnish, and paint your cannon.' This seemed an easy job so I got the paint and brushes, took the canvas cover off the cannon, hauled it out near the rail and set to work. It was very quiet. The elderly couple were dozing in deck chairs, the rest of the passengers were round the other side or below, with the exception of the roller skater. He came over and asked if he could help. I had taken the plug out of the muzzle and shoved my arm down to feel if I could reach the end with the paintbrush. There was a plug at the back, which felt like paper rammed in tight, so I left it. The young man started painting the after end of the cannon but then began fiddling with the plug rammed in the touchhole. I asked him to leave it alone. I continued painting and didn't see him get out the box of matches, but he must have lit one and dropped it down the hole. Flames shot out from the muzzle followed by blast, a deafening boom and a cloud of dense black smoke. The cannon leapt backward narrowly missing the elderly lady in her deck chair. She gave a start and her deck chair collapsed, as did that of the old gentleman. Fortunately we were both at the side of the cannon but the shock sat me down hard on the deck, the paintbrush falling out of my hand. That shattered the afternoon quiet and people poured out from everywhere aroused by the noise.

'What the hell has happened,' roared Mr Booth as he raced off the bridge. By that time the captain, Mr Fraser, the third mate and the engineers were there as well. The passengers, the Lascars from the fore end, in fact everybody. The elderly gentleman had a dazed look on his face and was holding up his wife, who had fainted from shock. Before I could say anything the young man spoke up.

'It was my fault, I dropped a match down the touchhole and the cannon went off.'

'Who loaded the thing?' demanded Captain McLean.

'Nobody sir,' I said. 'I was going to paint it and he wanted to help, and was just fooling around.'

'Sir,' chimed in Mr Booth, 'I gave young Donald a job to paint the cannon. He couldn't have loaded it as there is no gunpowder in the ship, except in the distress rockets.' That seemed to be the end of it and everyone dispersed. Then Mr Fraser saw the paint marks on the deck.

'God,' he said and turned white. 'Paint on the deck of an Anchor Liner, get holystones and scrub it off at once,' he screamed.

The old gentleman, I heard later, had an interview with the captain and claimed his hearing had been permanently affected, and he was debating whether or not to sue the company for damages.

Off the entrance to the Hoogly River, we boarded the river pilot. It was usual to anchor off Sagar Island Bar till the flood started to make and go up with it. The tide reached as far as Calcutta 80 miles up river. There we were moored to buoys in the river to await a berth at the wooden wharves, which lined the banks along the front of the city. Then we went alongside and discharged our cargo working night and day.

The purser advanced me some money, which my father had given him, to fit myself out with white suits (measured and made by a tailor established on the deck), shoes and a tropical hat, all at unbelievably cheap prices. The only trouble was that in a few months I had broadened out and the suits did not fit so well.

On this ship a number of people seemed to consider it their duty to look after me. Captain Black had mentioned to Captain McLean that he had got me into the firm and was to keep an eye on me. The second mate felt obliged because my father had known his father in Ceylon, and the third mate, Mr Jarvie,

A brand new apprentice.

13

had been warned by his aunt who lived across the road from us in Uddingston, to keep me out of mischief. He was the only one I was really friendly with. The person who actually did the looking after was Mr Fraser. He did so in order to make my life a misery, but because I was not of a nature to worry he did not succeed, which annoyed him considerably.

We two boys wandered around ashore of an evening and weekends but couldn't find much to interest us. Cinemas had not yet appeared and having almost no money we couldn't buy anything. Sometimes we met apprentices from other ships but they were in the same situation. It was through them I made my first acquaintance with the Seaman's Mission, the Flying Angel, which was situated not far from the dock in a suburb called Hastings. It was a very nice place, about the best I have known, and well run. In addition to the usual stage and billiard tables there was a boxing ring, and tea and sandwiches were available each night before leaving time.

Loading took a long time as there seemed to be some difficulty in obtaining homeward cargo but we loaded scrap iron for Genoa and also jute, hemp, tobacco and other items, including tea.

We left Calcutta around the second week in June and a week later we went into Colombo to complete loading and for coaling. I was allowed ashore to visit Bessie Morton, the daughter of one of my father's old friends. I knew her when she was at home in Glasgow, now she was married and living in a part of the city called Slave Island. Several people there remembered my father and I had a very pleasant evening during which I was taken round and shown "Hopewell", the house where I had been born. As there was a large photograph of the house at home I could recognise it, but found it much smaller than I had thought.

When we left Colombo the south-west monsoon was blowing and we had a rough passage across to the Gulf of Aden, and this meant no ports under deck level could be left open. I did leave the port open once and the sea got in flooding the room and soaking everything. The rolling made it unsafe to sleep on deck until the ship was in the Gulf of Aden, so we had to sweat it out below. We arrived in Suez on my 15th birthday, but I didn't remember it till sometime later.

We called at Genoa, Spezzia then the last Italian port, Leghorn, where I learned to swim properly, first with a lifebuoy and line attached to the foot of the accommodation ladder, then without their aid. We put down our own small boat and we two boys, and some of the male passengers, were taught to row by the second mate, my first introduction to an eighteen foot oar! Being very small at that time I was put in the bow with a short oar.

We left for London coaling at Gibraltar and, being July, we had fine weather all the way and berthed in the Victoria and Albert Dock, in a section called Custom House. I was not there long before instructions came from the office – I was to join the *Media*.

Chapter 3

Not wanted on voyage

I arrived in the early hours of the morning and had to wait until the office opened. I was told to go home for a few days. A week later I was ordered to report on board the *Media* berthed at Stobcross Quay, the same berth where I had boarded the *Algeria*. This ship was going to be something quite different.

When I reported to the chief officer, a Mr Guy Hamilton, he said, 'For Christ's sake not another one. What the hell am I supposed to do with you people in this kind of ship, you are a bloody nuisance, I'm not paid to be a teacher to apprentices.' I asked what I was to do and was told 'keep out of my sight.' This, I thought, is going to be an unpleasant ship and how right I was.

I found the apprentice berth and also met Alexander Cameron, senior apprentice. He informed me the *Media* was practically a new ship having come into service in 1911, about a year previously. Alexander had joined then, on her first voyage, so he had been a year at sea to my four and a half months. He considered I should do what he told me and fetch and carry for him, but I couldn't agree to that. He came from Dalmuir, down river from Glasgow, which further strained matters.

As usual there was no sleeping or victualling onboard. I was given 1*s* 6*d* per day as before, and went home at night. Arriving one morning I saw two bands being painted round the funnel, the lower one white and the upper one bright blue. On enquiring why, I was informed the Calcutta ships had been taken over by a Liverpool firm Messrs. T. & J. Brocklebank, and the two firms were now the Anchor-Brocklebank Line.

This was, undoubtedly, the most unhappy ship I ever sailed in. The old saying 'a ship takes its tone from the master' is true, but a more incompatible collection of men I have never seen gathered together in one ship.

Captain Roberts never to spoke to any of his ship's company except to give an order. The four deck officers detested each other and collectively had no use for the engineers and never, unless compelled, spoke to them. The engineers did not get on

S.S.Media of the Anchor-Brocklebank Line of Liverpool, on the River Hugli.

among themselves, and the chief steward was the enemy of all. The apprentices were totally ignored, except by the carpenter who lived next door, and he himself was ignored except for his duties. Cameron and I disliked each other and Captain Roberts loathed everybody.

We always had to be in full uniform when outside our berth and I got the impression, as time went by, that apprentices on this ship were regarded as an imposition and no one, from the captain down, had any interest in them whatsoever. If it was necessary to speak or make a report to an officer, one would approach, come to attention and wait until given permission.

Master's inspection, on a Sunday morning, was an impressive affair with the captain, chief engineer, chief officer, and chief steward, in that order. All catering staff had to be at their posts and the apprentice, not on watch, standing at attention outside the cabin. Similar inspections were carried out on *Algeria* without all this ceremony. I don't know if all this was routine in other Anchor Line ships, or whether Captain Roberts had thought it up himself but to me, blessed or cursed with a sense of humour, it was very, very funny indeed.

As expected there was no studying at all done and no signalling practice either. I once asked the second mate if I could take bearings and lay them off. He stared at me then said, 'Were you allowed to do that in your last ship?'

'Of course,' I said. 'I had to.'

'Peculiar state of affairs in that ship.' he remarked and walked away.

At that time of year in Calcutta, a low-lying wet mist would come in during the night. If one was caught in this, and got soaked, it seemed as sure a way as a mosquito bite to a dose of malaria. One night cargo was being worked and the third mate was on his settee leaving me in charge of the deck. I kept up on the bridge deck clear of the mist which then covered all the well deck to the height of the bulwarks. Around midnight Mr Hamilton came back on board, he had been drinking as usual. I was watching him following a cockroach up his door with his key thinking it was the keyhole. He happened to turn round and saw me watching him and demanded to know where the watchman was, and who was supposed to be looking after the ship. I was ordered to go down to the gangway and stay there. I went along to the poop where the watchman was but he refused to remain at the gangway.

'Fog no good, get wet, get fever.' he said.

So I stayed by the gangway until Mr Hamilton's light went out then went back on the bridge deck. By then I was soaked through and had to remain so all night. I tried to dry out in the galley but that didn't help. The next day I began to feel feverish, first hot then shivering with cold. The doctor took my temperature which was 104°. Afterwards I had a hazy recollection of being in some kind of conveyance and then a hospital bed. I was there 10 days and the only person who came to see me was Mr Osborne, the purser, and that must have been when the *Media* was leaving. I don't remember what he said as I was too ill. When I was allowed to get up I seemed to become a favourite with the nurses, they were all white not Indian. I was given the job of trolleyman pushing the trolleys round behind the nurses with medicines and meals. Others who were up had to sweep the floors, clean the toilets and bathrooms and any other jobs that required doing. Matron was a large, stout woman with a voice and manner that well earned her the title of *Bosun*. Then one day I was told I was well enough to be discharged, given a piece of paper with the address of the company's agents, Messrs, Graham & Co., and told to ask for Mr Barnes. My effects had not been delivered to the hospital and all I had was what I had arrived in, nothing else. I was given a hospital discharge paper and they had no further interest in me.

It was early afternoon when I walked out of the hospital. I was in a weak condition and a two mile walk in the blazing sun did me no good at all. When I got to Chowringee I was lost, and wandered down a street, which I thought might take me down to the waterfront at the Jetties, where the agent's office would be. I was lucky, I met one of the hatchmen who piloted me down to Graham's office. I know he expected a reward for this but I had nothing. Mr Barnes was very surprised to see me. He had been told I would be discharged the following day and had intended to come for me himself. He asked if I had any money and when I told him no, he gave me five rupees advance. He also said I was to stay at his house in Hastings until the next ship, Brocklebank's *Mahronda*, was ready to leave. I would sail home in her.

His home in Hastings was a pleasant, single storey house with plenty of room inside. All the rooms were painted with green distemper, as seemed to be the case in all the houses I visited in India and the East. I was once told that insects avoided the green colour but it did not stop small lizards from living on them. As they were harmless and kept the flies and other insects down no one bothered them.

The Mission, also in Hastings, was where I spent most of my time. There I met another apprentice who was also out of hospital. Plenty of apprentices and others came into the Mission in the evenings but we were the only ones during the day. One afternoon we had the boxing gloves on and were trying to box, but not making much show as we knew nothing about it. Watching us was a stockily built man with a beautiful black eye and a face that looked as if it had been trodden on.

'Ere,' he said after a while. 'Yer knows noffink abaht it, I'll give youse a lesson.' He certainly did. He put on a pair of gloves and I got my first lesson in the art of boxing and by the time I left I had a good grounding in how to use my fists.

The Brocklebank ship *Mahronda* was now loading in the nearby Kidderpore Dock and one day Mr Barnes told me that she would be sailing the following day. We went down that afternoon and I was turned over to the care of Mr Hart, the chief officer. She didn't carry apprentices and had no accommodation for them so I was put into one of the spare rooms. On this ship I was not ignored but treated as a curiosity. They really did not know what to do with me. I don't know what instructions were given but I was treated as an invalid, I must have looked in bad shape. I saw the scales when I left hospital and I was then only five stone. I hadn't grown and my small size heightened the illusion. Everyone was very kind but I was glad I didn't have to remain in that vessel, there was far more comfort on a tramp than there was on that cargo liner.

The day we arrived back in London I was sent off once more to join the *Media*, loading in Glasgow. I had hoped to miss her. She was lying in the usual berth. No one was pleased to see me or even enquired how I had fared after going to hospital in Calcutta.

That the ship was now under Brocklebank's control was becoming more apparent. There was living and victualling on board, officers and engineers' wives were allowed to live on board in port and, during summer months, undertake the passages between ports round the coast. Also a gentleman named Commander Jefferson, Brocklebank's marine superintendent, was giving orders, and there was no formality about him, even being ex-Royal Navy. He arrived in Birkenhead while I was on gangway duty.

'What are you supposed to be doing?'

I explained I was on gangway duty and what that entailed. He went away and came back with the chief officer.

'Get that boy out of uniform and into working clothes and give him something useful and constructive to do. We do not require an apprentice on gangway duty in this company, we are just plain cargo ships.

I was ordered to my room to change but, as I had no working clothes, I was sent down one of the holds to watch cargo. I would have to get dungarees, I could see that.

When we left Birkenhead around 1 a.m. and came clear of the river, we found a full north-westerly gale. It was then Mr Hamilton remembered the carpenter had not completed battening down the forward end of No. 1 hatch when he was called away to work the windlass. I was sent forward to give a hand and, just as we got the wedges hammered home, the ship picked up speed into a heavy sea. I heard someone shout but I couldn't make out what was said, and then a large wave lifted over the forecastle head. I felt myself buried under water and washed along the deck, then I struck something.

When I came to, it was sometime in the forenoon and I was in my bunk strapped up with sticking plaster. I had struck one of the bulwark stanchions in such a manner that two of my ribs were pushed up and were projecting, the strapping was to force them back into position. The second mate, Mr Monro, had run off the bridge as I was washed along and picked me up. I had no other injuries but I was half drowned. The carpenter had escaped with abrasions and bruises. It was quite a long time, years in fact, before my ribs went back into position, though the strapping was only on for about a month.

During the passage out to Calcutta I became more certain that I had to get out of this ship, but how? If I stayed, beyond studying navigation myself nothing would change, not one of the mates bothered to explain how or why things were done.

It was while we were in Calcutta that I first saw Brocklebank's old steamer the *Montgomeryshire,* and I took a great liking to her. Her only apprentice was Edward Ward, on his first voyage, and I got to know him well. It was then I made up my mind to transfer to that ship if at all possible. There was an entirely different atmosphere there and she carried white quartermasters, and I knew they were the ones to teach me seamanship.

Back in Glasgow I took a chance. I was determined I was not going to remain on the *Media* whatever happened, so without being noticed I removed all my effects and took them home, then I kept a lookout for Commander Jefferson, Brocklebank's superintendent. He arrived one morning in company with the Anchor Line superintendents and they stood talking at the bottom of the gangway. I was lurking in the shed and thought *it's now or never*. I walked into the middle of the group, touched Commander Jefferson on the arm, and asked if I could have a word with him alone when he had time. They stared down at me as if they couldn't believe this was happening, a mere apprentice, the lowest form of life in the Anchor Line heirachy.

Commander Jefferson looked down at me and said, 'Remain here till I come down again.' Then the party went on board. Sometime later he came down the gangway and called me over. I told him I wasn't happy in that ship and was learning nothing. 'So,' he said, 'you want to be a sailor not a bridge ornament. Well,' he continued at last, 'pack up your gear, go home and I will send for you when I see what can be done.' As I didn't have any gear on the ship I was on my way home as soon as he had gone.

When I got home I told my father what I had done. 'You have your own life to live,' he said, 'I hope you know what you are doing'.

Chapter 4

Double trouble

I was at home until the third week in July when I received a letter instructing me to call at the Anchor Line office that day; I was again directed to Mr Hendry.

All he said was, 'You are being transferred to Messrs. Brocklebank's *Montgomeryshire*, now loading in Liverpool, and are to join her tomorrow morning which means travelling down there tonight.' He paid me up to date, gave me an envelope containing my indentures and, I presume, a letter to the captain of that ship and a third class rail fare. We shook hands and that was the end of my connection with the Anchor Line.

I went down to Liverpool that night and crossed to Birkenhead. On board I found a quartermaster on the gangway with Brocklebank Line across his jersey and *Montgomeryshire* on the ribbon round his cap. I asked for the chief officer, Mr Cornish, and he pointed to a small man some way along the deck. In correct *Media* style I saluted him and stood to attention. He stared at me. Finally he said, 'What the hell's the matter with you, cut out that saluting stuff, you are not in the Anchor Line now. I remember you, the boy from the *Media*. Commander Jefferson told me you were coming and wanted to be a sailor. I will do my best but you will have work hard. Go and get your mate, young Ward, he will give you a hand with your gear into the half deck.' This was the first time I had heard apprentices' accommodation called by its old sailing ship name. I found Edward Ward and he took me down to our cabin. I had just passed my 16th birthday and he was a few months older. We were together on that ship a year and eight months and got on well enough, but were never over fond of each other.

Our cabin, or half deck, was at the bottom of the captain's stairway so that he could partly see into it when he came down to the saloon for his meals. If the door was shut he would pull it open as he came down for breakfast and inspect the place. It was the cleanest and tidiest room in the ship, it had to be. It was only six feet fore and aft and eight in width, but I lived in that space for two years and ten months, some of it by myself.

No longer was I down in the holds watching cargo. When we got up in the morning it was into dungarees. We were allowed, when working, to breakfast and lunch in our room without having to change into uniform and back again. That would lose valuable working time and we had plenty to do.

Mr Cornish looked upon us as his special hobby. I don't think he had had any apprentices since he had been a chief officer and he made the most of us. There was no atmosphere now of not being wanted, we were part of the personnel of that ship and had our place in running it. He thought up an ingenious schedule for us so that each apprentice got eight hours' sleep, four hours on watch, some time to himself, and the chief officer six hours' work out of us.

This ship had a great deal of canvas and consequently plenty of awnings to be kept in repair and it took a great deal of work. All that, along with wire and rope splicing, kept us busy. I had, of course, never done any canvas sewing or splicing before joining this ship, so naturally I was not given any to do. I asked Mr Cornish about this.

'Can you sew canvas and splice?' he asked.

'No,' I said.

'When you can I will give you those kind of jobs.'

'How am I going to learn?'

'You have brains haven't you, go and find out.'

I thought this over. The only ones who could teach me were the quartermasters, so I approached McNay and he agreed, but not for nothing. I would have to supply him with hard tobacco and, as we were not allowed to buy any, I had to give him money. It didn't cost much, as on board the tobacco was duty free, but with only 5s per week every penny counted. Later Ted Ward made the payments as well, and we spent a lot of money in this way, which eventually had to include the carpenter as well.

Quartermaster McNay was a sailmaker by trade and had gone to sea for a while in a tea clipper. He taught me to sew and splice as well as all the knots and fancy work. According to him a journeyman sailmaker had to sew 60 feet per hour. He could, I had seen him do it, but at my best I could only do 30, and that I found, was more than most. When McNay allowed I was good enough to do these things by myself, I approached Mr Cornish again and passed all the tests he gave me, so I was put on to real sailor work at last.

The carpenter, Chips, was a great friend of McNay. He had built a model sailing ship, some four feet in length, complete in every detail. He had made the sails and rigging and everything worked. It was the most perfect thing of its kind I have ever seen. Chips would put his sailing ship on the hatch and, with a seamanship book, we would be taught by these old experts the names of masts, yards, sails, blocks and every rope and tackle. Shown how to send up and down topmasts and topgallant mast, yards and sails. In fact, under their supervision, we stripped the

William (on the right) on board the Montgomeryshire.

vessel down to a sheer hulk. Starting with rigging sheerlegs, then taking in and stepping the lower masts, and rigging her up again. Then we had to make sail, shorten down for bad weather, heave to, tack and wear ship, come to and leave an anchorage under sail, load and discharge using the yards as derricks. That model tacked and ran, wore and hove to all over No.1 hatch. I got such a grounding that, as far as I myself was concerned, I could argue with men who had served all their life in sail, and they would not believe that I had never been in a sailing ship. That knowledge stood me in good stead many a time. This continued for about eight months until McNay's illness put an end to it.

The company had decided to give us season tickets for the Eden Garden swimming baths while we were in Calcutta. These were fine baths, as good as the best anywhere, and all the Europeans used them. Sports, such as racing and water polo were held there, and it was the coolest place to be in that heat.

Our sister ship the *Glamorganshire* was next ahead of us, which meant she was loading while we were discharging. The third mate of that ship had organised a football team and Ted and I were usually called on to play. These matches were mostly against other ships' teams, but sometimes with shore teams like Burns Repair Yard, the Police or Berthing Pilots. Being small and, at that time able to run fast, (the result of getting away from the police before coming to sea) and being a left footer, my place was on the left wing. We won and lost in equal amounts and usually had two matches each time we were there. The football ground (it could not be called a field as it had no grass) was close to the Mission. The matches commenced

23

at four when the heat was cooling, and ended at five-thirty after which it got dark very quickly.

At the top of the ground was a grove of trees in which lived a tribe of monkeys. It was a recognised thing, when going to or coming from a match, to have a stone throwing battle with them. They were led by an old bearded warrior and appeared to be properly organised. They were very accurate marksmen, probably through constant practice, and before long we had to give up as we always got the worst of it. I don't remember any of the monkeys being knocked down but we certainly got some hard cracks.

Our chief steward, Mr Thomas Madden, was a large fat man with a permanent thirst for whisky and, being purser, he had to keep the ship's accounts. On the homeward passage, after leaving Colombo, he suddenly got an idea prompted by the two apprentices berthed next door, and the the fact that no one else was in that corner of the ship. These boys, he reasoned, having not long left school should be good at figures and, if so, why should they not with supervision, do all his accounts, crew lists, store lists, custom manifests, etc. They should be grateful for the opportunity to learn and practise the ship's business. We couldn't see it in that light at all but, if Mr Madden was prepared to make a deal, we would consider it. Finally, after protracted negotiations, it was agreed we would receive hard tobacco, in quantities according to work done, which he would book out against himself. By this means our supply of tobacco for McNay and the carpenter was assured.

Who started the idea was not known, most probably Commander Jefferson, but we were both ordered to attend Captain Tait's Nautical School in Oswald Street, Glasgow, which ran between the Broomielaw and Argyle Street. This school had, at that time, the best record of examination passes of any, due to the personal supervision given by Captain Tait himself – he was a born teacher. A feature accounting for most of the success was a book in which every candidate, whether passed or failed, wrote down what problems and questions he had been asked. This kept Captain Tait up to date with all the examiners' favourite questions. He also gave a demonstration of the character and methods of each examiner so that one knew what to expect. As we were usually only about eight days or so in Glasgow this didn't give us much time in the school, but we discovered which textbooks to buy and what to study (which we didn't do) but a few days every three months mounted up.

In Birkenhead we encountered another new working practice. Apprentices standing by ships in Birkenhead now had to work in the rigging loft while the ships were in the berth. Brocklebanks, being a very old shipping firm, had retained a lot of practices from the old sailing ship days, and one of them was a sailmaking and rigging loft of their own. I was kept busy splicing mooring wires in the period I worked there. I was shown several different ways of splicing but I only managed, by myself, an eye splice and short splice in wire, but in rope I could do a long splice as well. It was wonderful training but very hard work.

This voyage we had a new quartermaster, Thomas Winter. He had a parrot reputedly from the Amazon and, to pay his debts, he was offering this bird for sale. Ward and I thought we could sell the bird and cage to the owner of a fish and chip shop in the main street and make a good profit. So we became the owners of Cocky. He was a problem from the start. The sale to the fish and chip shop didn't come off, though we did make a deal that the parrot would stand on the counter, while we were in port, to attract custom. In return we would have free fish suppers, but we had to take him with us when we sailed.

This ship was overrun by rats and it was now a case of the rats being got under control or they would take over altogether. Captain Montador put up notices to the effect that, on the night before sailing, anyone who was ashore had to look for, and capture, a cat on their way back. Ted and I went ashore to bring the parrot back and managed to waylay the fish shop cat, which I managed to carry inside my coat. Then we got another one, a grey of some kind, and I had to keep them out of sight until we passed the gate policeman. It was never known exactly how many cats had been collected, but by checking up on everyone who claimed they had brought one on board, the tally was agreed at 13. We were ordered not to feed them. A hatch cover was taken off each hatch and the cats put down. They eventually did a good job and we were not troubled by rats afterwards. Unfortunately the cats were a mixed lot, the toms got to work and by the time we were homeward bound we had a plague of cats and kittens. The orders were to throw overboard every cat and kitten we could catch, and the homeward track was marked by floating bodies. It was a cruel business all round but something had to be done.

It was now getting on for the middle of November, and crossing the Bay of Biscay we had a full north-west gale, and how the *Montgomeryshire* could roll. With a loaded ship, and a heavy sea just abaft the beam, she was rolling so far over that the well deck rails were dipping under. It was impossible to move around without hanging on to lifelines which had been rigged all over the ship. Just before 2 a.m. one day the standby quartermaster came racing on to the bridge calling out to the second mate that some cargo had come adrift in No.4 'tween deck. He went down to listen and came back to call Captain Montador. Then the chief officer and all the deck hands were called out. The captain came up on the bridge, reduced speed and hove the ship to, in an attempt to reduce the rolling as much as possible. By this time, a section of hatches were off and with the 'tween deck lights on and cargo clusters rigged, we could see what had happened. A consignment of wagon wheels, one on each end of an axle, had been stowed pointing fore and aft. Whether they had been properly secured, I don't know, but with the heavy rolling they had started moving and gradually smashed everything in their path. They were crashing so heavily against the ship's sides that, left to themselves, they would have damaged the ship's side plating while smashing themselves up. The idea was to get wires round them and lash them to the hold stanchions, then swing them round broadside forward and, when all secured, bed them down. This was done eventually, but it took some time. Finally everything was secured but a lot of light cargo had been badly damaged. As all Birkenhead cargo was loaded by the firm's own stevedores, the responsibility for the bad stowage was theirs. Apart from that, the outward passage went as usual and we had good weather from then on.

On the passage back from Colombo to Suez, McNay became very ill and got steadily worse. I went in to see him one morning and was surprised to find his hair and beard a dirty white not auburn as they used to be. It dawned on me then that he must have kept his hair and beard dyed to conceal his real age, and he must have been much older than we thought. In Suez Bay he was taken to hospital and the following day in Port Said we heard he had died during the night. To my surprise he had left me all his sailmaking kit plus two books, one on sailmaking and canvas sewing and the other on rigging, knots and splices. In the course of time I had one item and then another stolen until finally the whole kit had gone.

When we arrived in Dundee, a steamer belonging to Gardiners of Glasgow, called the *Glendevon*, was discharging at the shed next to us. When she sailed her cargo of jute, some 30,000 tons, was stored there. The following afternoon Ward and I were painting in the draught figures on the stem (punishment job). It was very cold. The berth ahead was empty and everything was quiet. I was looking around, instead of getting on with the job, when suddenly I saw a sheet of flame which seemed to be coming from the upriver end of the shed. Then I saw the watchman race to the telephone box. I went up the ladder and called out to Ted.

'Look that shed's on fire.' By then we could hear the flames roaring and the man who had telephoned was getting a hose from a hook on the shed wall.

Ted said, 'Lets go and give him a hand.' It was none of our business but we raced along to the gangway and down the wharf to the shed. Being the middle of the afternoon no one saw us go. As we reached the shed the Fire Brigade arrived and got busy. Jute is highly inflammable and burns like paper, so by this time there was no hope of saving the shed and the bales of jute, so the firemen concentrated on saving the wooden wharf and the shed down wind, which was ours. The next thing we knew was a fireman ordering us to get onto a hose and help out. There were four of us on that hose and it was jumping around as if it was alive. Then we noticed our ship dropping off the wharf to an anchor – harbour master's orders we heard later. The fire didn't last long, and the firemen managed to keep it from spreading, but the whole shed and 30,000 bales of jute were reduced to ashes. Then everyone began to arrive, police, newspaper reporters and photographers. The Fire Brigade chief took our names and told us to call at Brigade Headquarters the following day to collect our pay, which would be about 5s. In the meantime our ship had hauled back alongside – we hadn't been missed at all. The following morning at breakfast Mr Cornish came storming into our room and demanded to know where we had been the previous afternoon.

'Painting draught figures on the stem, sir, as you told us to do.'

'Oh you were, were you, well have a look at this.' He held up the morning newspaper. There was a photograph of the blazing shed and Ward and I holding a hose with two firemen. He pointed to the description, 'Ably assisted by crew members of the *Montgomeryshire*'. Captain Montador was rather pleased and I expect he sent the photo and cutting to the Liverpool office. That evening we presented ourselves at Brigade Headquarters and duly received our 5*s* each, we were in the money!

While in Glasgow the ship's name was changed back to the original *Bengali* but why no one seemed to know.

Chapter 5

Cockroaches and Cocky the parrot

*I*n Birkenhead the *Montgomeryshire*, now renamed the *Bengali*, underwent survey. Ward went home for a few days, I went into the rigging loft, and Cocky went back to his job in the fish and chip shop. Captain Montador was relieved by Captain Witham, as he was to stand by the fitting out of one of the two new ships that were being built.

Being on the point of completing two years of my time I had been told to get a sextant as I would have to take and work out sights every day, and also take the sun at noon. This was Captain Montador's idea and Captain Witham carried it on. Knowing nothing about buying a sextant I had asked Jim Embley, the third mate, for advice and he agreed to help me find a second-hand one. Somewhere near the Custom House I finally ended up with a new octant, that is with arc marked to 152 instead of 102 as is a sextant. It is just as good although it has only 90° of arc instead of 120°. It cost £2 10s.

In due course we sailed for Calcutta again, and there were plenty of real seamanship jobs to be done getting everything back into shape after the survey.

At her launch the Bengali had been fitted out with sails. The staysails and trysails, together with blocks and tackles, were still in the ship. Upon reaching the Gulf of Aden, they were brought out when conditions permitted, for practice in setting and handling canvas. I don't think they added even a fraction of a knot to the speed but they did check the rolling considerably.

A craze had taken hold some time previously for cockroach racing and soon everyone had their own stable. The whole idea was based on the fact that a cockroach wouldn't cross a chalked line; why has never been explained to me, but apparently this is so. The racecourse was laid out on the engineers' mess room table. A series of heavy chalk lines were drawn down the table in pairs two inches apart, a line across the bottom of these and one across the top. The contestants were held with their rears to the top chalk line and the starting signal released. To make their

S.S.Bengali under canvas.

escape, as they thought, the 'roaches ran down the table between the lines, reached the bottom line, then in panic turned and ran up again seeking a way out at the top. The one that arrived back at the top first was declared the winner. Some notable racers emerged and a lot of money changed hands. I didn't enter any of the races. As I was in charge of the cleaning gangs for the after holds in Calcutta, I went into the supply side and had my gangs looking for, and bringing me, all the cockroaches found from one and a half inches upwards. I developed quite a nice business and always had a good selection available. Races were arranged in Calcutta between ships and it was as exciting as real racing.

It was an accepted thing that any bird found on board was handed over to us, no one else could be bothered with them. Once the deckhands found a small grey owl which had been sleeping somewhere on the boat deck. It was only eight inches in height and quite tame. It took up its abode on the upper bunk curtain rail but refused to eat anything. It is said that where there is one owl there is usually another, so the following night we put the little owl in a potato basket on the hatch and, in the morning, sure enough there was another one perched on top of the basket. So now we had two. They began to eat but made no attempt to fly away, perhaps they sensed land was too far away for them to reach. Later on, off the Ceylon coast, the washing down gang surprised a large white crane asleep on one of the boat spans. This was a nasty customer, too large to have indoors so it was fastened, by a line round one leg, to a ring bolt in the deck. His diet was fish but he would eat anything he could get. When we got to Calcutta, on Captain Witham's advice, we wrote to the Calcutta zoo and offered them the birds. They accepted and sent down a van and uniformed keepers to collect them, and we were given a free pass for the zoo while we were in port.

During this particular voyage, and to the astonishment of everyone, I suddenly grew five inches in three months. I was now five feet six and a half inches, which height I remained, and I was no longer wee Donald.

By this time I was becoming quite good at Lascari-Bat, which was a mixture of Arabic, Hindustani and Malay spoken by all the sea-going natives from Aden to Singapore. By the time my apprenticeship was completed I had a good working knowledge of the dialect. The ships' officers, some of whom like Mr Cornish had spent most of their lives with native crews, knew hardly any. So the curious situation arose that an apprentice, only two years on the run, had to act as interpreter.

In this ship the senior apprentice had to attend the captain when he went ashore on business. On this occasion I was with Captain Witham in the Calcutta Shipping office while the Lascar and Goanese crew were being signed on. The captain spent most of the time talking to a tall, thin man in a white uniform with the German Hansa Line's badge on the front. When we came out Captain Witham said, 'Do you know that man is a captain in the German navy, and is at present in command of the Hansa Line's *Hohenfels.*' I was not really interested and only remembered this when Count von Muller, of the *Emden*, became a well-known name around the Indian Ocean after the outbreak of war. I was told later that, if a German naval officer specialised in commerce destruction, he had to serve in merchant ships to get to know them and their habits.

Malta was a permanent port homeward bound, and was a centre for trade in monkeys of all shapes and sizes. These animals could be caught, or bought for next to nothing, in Calcutta and a good price obtained in Malta. As we were always trying to think up ways of making money we decided to get into this monkey racket as well. On the roof of the cargo shed lived a female monkey. What she lived on I don't know but she seemed to make a living along the quay somehow. We decided to capture her as there was no point in paying out money when one could be got for nothing. We tried leaving part of a mango, or banana, at the foot of the drain pipe, then enticing her to come down. I nearly got hold of her once but she was up the drainpipe like a flash after grabbing the fruit. Brocklebanks had a permanent night watchman, old Abdul. I had always been friendly with him and he could speak very good English and sometimes used to read the Koran to me in Hindustani. I asked his advice on how to catch the monkey.

'You give me four annas sahib, I get small boy to go up on the roof at night when monkey asleep and bring her down.'

We hadn't reckoned on paying for a monkey but I gave Abdul the money and a night or two later he presented us with Jinny. She was dirty and smelled so much she had to be washed. We got a box for her, and a line round her middle made fast to a stanchion on the boat deck would serve for the time being. Once the ship was at sea having the monkey on the boat deck was no longer feasible. With the heat from the stokehold, ash and coal dust, the poor animal would not have lasted long, so she had to be brought down to the bridge deck during the day and our room at night, which meant she had to be frequently bathed otherwise she smelt.

At 8 a.m. one Sunday Ted was giving the monkey her daily bath and, to save himself trouble, he attempted to bath her in the wash basin. The monkey, though still with the line fast round her, was not tied to anything so he had to hold on to the line as well. I was not a witness to what followed, as I was on watch, so I only quote from hearsay.

The room door was hooked back as usual and only the curtain drawn across. This being Sunday Ted had on a pair of white trousers instead of working clothes. The monkey hated being washed and in the ensuing struggle Ward let go of the line and the monkey slipped out of his grasp. The drop table was up for breakfast and, on a small stand just above the table, was a bottle of ink with a cork stopper which the monkey grabbed as she leapt across the table into Ted's bunk. The bed linen had just been changed and everything was clean. He tried to get hold of her again but the monkey pulled the cork out of the bottle and, as it was nearly full, there was an unholy mess as she dodged around still holding the bottle. The ink got everywhere. Mad with fear the monkey leapt across the alleyway and into the chief steward's room. Tom Madden was sitting on his settee when the monkey ran over him, giving him the benefit of some ink over his clean white suit, then leapt into his bunk. Glasses and bottles went crashing as the maddened animal tore round the room then out into the alleyway and into the saloon. Ward told me later he never knew Tommy Madden could move so fast as when he raced after that monkey. Captain Witham, the officers and a couple of passengers, had just sat down to breakfast when the monkey leapt on the dining table getting its feet into everything. The second mate's coffee cup got knocked over and he got the contents over his white suit, before she scrambled over Captain Witham and out through the open port and along the fore deck, finishing up in the rigging of the foremast. The amount of ink that bottle held was unbelievable. Captain Witham was demanding to know where the animal came from and who was responsible for it, the apprentices of course.

'I will talk to those two later,' he said, and he did. When we told him we had bought the monkey for selling in Malta he went off the deep end and ordered us to get rid of it. If ever it came round this part of the ship again he would take action. There was a painful scene with the chief steward over the ruined bed linen, the wreckage of his room, and the spoiled white suit, which he said we would have to pay for. Fortunately he wasn't in a position to enforce anything as we would have refused to do his accounts. Jinny was loose round the ship till hunger drove her to the poop among the other monkeys. Who took possession of her, and sold her eventually in Malta, we neither knew nor cared, we had had enough of trading in livestock.

31

Our parrot had become a fluent talker and at sea his cage was on the bridge deck hatch all day. He could mimic perfectly the various whistles from the bridge for the stand-by quartermaster, even to the tones of the different whistles. As a result the quartermasters often went up on the bridge or ran for the log when the officer on watch had not blown at all. He also developed a loud mocking laugh, but only did this when the captain went past, which infuriated him but amused everyone around. I could do anything I liked with him, and when I picked him up he would sit on my wrist or shoulder, and never at any time attempted to bite me, but I was the only one. He had grown to full size and was now the largest parrot I had ever seen. He was dark green with red and blue bars on his wings and tail. I learnt later that South American parrots always had red shoulders, but this one had bright yellow. Just above its beak was a patch of bright blue feathers, then yellow and the basic green, a very gaudy creature. The blue patch above his beak caused people to greet him with 'Hello you blue nosed bastard' and he copied this perfectly, causing more trouble when someone got that greeting from him. One day Captain Witham called us both up on the lower bridge and asked who was the owner of the bird. We told him we were joint owners.

'That bird,' he said, 'has to be taken out of this ship before she leaves on another voyage, that is an order.'

I had written home to ask my parents if they would like to have the parrot. My mother said she would and what she said went. She was always very fond of birds of all kinds. After a lot of arguing Ward finally agreed to be bought out of his share in the parrot for 25*s*. I was allowed to go home on weekend leave while in Dundee. I suspect Captain Witham had got to know I was taking the bird home. He was in such a fever to get Cocky, and his laugh, out of the ship that he told Mr Cornish to let me go.

The cage was too large to go in the compartment with me and, in any case, Cocky's vocabulary was such that he could cause trouble if he got into a talking mood. With a suitcase and a large parrot cage I had my hands full getting to the station. I had wrapped several layers of brown paper round the cage to keep him quiet and he didn't make a sound. I bought a ticket for him and put him in the guard's van. While the train was waiting in Perth station the guard came along the train demanding to know who owned that parrot in the van. I said the bird was mine. The guard was in a state of frenzy.

'Take that bird out of there at once,' he screamed. 'I am a God-fearing man and I have never been spoken to like that in my life, the foulest language I have ever heard.' I knew what had happened. Cocky restless and wanting to see what was going on had torn away part of the paper wrapping and engaged the guard in conversation, opening with the greeting he was used to hearing, 'Hello you blue-nosed bastard.' By the look of the guard's nose I could see why it had hurt so much. I told the guard I had paid the bird's fare and was not going to remove it until we arrived in Glasgow. He stalked off. I wondered what was going to happen when I got the bird home and the family heard his language. I might have to wring his neck after all. When I got him home the first thing my mother did was to open the cage, lift him out and put him on her shoulder. It scared me. I thought she would get badly bitten, but no, she could do anything with him then and ever after, but no one else. Right away he turned on me, so he was a one person bird. I couldn't believe it but he never spoke until he had picked up the words being used around him, except on one occasion. The minister was visiting and he liked his drop, and the colour of his nose showed it. Cocky gave him the greeting. He never visited again, which pleased my father. That bird was with the old people for 14 years.

Since we had been in Calcutta there had been rumours of war. We had nearly completed loading by 4th August and the news from Europe was getting worse by the hour. While walking back to the ship one evening a babu (native clerk) stopped me crying 'Sahib war, war, the British Raj fight Germany.' When I got on board I found all loading had ceased. I was told France and Britain had declared on Germany. Orders had come from Graham & Co., to cease loading and all sailings had been stopped. There was great excitement at the Mission that evening and a great deal of boasting about what we would do to the Germans. The usual closing time of 9.30.p.m. was ignored and it was midnight before everyone dispersed.

After a couple of days orders came to discharge No.3 lower hold and fill it up with bunker coals. This was to take us home, but it wasn't until 20th August we were allowed to sail. The German cruiser squadron based in China had vanished and, until information as to their movements was available, all ships were to be held in port. We had to proceed direct to Suez.

One night, in the Gulf of Aden, I was relieving at the wheel. The ship had no navigation lights on but was showing plenty of light round the decks, no one had heard of blackout at that time. It was pitch dark with no moon when I saw, practically alongside us, a black mass looming up. Out of the blackness a voice roared.

'What ship is that?' Charlie Owen, the second mate, nearly jumped out of his skin. Again the voice came. 'What ship is that, answer immediately.'

We answered, '*Bengali*, Calcutta for Hull.'

'Have you sighted any ships between the Ceylon coast and here?'

'None.'

'Thank you, HMS *Yarmouth* speaking, do not report contact with me.' Then the black shape faded away.

We arrived in the Humber at the end of September and moored stern on in the Alexandra Dock, which was a long way from the town. Discharge was very slow, everything was disorganised owing to the war, and we were there some three weeks. One evening Ward and I were up town and, being in ordinary clothes, were accosted by a recruiting sergeant who asked us to join up as 'your King and Country needs you'. We thought it would be a nice change as there seemed to be nothing much doing in the merchant service, so we took the 'King's shilling' and were told to present ourselves at the recruiting office the next morning to pass the doctor and sign up. I think we had volunteered for the East Yorkshire Light Infantry. The next morning we didn't turn to but got dressed in shore suits again. We were just coming out of our room when Mr Cornish appeared. We informed him we had nothing further to do with this ship, we were soldiers now, joined last night, and are going up to have the medical.

'You crazy young fools.' he shouted. 'You are indentured apprentices, get your working clothes on at once.'

'Sorry Mr Cornish, but we are in the army now, our King and Country needs us.

'You might be some slight use at sea but no use at all in the army.' he said, then he went upstairs to the captain.

When we arrived at the recruiting office there seemed to be hundreds waiting to be examined but after about an hour and a half an NCO came in.

'Anyone by the names of Donald and Ward here?' We answered and were taken into a room where an officer was sitting behind a desk. Captain Witham was also there, and on the desk were our indentures.

'Get the hell out of here,' he said. 'You can't join anything, army or navy, unless your indentures are cancelled.' We were taken back to the ship in a taxi and that was the end of my service in the British Army.

While in Glasgow, gun mountings were installed on the after end of the poop. These consisted of three rings, the outer for a 4.72- inch, then a 6-pounder and the inner one a 3-pounder. There was also the necessary stiffening on the deck and inside the steering engine house. A naval reserve rating would join the ship as gunner and the gun was to be mounted in Birkenhead.

The morning of the day we left Glasgow I was sent up to Queen Street station to meet, and bring down to the ship, the naval gunner. I had to report to the transit office and enquire for the rating posted to the *Bengali*, but I was not told when he would be arriving. However, as soon as I reported able seaman McLeod was called out. An elderly man came forward, he had West Highlandman written all over him, and looked quite lost. When we set off I discovered he knew very little English, Gaelic being his language. I did manage to find out he was a fisherman, 56 years old, from Stornaway in the Hebrides, and had finished his Royal Naval Reserve (RNR) training 20 years ago. Apart from that he had never been away from the fishing, as he called it, until now. He did not know what kind of a gun he was to have or what he was to do. I had to act as shepherd to Jock all the time he was on the ship. It was always, 'ask the boy,' which was me, and he would not listen to anyone else, always, 'the boy will tell me what to do'. Somehow I seemed able to make him understand, but no one else could.

There were other changes made while we were in Birkenhead. Mr Cornish left to stand by a new ship, and Tom Madden, the chief steward also left. A Mr. Sandeman, a big burly Scot from Dundee replaced Mr Cornish, but despite a rough manner he was a very nice person. The new chief steward was an entirely different type of man, by the name of Barson. He knew his job and did all the paperwork himself, so we no longer had a source of revenue from doing accounts.

One morning we reported to one of the Anchor Line Bombay passenger ships for instruction in gun drill. The party consisted of three mates, four quartermasters, two apprentices and old Jock. That ship had been fitted with a 4.72-inch gun firing a 60 lb shell, and in charge were two Royal Marines. We were instructed how to make up a gun's crew and set watches, then watched as the *Castilia's* gun crew were put through the drill. Then came our turn which took all morning. Old Jock, I could see, did not get the hang of it at all.

Our gun didn't appear until almost the hour of sailing. A lorry arrived with a long narrow box, a cone shaped mounting, several smaller boxes and a number of cases marked ammunition. All had blue and white stripes painted on them and stencilled Brocklebank Line, so it appeared the firm bought the gun. It was a 3-pounder the rating in charge said. His instructions were to deliver – nothing about fitting up the gun, the gunner would have to do that. We sailed with the gun still in its boxes. The following forenoon the gun was assembled. Fitting the mounting was easy but then things began to get difficult. At the first try the gun barrel would not remain horizontal but drooped down touching the platform. Up to this time the chief officer, Mr Sandeman, had been in charge with Jock watching. Then it was decided to call in the second engineer for technical advice. At the next try the barrel would not move up, down or track round, but finally everything was in order. The trouble was no instruction leaflet had been included. We then decided to fire a round to see if everything really was in working order. The report of that gun was the nastiest bang I have ever heard, the crack nearly split my eardrums.

In Glasgow a platform had been built with drop rails around it, with ammunition lockers, hooks for the sponge rammer and so on, but no magazine. To be near the gun the cases had to be stored in the steering engine house, underneath the poop and the shells handed up through the skylight. Later on a magazine was built in the port corner of the steering engine house. This backed on the fireman's forecastle which they didn't know, perhaps just as well.

In Port Said Jock McLeod and the popgun were landed as it was deemed unnecessary for the rest of the voyage. During the passage I had written out a request for Jock to be transferred to trawlers or minesweepers, and he handed this in at Port Said. Some months later I received a letter from him (someone had written it for him) informing me he had got his transfer and was now in trawler minesweeping – where he had always wanted to be.

On the homeward voyage we loaded a mixed cargo for London and Dundee and also accommodated the Lascar crew of another new ship, some 120 of them. With four passengers, we were now 220 all told, and only four lifeboats!

We left Calcutta around 11th December 1914, and passed through the Suez Canal the day before New Year. An attack on the Canal, by the Turks, was expected and in case snipers were around we had sandbags stacked along the starboard side fore and aft, and the lower and navigation bridges. The weight of the bags gave the ship a starboard list, but all ships had to have them. Actually the Turks did attack some time in February 1915.

The gun put on board in Port Said was an advance on the previous one, it was a 6-pounder and a gunner came with it. It didn't take him long to fit it up and have everything organised before we left.

The *Bengali* was 60 miles south-south-west of Vigo pitching into a strong northerly wind and stiff head sea, and had been doing this all the way up from Cape St.Vincent. It was around 8.30 a.m. on the 9th January 1915, one day in my life I never forgot.

The deck serang had finished eating his breakfast, out of a large circular tin, alongside No.6 hatch. He filled the dish with water and went to his room for a cloth to wash the dish. When he picked it up it was hot. Puzzled, he felt the deck underneath and found that too was hot. Being an experienced seaman he knew what was wrong and gave the alarm.

'Captain sahib, ship on fire.'

Everyone poured out on deck and ran aft to No.6 hatch where smoke was coming out of the starboard forward ventilator. The serang and the deckhands unbattened the starboard fore-end of the hatch and, as soon as the air got in, a dense cloud of smoke poured out and the fire could be heard crackling. According to the book, everything had to be battened down to smother the fire, so the hatches were replaced and the task of unshipping the big heavy ventilators was started. In the meantime deck hoses were rigged. The gunner told Mr Sandeman the ammunition must be got out of the steering engine house magazine or the heat would set it off. We got it out, fortunately it was not heavy stuff.

By this time everyone was out of the poop. I was helping to run the deck hose along to the hatch when the hatch blew up, and everything including No.6 derrick, went sailing high into the air and over the side, followed by a pillar of fire and a smoke cloud that must have been visible for miles. The explosion had hurled everything out of the square of the 'tween deck hatch and, with the hose playing down there, it looked as if we might hold the fire, but the copra further aft was well away, roaring like a furnace. When the hatch blew up the Lascars made a rush for the boats. The chief engineer had an idea this might happen and had the engineers rig up a steam hose on the boat deck where he stationed himself with one of the quartermasters. He cleared the boat deck with his hose. I don't know how many Lascars got skin flayed off them, but it must have been quite a few. They didn't try that again.

We were now flying distress signals, and two vessels were stationed nearby ready to help if we had to abandon ship. This would not have been allowed later on in the war, if a German submarine had come along he could have bagged all three of us.

The main deck was getting hotter and commencing to buckle. The hoses were getting charred, as well as our boots and shoes, and it was impossible to control the fire. By now it was noon and the fire had been raging for three hours when the chief engineer, old and ill that he was, had an idea. It would take far too long to explain exactly what he did, but suffice to say he managed to get the shaft steering gear cooled down and working again, and the ship underway for Vigo, a Spanish port. We anchored off the town just after daylight with signals flying for the Lloyd's agent. We must have looked a forlorn sight.

Late in the afternoon, with the salvage tug *Leon* attending, the anchor was hove up and we proceeded to the head of Vigo Bay, where the ship was run into shallow water. The anchors were run out as we went in, and the ship settled on the sandy bottom. Then *Leon* came alongside and pumped water into Nos. 5 and 6 holds to the hatch coamings. When the holds were full, about midnight, the water in No. 5 was scalding hot.

The next evening *Leon* started pumping out the holds. Sometime the next morning the water was out, or as much as could be got out. By late evening No.5 was blazing again. It was flooded again and this time left for four days, then pumped out and this time the fire appeared to be out, but the jute was still smouldering when taken out in Dundee two months later.

Now we had to wait for a Lloyd's surveyor; we were told one was on the way. He informed Lloyds that, in his opinion, the vessel could proceed to London. The reply came back saying if he was satisfied he was to make the passage to London with the ship. It was now February 1915 and we were a crippled ship down by the head, even with after ballast in, with uncertain steering gear and no hand gear. We left Vigo early one morning with a covering of planks and tarpaulins over Nos. 5 and 6 hatches, enough to keep out a shower of rain but not a sea. Crossing the Bay of Biscay it began to blow hard from the north-west right on the beam, but by the evening of the next day fortunately it was clear. Once round Ushant the wind was on the quarter and weather remained fine all the way to London.

I was sent home on leave and about three days later arrived in Glasgow. The last train stopping at Uddingston had gone but I managed to get on the last one to Tollcross – four miles short of Uddingston. There was nothing else for it, using my woollen scarf I slung my suitcase on my back and tramped the four miles home. The only person I met was a policeman, who took some convincing I was not a burglar with a case full of loot, and followed me until I reached home. My parents and the rest of the family got quite a shock as I hadn't been able to let them know I was coming.

I rejoined the ship in Dundee on 17th March, and on arrival in the Mersey she was berthed in the Basin for survey and tenders for repair, and laid there for a fortnight. The underwriters would not agree to her being scrapped as it was cheaper to repair the vessel and, being at war, every ship was valuable. Finally Graysons of the West Float were awarded the job, being the lowest tender. Then we moved up to the West Float and berthed just outside the dry docks.

Officers, engineers and crew were given a month's pay in recognition of their efforts to save the ship. The Lascars and Goanese, who never lifted a finger to help when the fire was raging, got a month's pay for nothing. Ward and I, when we heard of this, went to see Captain Witham. He said no mention had been made of apprentices but he agreed we had earned a reward. Ted and I went across to Liverpool one morning to the office in the Liver Building and requested an interview with Mr Williams, the manager. He listened to what we had to say and promised to look into the matter. A day or two later we were called to the captain's cabin and solemnly handed £2 each.

When instructions came, by letter, for Captain Witham as to the disposal of officers and crew, the sentence concerning apprentices read, *apprentice to be sent on leave to await instructions for joining another of the company's vessels.* Actually a typing error left out the 's' at the end of apprentice, it should have read apprentices. Captain Witham didn't query this, and disliking Ward, sent him home. That two and a half months was the dreariest time I have ever spent. I was in a state of complete poverty, and for three weeks all I had was half a crown (2s 6d). I was now in the fourth and last year of my apprenticeship and in receipt of £2 per month. Out of that I had to buy toilet articles and keep myself in clothes. The £2 bonus had gone in buying oilskins and other necessary items.

When loading commenced there were some changes. It seemed white quartermasters of the type Brocklebanks wanted were not now to be had, so the office decided to ship native quartermasters for the time being, but they could only be obtained in Calcutta, so for the passage out apprentices were to act as quartermasters.

I suppose Mr Sandeman had informed the office that only three apprentices were required, for according to their records I was supposed to be on the *Manipur* with Ward. I found this out when I went over to Liverpool on the morning of sailing day, and was waiting in the outer office for papers when Mr Williams came along. He stared at me.

'Good God where did you come from?' he said.

'From the *Bengali* over in Birkenhead,' I replied.

'But you are officially on the *Manipur*.'

'No,' I said, 'I have been in the *Bengali* all the time.'

'Come into my room, I don't want anyone to see you, there must have been a mix up somewhere. So that's why Mr Sandeman said only three apprentices required to make up the complement as quartermasters.'

When we came to leave there was still no suitable carpenter available, so I had to carry out the carpenter's routine for this voyage as well. I was now, with the exception of Mr Owen the second mate, the longest serving person on deck.

Our 4.72-inch gun arrived and so did two gunners, ex-Royal Navy, called up from the reserve. Gun watches were now kept day and night as submarines were taking an increasing toll of shipping, but there was no escort to take us clear of the danger zone, and the submarines were now down as far as the Gibraltar Straits.

For the Canal passage the bridge had to be sandbagged as before. The two youngest apprentices had never done any steering in rivers or narrow waters, so Grieg and I had to take the wheel the full four hours of our watches. Fortunately it was a daylight passage with no tying up.

We loaded our usual jute in Calcutta, but this time had a part cargo consigned to Alexandria. I have been in Alexandria many times since but can remember very clearly the first time I saw that harbour, full of troop transports. There seemed to be a large number of Australian and New Zealanders as well, the troopship ahead of us was full of them.

From Alexandria we sailed to Malta as usual for bunkers. The harbour was full, naval vessels and troopships moored all over. We berthed early in the morning and by 4 p.m. had completed coaling and were ready to leave. However the signal went up that no movement of vessels would be allowed until the convoy had cleared the harbour. The naval escorts went first and the troopers followed, rails and rigging crowded with soldiers. Bands ashore were playing *Auld Lang Syne* and the soldiers were singing. By the time they were all out it was sunset – the most impressive sight I had ever seen.

Still sailing on our own we arrived in London without being molested and berthed in Tilbury Dock, then to Dundee to complete the discharge, and finally an uneventful passage to Glasgow. The nautical school attendance had now been dropped owing to the war, but I managed a few days leave.

Now at last we had a carpenter, Samuel McLean, and he and I became great friends. He was originally from Stornaway in the Hebrides and had served an apprenticeship in the boat building trade. He emigrated to Canada and, in the course of time, developed his own business building and repairing boats and yachts. When the war broke out he decided to come back and do his bit and thought he would try going to sea as a carpenter, hence his appearance on the *Bengali*. He hadn't been to sea before but, as he was expert at his trade, all he had to learn was to take soundings, work the windlass and batten down the hatches.

One afternoon I noticed something very curious. A battleship, which looked to be one of our latest, had just berthed at Stobcross Quay astern of us. I thought it funny a battleship would berth there, and what was more curious only a few riggers appeared round the decks. After dinner I went on the poop for another look – she appeared deserted, no sign of life anywhere. Then a workman came out from amidships, walked along to the forward gun turret, put his arm round a 16-inch gun, pulled it out, dropped it on the deck and rolled it into the scuppers. I watched with my mouth open. He did the same to the other one, then I realised they were only made of laths and canvas. More workmen appeared and began pulling down gun turrets, superstructure and bridges. I watched fascinated as an ordinary cargo vessel gradually emerged then, with a shock, recognised one of Brocklebank's steamers the same type as the *Mahronda*. She must have been one of the dummy fleet used to make the Germans believe the fleet was always at sea waiting for them. Even at close quarters she would have fooled anyone.

At Birkenhead there were more changes in the crew. Charlie Owen had been promoted to chief officer of the *Matra* and was full of apprehension at having the responsibility of looking after a ship. The third mate was promoted to second mate, and another third mate joined. We all had to attend gun drills in one of the sheds run by naval gunnery instructors.

Schofield and I were now the only two apprentices left on the ship. There were gun watches all the way out to Port Said where we landed the gun as usual. From there to Calcutta we were put on day work and most of my time was spent with Sam. I was learning to use carpenter's tools properly, and Sam had the finest tool chest I have ever seen, all American made. He seemed to have taken a fancy to me, and I took a great liking to him.

On 26th January 1916 we arrived back in Birkenhead, via Dundee and Glasgow. I would be out of my apprenticeship in seven weeks' time. It had always been firmly fixed in my mind that I had commenced indentures on 21st March 1912. Between Calcutta and Colombo, I informed Captain Witham that I had now completed indentures whereupon he called me into his room and handed them to me.

'Have a look at that,' he said. The date was 27th March 1912, I must have had the wrong date in mind all that time. The day after we left Colombo he called me into his room again. 'It is now 27th March and you are a free man. I will put you on the articles as an able seaman (AB) at £7 10*s* per month. That's more than the white quartermasters are now getting. I can't sign you on as a fourth mate as we don't carry one, but from now on you will be acting fourth mate and keeping watch with Mr Sandeman.' I had now been on the ship two years and four months.

Since obtaining the octant, I had maintained my practical navigation with the other mates whenever possible, and, by what I had seen at Tait's Nautical School, I did not have much to learn. I was also good on signals. My weak point was what was known as memory work. Captain Montador had bought a pack of *Captain Jutsom's Rule of the Road* cards and somehow these had passed into my possession. I happened to mention to Sam that unless I got these committed to memory, I could not get through the examination no matter how good I was at other things. That started something. When he was put into the half-deck with me he made it his business to see that I did learn them off by heart, and had me repeat them every night when we were on watch. I could not get out of this under any pretext, and the result was I got them off word-perfect.

When the gun came on board at Port Said as usual, there were four naval ratings. This was because too many guns were being landed and not enough ships returning, so the surplus had to be returned to the UK where there was a shortage. This was fortunate for me as I was no longer involved in those never-ending gun watches. A passenger gun was brought on board in a crate with its ammunition, and stowed on the after deck.

I finally signed off the ship in Glasgow on 15th May 1916. I had asked Captain Witham for a reference for my time as AB, a necessity for the second mate's examination.

'I will send you one from Birkenhead when the ship pays off,' he said. When I went to say goodbye to him he wished me the best of luck for the future and said, 'Some day you will be a shipmaster yourself.' I hoped he was right.

I subsequently received the reference from Captain Witham and a cheque from Brocklebanks. The princely sum of £8 was a war bonus, and with my wages as apprentice and AB I now had approximately £25. I was a rich man.

The Anchor Line finally returned my indentures, with a fine endorsement three weeks after signing off, by which time I was at Captain Tait's Academy.

Chapter 6

Captain Tait's Nautical Academy

I decided to give myself a few days holiday before starting at Tait's Academy. There was hardly anyone around of my own age, only the few who had not been accepted for the services owing to failure in the medical examination.

After my holiday I settled in to study for the second mate's examination, but soon discovered I had almost nothing to learn. I went through all the navigation papers, and the chartwork. Captain Tait gave me a test in seamanship and rule of the road, also signalling, and told me there was no point in remaining at school – I was ready now. I was to take my papers in to the examiner at the examination rooms, and enter for the following week. I had been exactly 10 days at school.

While there I became acquainted with a young man by the name of Thomas Templeton, who came from Gatehouse-of-Fleet in Kirkcudbrightshire. We travelled in the same train each morning and evening. He was staying with an aunt who lived in Uddingston and it turned out that my mother knew his aunt, she knew everyone. After passing for second mate he had joined a Glasgow Firm, Andrew Crawford, Barr & Co., as third mate in the *Galavale* and was to join another of their ships, the *Gryfevale,* as second mate. He was sitting the first mate's examination a week or two later.

I had told him I was not going back into the Anchor Line or Brocklebanks as I wanted to get into *tramps* until I obtained my master's certificate, to see something of the world and gain experience. He suggested I apply to the firm he was in as a third mate was required for the ship he was to join. Anyway, if I got through I intended to look around for a bit before applying to any firm.

We assembled in the passageway underneath the examination rooms well before 9 a.m. on the Monday morning. There was a large number of second mates, a smaller number of first mates and a few masters. The fee for second mate was £1. Everyone appeared to be in a highly nervous state. As our names were called we went into the examination room and found the desk which had our name on a card.

The first test was spelling for which no marks were given. The examiner, an elderly gentleman, must have had quite a sense of humour. The paragraph he read from the *Glasgow Herald* was a description of a flower show and spelling the names of the different flowers was beyond me and, I learnt later, beyond the others as well. We knew that this test was not a failing subject, but all the second mates were badly shaken.

Then followed a navigation paper. A look down this paper restored my confidence as I knew I could complete it. When we came back from lunch we were given a second navigation paper which didn't bother me either. This marked the end of the first day.

On Tuesday morning, before anything commenced, the examiner read out a list of names and then asked the candidates named to stand up.

'I regret to inform you unfortunate gentlemen that, on the basis of the papers you have handed in, there is no point continuing with the examination, the clerk will hand you your papers as you go out.' The number that walked out surprised me. This procedure was repeated each morning and the number of candidates shrank till only a small number were left on the last day.

On Wednesday morning, with a much depleted number of candidates, everyone was taken separately in oral seamanship (known as the chamber of horrors) and it was a long process. Each person left the room directly afterwards with a blue paper which was either the pass that entitled them to a certificate, or a sentence of further sea time. I was not called that day, my turn came on the Thursday forenoon and included in my examination was the international code of signals. The dangerous part was the rule of the road, as hesitation in this was fatal, and the relative article to the question asked had to be given word-perfect. Thanks to Captain Jutsom's *Rule of the Road Cards* I had no difficulty. The rest of the seamanship was only reading the marks on a hand and deep sea lead, barometer and thermometer, the various tackles and ordinary routine of running a ship. Before I realised it the examiner was shaking hands and wishing me luck, and I was out with a blue paper in my hand, but not quite finished. The clerk handed me a sheet of foolscap with my spelling test attached, and the newspaper with the article in question boxed in pencil. I was told to write it out again and then to destroy the original. Finally I walked out with a paper which entitled me to a certificate stating I was competent to fulfil the duties of a second mate of a foreign going steamship. Back at the school I had to fill in the examination book and stand drinks all round.

Chapter 7

The first taste of war

After the examination results were published I received a number of letters from shipping firms; ship's officers were a scarce commodity in those days. Most of them were from firms trading abroad on the Indian and Chinese coasts and some from oil tanker firms, but I had no desire to join any of these. Then Tom Templeton got hold of me. He was to join the *Gryfevale* in two weeks' time and had been asked by his company if any of the second mates who had passed could be persuaded to take the third mate's berth. He mentioned my name and was asked to contact me.

The *Gryfevale* was on charter to Norton Lilly of New York, who ran the American Australian Line, trading between the USA, Australia and New Zealand. I wanted to get on the Australian run and it would be better for me, sailing with someone I knew, when making a start as a ship's officer. I called on Messrs. Andrew Crawford, Barr & Co., at 53 Bothwell Street, Glasgow and was sent in to Mr Crawford himself. He asked me why I didn't return to the Anchor-Brocklebank Line. I told him I didn't care for the Indian trade and wanted to move around and gain experience until I had my master's certificate. He offered me the third mate's berth at £12 10s per month, the 10s being for checking and looking after the steward's stores. The chief steward, being Chinese, could not read or write English. This firm paid the officers and engineers overtime at the rate if 1s 6d per hour – the first time I had ever heard the word. I accepted the berth and was told I was on pay as from then. Mr Crombie, the manager, would let me know when to travel to join the ship in Cardiff, where she was lying outside the Mount Stuart dry dock.

Several days later I received a telegram to proceed to Cardiff the following morning, calling at the office before catching the train. I now had more luggage than ever as I had to bring bed linen, blankets and towels. Templeton had told me I could buy a mattress and pillows in Cardiff. The train left Glasgow at 10 a.m. and was the longest train journey I have ever made in the UK. It was late the following afternoon before I arrived in Cardiff. Every hour or two we were shunted into a siding to give priority to troop trains going south. The commencement of the Somme offensive was, I suppose, the reason for the heavy troop movements.

By 2 a.m. the following morning we had only reached Crewe and had to wait for hours for the next connection. There was no restaurant car and the tearoom only opened when a troop train arrived. Then the rush of soldiers to get cups of tea made it nearly impossible to get anything. I had to make several more changes before arriving in Cardiff and, apart from having had no sleep, was absolutely starving on arrival. I managed to get a meal of some kind in the town before getting a station taxi to take me down to the Mount Stuart dry dock.

The *Gryfevale* was a drab looking vessel lying on the mud outside one of the docks. I don't know what I had expected but I got a considerable shock at my first sight of the ship. Her stem was, at that state of the tide, 20 feet from the quay and the only means of getting onboard was by a long ladder up to the forecastle head. How, I wondered, was I going to get my trunk and seabag up that ladder. I walked round and finally found the night watchman. The mate was not on board and would not be back till late. His advice was to get into the pub near the dock gate for the night. That seemed the only thing to be done, so I thanked him and went ashore. The gateman agreed to store my gear in his office for the night, so I went over to the pub and got a room and some sandwiches. I was up early next day and down to the ship before 7.30a.m. I found the mate, Mr Jakes, and reported to him, handing over the letter I had received from the office.

'So you are the new third mate,' he said. 'Just got your ticket, what type of ship have you been used to?' I said I had served my apprenticeship in the Anchor-Brocklebank Line.

'So', he said, 'you are a coolie ship man, you'll find things a lot different here. You can't boss a white crew like you can coolies.' He obviously thought I would be a bridge ornament and no use around the decks.

'Well', he said, 'here is the key to your room.' I found some riggers willing to collect my bags from the gatehouse, at a price, this business of joining the ship was turning out to be expensive. After I had put my gear in my room and changed into uniform I found Mr Jakes again and enquired what he wanted me to do.

'There is nothing to do at present,' he said, 'the ship's under survey and waiting to go into dry dock, just look around and get to know the ship.' Later he told me he had been in the *Galavale*, the ship in which Tom Templeton had been third mate, and had been promoted to this one. He had joined the ship in Cardiff and had only been on board a few hours when the previous mate, Daniel Clayton, went home on leave. He would be rejoining the ship as master. This was interesting as it appeared everyone on the deck side had got a step up and would be new to their various duties. All the engineers with the exception of the chief, who had been in the ship since she was built, were making their first voyage in her.

When I took over the third mate's room I found a perfectly good hair mattress in

S.S. Gryfevale

the bunk. As a mattress was always encased in a washable cover and a sheet, a change of ownership did not matter, but I had to obtain a couple of pillows. My £25 had lasted very well but I was now about broke. I asked Mr Jakes about harbour wages and my expenses. He said he was making up the harbour wages on Saturday, and as this was now Wednesday, I had two more days to get through. The expenses would have to wait until Captain Clayton came back from leave.

The food came as a shock to me. Afterwards I knew by experience it was just the usual fare served on all British ships of the tramp class. The saying *The Lord sends the food and the devil sends the cooks* about sums it up; you could tell what day of the week it was by what arrived on the table. The baking of bread was the acid test of a cook's ability, very few of them could make a good loaf of bread.

On the Friday afternoon the ship was moved into one of the dry docks. After being used to a dozen or more Lascars, carpenter and quartermaster on the forecastle head for mooring and shifting ship, it was a revelation to me that only three men could do everything necessary by themselves with no orders given. Each man could see what had to be done and they just went ahead and did it.

On the Monday morning the voyage stores began to arrive, and the rest of the crew. The repairs were completed and we moved out of the dry dock into the Queen Alexandra Dock, to fill up with bunker coals for the passage to New York. No gun mounting had been fitted aft. It was now July 1916, but this ship was going out again as if no such things as submarines existed.

The crew were signed on in the shipping office; eight deckhands, six ABs and two ordinary seamen, bosun and carpenter. Some one said the ship was well manned, but I was used to 32 on deck, not counting quartermasters, and it seemed impossible this small group of men could watchkeep, steer and work on deck. But they could, as I found out. There were no quartermasters. I didn't realise that the four apprentices were reckoned as part of the deckhands and worked with them. Including the apprentices and the master, 41 crew, the *Bengali* crew totalled 96!

Being used to double watches in the Channel and around the coast I was expecting the same on this ship.

'We do not keep double watches in these ships,' said Mr Jakes, 'each officer is supposed to be capable of keeping his own watch at all times, it's only the liners that get Channel jitters.' When I came up to relieve Mr Jakes at 8 p.m. Captain Clayton was on the bridge. When the mate had gone down he said, 'This will be your first time in charge of a watch, have you any experience of bridge work?' I told him what I had done during my apprenticeship. 'Well you will be all right,' he said. 'The way you were trained is a darned sight better than boys get in these ships. We have to use them as deckhands so have no chance to give them bridge training.' It was fine weather with the sea like a millpond. The ship was blacked out with no navigation lights, boats swung out, but otherwise there was no sense of a war being on. Once passed Lundy Island we were clear of the land. 'Just carry on,' he said. 'You are in charge of the watch, but I will stay here till we are clear of coastal traffic.'

The fine weather continued and the following night the captain was not on the bridge. For the first time I was on my own in charge of the ship's bridge. There was nothing about but for a while I imagined I saw dark shapes everywhere. One night five days out I saw what I took to be a bank of cloud rising up ahead. As I could still see, as I thought, the horizon, I took this to be a change of weather. Suddenly, close to on the starboard bow, the fore part of a sailing ship appeared, she had all sail set but was motionless, not a light to be seen.

'Sailing ship close on the starboard bow.' yelled the lookout. There was no danger of collision, the ships were parallel to each other and about a quarter of a mile apart. I stood gazing at her and by the time she was just abaft the beam she disappeared and we were immersed in dense fog. I had just got to the speaking tube to call the captain when he came up on to the bridge having heard the lookout's shout, and I told him what had happened.

'Good God,' he said, 'that was a near thing, didn't you see the fog bank coming?'

'I thought,' I replied, 'it was a bank of cloud as I could see what I took to be the horizon underneath, it must have been the bottom of the bank reflecting the moonlight.'

'That is how fog usually comes in the North Atlantic,' was all he said, 'you will learn by experience.' From then on the fog was intermittent until we got on the

Newfoundland Banks, where it became continuous. Every now and then I had to blow three long blasts on the whistle, then listen. The theory was that if an iceberg was close the echo would come back. I also had to watch air and sea temperature for a sudden drop, this was another indication of the proximity of a berg. Approaching New York the fog lifted just as we arrived off Staten Island to await a loading berth.

Altogether we were a month in New York, 11 days were spent at anchor off Staten Island. At 2 a.m. one day the ship shook so violently everyone turned out on deck in the belief we had been rammed by another ship. Tom Templeton, who was on anchor watch, said there had been a tremendous explosion on the west side just above Staten Island. He had taken a bearing and found it was Black Tom Island. Another series of explosions broke out followed by what appeared to be a fireworks display which settled down into a raging fire. The ammunition and explosives depot had blown up and what we thought was a fireworks display had been shells and bullets flying round.

From Staten Island we moved to the Bush Terminal at Brooklyn to complete loading. I made one visit to Manhattan Island to look at Broadway and up town theatre district, but was not impressed; it was just streets and hurrying crowds.

We loaded for four ports Wellington and Auckland in New Zealand, and Melbourne and Adelaide in Australia. Apart from case oil the cargo was general. I had never made up a cargo plan for a general cargo, so to keep track of what cargo and separations were going into the forward holds I made up a plan in the same way I had been taught to do on the *Bengali*, giving each port its own colour. Mr Jakes saw me filling these in and asked to have a look.

'Who taught you to do that?' he asked.

I explained and said, 'I must have been taught something in a coolie ship after all.' He made no reply but later I found myself making up cargo plans for the whole ship, and it was my job from then on.

The run down to the Panama Canal was interesting, but from there to Wellington was the longest passage I had yet made and it seemed endless. During the passage from Panama Tom Templeton and myself were engaged, while on watch during the day, in making a tarpaulin hatch cover. I had heard that on tramps the mates had to work like deckhands and did not quite believe it, but here it was and in wartime too. This was another shock for Mr Jakes – the coolie ship third mate could sew canvas, and by the way he went about it seemed he had more experience than any of them! I told him I had been taught by a sailmaker and could do anything in canvas, and that was not a boast, but a fact. His dislike of me grew, so far he had not found anything I was unable to do, and this was not at all in line with his ideas about liner ship apprentices. He watched me like a hawk in the hope of catching me out.

We had a short stay in New Zealand before crossing to Australia. The Tasman

Sea is famous for bad weather and being winter we caught, about half way across, what was called a southerly buster. This was dead on the beam, and only lasted for a few hours, but that was some experience. The bulk of the cargo was now in the lower holds and the ship, in light condition with sea on the beam, was rolling rail to rail. Most of the time that gale lasted we spent in the 'tween decks chasing cargo around which was supposed to have been properly secured. In No.1 'tween deck barrels of crude oil had broken adrift and were charging from one side to the other, colliding and smashing themselves and also cases of other goods, among which were cased plate glass windows. Eventually we got them secured by standing them upright and herding together what was left of them, but the 'tween deck was inches deep in oil and quite a quantity of cargo was damaged. After that dust up we had fine weather to Melbourne and in due course berthed somewhere in the river along Melbourne Wharf.

There was a not great deal of cargo to be discharged here but as everything occurred in fits and starts we were there for a week. Sometimes after the dinner break the wharfies didn't come back at all and the crew had to close the hatches down. I asked Templeton, as he had been trading out here all his apprenticeship, what was the matter.

'You are in Australia now,' he said. 'The Aussies don't like work and will knock off at the slightest pretext, we'll be lucky if we get discharged at all.'

We arrived in the Roads off Port Adelaide one day around noon. Sometime earlier, as we steamed along the coast, I suddenly saw abeam a number of houses and what appeared to be the entrance to a river with a buoyed channel leading to it. This I thought must be Port Adelaide, but we were not due off the entrance for another couple of hours. I called Captain Clayton, he came up and stared in bewilderment.

'I don't understand this,' he said, 'the last set of cross bearings put us still 20 miles to go to the Roads.' He rang STAND BY on the engines. Then we saw houses, river entrance and buoys slowly fade away. 'I have never seen a mirage like that before.' he said. It was the first one I had ever seen, I have seen plenty since then but never one as real. When we did arrive the scene was exactly as depicted.

Port Adelaide was a small place some two or three miles up a river, the city of Adelaide being about six miles inland. It was situated on the northern bank and consisted then of only a few berths along a wooden wharf, and some sheds. This was the last discharging port but we loaded a cargo of bagged wheat for Naples. Ships were scarce now and it appeared the Australian Wheat Board had taken over the ship from the American-Australian Line, as a cargo of food was more vital than the luxury stuff we had brought out. There was so much wheat on hand, and not enough ships to take it away, that all the way up to Port Adelaide, and to Adelaide itself, were large stocks of bagged wheat alongside the railway lines just rotting away. The rats were having a glorious time. The bags we loaded were so rotten that it was more like a cargo of bulk wheat than a bagged one.

I had been given the address of a family who had emigrated to Australia and were now living in Adelaide, a Mr and Mrs Grey. Mr Grey was something on the railways. Shortly after arriving I wrote a note to him asking if I could call. I didn't receive any reply but one day a gentleman came on board inquiring for Mr Donald. This turned out to be Will Grey, the son, who was at that time at school in Port Adelaide preparing to sit the examination for master. He took me home to Adelaide with him that evening. Mrs Grey insisted I should come up every evening when I was off duty, but I couldn't afford to do that as the train fare would be too expensive. I did go several times and also spent a couple of Sundays with them, but as Will was studying I did not want to distract him. Mrs Grey gave me a lecture about going around with the girls in Port Adelaide, they were a bad lot she said, and one would be quite likely to pick up some disease. The weekend I did not go up she cross-questioned me closely as to my doings, much to the amusement of Will.

'Mother is very concerned about our morals,' he said, 'I get this regularly.'

We only saw Captain Clayton and the chief engineer at intervals during our stay in port; it seemed they were well known here. The place swarmed with women and girls and it was not long before everyone except me had a girl friend. I was under the eye of Mrs Grey.

When we had completed loading, and the vessel was due to leave, all but six of the ABs were missing. Also the carpenter had gone – bag and baggage. Captain Clayton now had to obtain replacements. Finally, some time during the afternoon, he returned with an odd assortment. All he could find were an old Italian fisherman who wanted to return to Italy, a young Japanese who had stowed away on a ship from Japan, and a couple of ABs who had deserted and wanted to go home, but no carpenter.

Where the liquor came from I don't know, but in the case of the mate and Tom I suspect it was supplied by the stevedore as a farewell present. By that time the bosun could only get around by holding on to something. I was fully occupied checking the steward's stores and battling with customs over what had been used in port. The chief engineer had been giving a farewell party to his friends with an exhibition of Highland dancing on the after deck. It was a miracle the engines were got ready for sea as the second, third and fourth engineers spent most of the day in the pub. I knew the catering department were sober as I had to check them over with immigration. Of the rest, by the time we got under way, only myself and the apprentices were sober. Captain Clayton had been saying 'goodbye' to his friends while ashore getting replacements. He seemed all right when he came on board but, by the time the stevedore, agent and ship chandler had gone ashore, he had more than he could carry. This was apparent when he came on the bridge.

Getting a ship away with drunken deckhands and firemen was no uncommon occurrence in British ships, but this was the one and only time I have seen a ship leave with master, mates and engineers so drunk they did not know what they were doing. I had said 'goodbye' to the Greys the previous evening and was glad Will was not on the wharf to see us leave. With the four apprentices I got the gangway in and then went on the bridge. The unmooring and making the tug fast was, the pilot said, the most disgraceful performance he had ever seen. Mr Jakes was hanging on to the jackstaff shouting orders to which no one paid any heed. The moorings were got in, that's all that can be said, nothing was even coiled down. What went on aft I don't know but they unmoored somehow. Captain Clayton had come on the bridge and was holding tight to the forward rail, saying nothing. We moved off and, clear of the berth, let go tugs and proceeded. The engine movements were being carried out as usual and an apprentice was at the wheel. When the tugs had gone, Mr Jakes came off the forecastle head – I don't think he touched a rung of the ladder on the way down. He progressed along the deck with a series of staggering runs and then crawled on hands and knees. He did not come on the bridge. About half way down to the Roads Captain Clayton let go of the rail and, smiling like a cherub, staggered slowly backwards, watched in amazement by the pilot and myself. He arrived at the top of the starboard bridge ladder and, before I could reach him, suddenly sat down on the edge of the deck. There was so much of him over the edge that he slid backwards, maintaining a sitting position, down the ladder and landed like a rag doll on the deck, holding on to the ladder, still smiling.

'For God's sake get him to his room,' said the pilot, 'he's no use up here.' I went down and pulled him to his feet. He came as quietly as a child, and I got him into his room and on to the settee, then went back on the bridge.

'I can only turn this ship over to a master's certificate if she is going to sea,' said the pilot. 'Ask the mate to come up here. Oh God no, was that the mate crawling along the deck; what ticket has the second mate?'

I told him, 'First mate, but he is out on his feet.'

'In that case I must anchor this ship before I leave, what happens after that is not my responsibility. I will leave her anchored in a safe berth, go forward and stand by to let go the anchor.' I had no alternative but to do as he told me. So in due course we anchored in the Roads and the pilot boat took the pilot away.

'What are you going to say when you get ashore?' I asked him before he got into the boat.

'I will report "anchored through engine trouble", but for Christ's sake get the captain or mate sobered up and get out of here before daylight or somebody will be here to find out what's wrong.'

I got hold of Haslam, the senior apprentice, and told him to collect the other boys and anyone else capable, and get the moorings down fore and aft ready for going to sea. I had a look round. Captain Clayton was out cold. Mr Jakes had made it to his settee but no amount of shouting or cold water would bring him round.

Tom Templeton had not reached his settee – he was stretched out on the floor. Next to the engineers' quarters. What the chief was like I don't know, he had locked himself in his room. The third and fourth were flaked out on their settees and the second was not in his room, he was in the engine-room dead to the world. An old Chinaman was there, smiling like a Buddha.

'Who makee engines walk?' I asked him. He pointed to himself.

'You savee engines?' I asked.

'Me plenty savee, me engineer one time China.'

'All right we go, you makee engines walk, one hour I ring telegraph'.

Well, I thought, he brought the ship out so he must know what he is doing, and I have to take the chance. I went back on deck. When the moorings were all down I told Haslam and the other apprentices to have their tea. 'Then,' I said, 'we will go. No one will be sober till morning and if we are still here there will be trouble, and perhaps certificates involved.'

At 7 p.m. it was quite dark. I put the four apprentices two on each watch. I would have to keep the bridge all night, or until someone could relieve me. The anchorage was open and only one alteration of course to be made during the night. I rang STAND BY and was answered from below, so that seemed all right. I had sent Haslam forward to heave up, and when the anchor was aweigh, we turned on to the first course. Everything went smoothly and the weather was fine. I wondered what would happen when the captain and Mr Jakes came to. I had made up my mind to say nothing at all and cautioned the apprentices to keep their mouths shut. I hadn't logged the anchoring, although we had been anchored for one and a half hours. I logged half an hour waiting for pilot boat and a speed adjustment took care of the rest of the time.

Just before 8 a.m. Mr Jakes staggered on to the bridge, he was a wild looking sight. He opened his mouth to say something but with a violent effort restrained himself. The course is on the board, I told him.

'Alright,' he said, 'go and get your breakfast.' I went below.

Tom Templeton had just come to but I didn't say anything to him. I had my breakfast, a wash, and went back on the bridge to take my watch. It appeared Mr Jakes had just made it ahead of Captain Clayton by a few minutes. As it turned out none of them said anything at all to each other about how the vessel came to be at sea. Each one knew he had nothing to do with it, but did not know just what part, if any, the others had. What they thought they kept to themselves and carried on as normal. The departure from Adelaide was never mentioned. Later the fourth engineer asked me to give him the times of engine movements when leaving as he had been too busy to note them down himself. One good thing did come out of this for me, I had no more trouble from Mr Jakes for the rest of the voyage, his attitude towards me had completely changed.

Being late spring in the southern hemisphere we had fine weather across the Australian Bight to Colombo where we called for bunker coals. When I looked round the harbour there was the *Bengali*. I went over to pay her a visit and it was like going back into another world. It was hard to believe that until May of that same year I was still part of that ship's company. They were all pleased to see me, and I spent a very pleasant couple of hours on board. There was a new addition to the crew, a wireless operator. The wireless office and operator's room combined had been built on the after end of the boat deck and they were astonished to hear we had neither gun nor wireless. I never saw the *Bengali* again. I later heard that she had been torpedoed off Cape Bon in the Mediterranean. She must have been carrying a cargo of jute because according to the story, she had three torpedoes in her, the last in the engine-room, and still floated. While being towed towards Alexandria she was torpedoed again, and yet remained afloat. Off the entrance to Alexandria Harbour she got the fifth one and that finished her. The poor old ship just turned over and sank.

We had a quiet passage to the Suez Canal and arrived safely in Naples. I had the watch approaching the Messina Strait and had a good view of Mount Etna which was active at that time. The red glow over the crater was plainly visible at night and it was a fine sight.

We laid in Naples for some time, discharge was very slow. Mount Vesuvius was erupting and night was like day. From there we were ordered to Segunto, a Spanish iron-ore port, 11 miles north of Valencia, to load for Glasgow. Ore was now top priority. We had to lay at anchor for a few days but when under the shute the loading was fast. About 1000 tons went in to the deep tank, which surprised me. It was easy enough to fill but getting the ore out with buckets or grabs would be a long job. It was a scheme, as I found out later, to keep the vessel as long as possible in Glasgow, and it certainly worked.

We were still on our own and seemed to be following the same courses as we would in peace time. There was heavy weather all the way and the cargo of iron ore caused a sickening pitching and rolling, but at least any submarines would be too busy looking out for themselves to bother with other ships. It eased off when we got under the lee of the Irish coast and turned bitterly cold.

I was in two minds whether to remain with the ship or not, I didn't care to be shipmates with Mr Jakes again. Tom Templeton, however, advised me never to make only one voyage in a ship, it didn't look well in a discharge book; always make two, otherwise it might give the impression you had been sacked. So I decided to stay another voyage, after which I would have enough time at sea to attempt the first mate's certificate.

We then moved into the dry dock at Elderslee, Clydebank. I wondered why as it was only some eight months since she had been in dock in Cardiff. Apparently the ship had been taken over by the Admiralty as a fleet store ship or, as it was called a

Merchant Fleet Auxiliary. Naturally they wanted to survey the ship and sight the bottom, hence the need for the dry dock. While there a gun mounting was installed aft for a 4.72-inch gun, a magazine built in the poop and a wireless office and operator's berth constructed on the after end of the boat deck. Mr Jakes left to join the second new ship which Captain Clayton was taking over, and I must admit I was glad to see him go.

Mr Simpson, the chief engineer, remained with the ship, with Tom Templeton as second mate and myself as third mate. One afternoon, while we were still in dry dock, an odd looking character came on board. He was short, and nearly as broad as he was long, with arms that appeared to reach his knees. He could have been anything from 25 to 45.

'Are you the third mate?' he asked.

I told him I was and asked 'Who are you?' By his accent I knew he was a Glasgow man.

'I have been offered the mate's job on this ship and have come to look her over. Where are you from?' he asked.

'Uddingston,' I replied.

'That dump is where all the sheenies live, I am from Rutherglen.' he said proudly. I was not going to let him get away with that.

'I thought by your appearance you came from there.' Sheenie was the Glasgow name for a Jew boy. I had heard Uddingston called many things but never before referred to as a ghetto.

'Well anyway Uddingston is only three miles from Rutherglen so you're near enough,' he said. I couldn't make out what he meant by that but came to the conclusion the remark was only meant as an insult.

'Who shall I say called?' He looked at me.

'Mr Angus McNeil,' he said, and walked down the gangway. He joined the ship when we came out of dry dock.

The last to arrive was Captain Hunter. Of all the unusual people with whom I have been shipmates Adam Hunter was in a class by himself. I knew only that he was a Shetland Islander and one of six or seven brothers, all in command in various companies. He was always referred to as Captain Adam Hunter, presumably to distinguish himself from the other Captain Hunters, his brothers.

Our orders were to sign the bridge deck personnel on voyage articles before leaving for Cardiff, and the remainder of the crew on coasting articles for the passage to Cardiff. The signing on took place on board, in the saloon, on 10th April 1917. Seated at the table were a RNR officer and a lieutenant in addition to the shipping clerk. Being young and inexperienced I naturally considered I knew all the answers. When I signed the articles and copy, the lieutenant pushed across to me what looked like another copy.

'You are required to sign this as well,' he said. I did notice this one appeared to be printed in red. Before I signed he said 'Are you satisfied you know what you are signing.' Believing this was only another copy, I did not wish to appear ignorant.

'Certainly,' I said and signed the red copy, which was not a copy at all but a contract of service with the Merchant Fleet Auxiliaries for the duration of hostilities. If I had examined the document I would have seen that, but I only found this out at a later date. I was rated as a sub-lieutenant, the mate a lieutenant-commander and the captain a commander.

Apparently white deckhands were not to be found in Cardiff so we finished up with Malays on deck and a Malay bosun. The firemen were, as usual, Chinese, but not like the last lot, I didn't like the look of these at all. The catering staff, also Chinese, were not impressive either. It seemed all the best men were away now and only the dregs left. Two gunners joined and were berthed in one of the spare rooms.

No one had the slightest idea where we were going. Captain Hunter had received sealed orders but it was the general belief, as we had loaded a cargo of coals, that we were going to coal naval ships. This time we had an escort for a couple of days, some kind of an armed trawler I think.

Our gun crew was made up of the two gunners, four apprentices, myself and the fourth engineer. Tom Templeton was appointed as gunnery officer, because of his seniority not because of what he knew. I was considered a veteran gunner and appointed as spotting officer and my station in any action was to be the main cross trees. I was also assistant gunnery officer.

We had been presented with a book of zigzag courses. When on our own, we had to carry them out until we were clear of the submarine area which now extended well past Gibraltar. Captain Hunter opened his orders when the escort left and we proceeded to Dakar, a French port in West Africa, to replenish bunker coals. After leaving there another sealed envelope had to be opened. The escort left us during my watch and I asked Captain Hunter what number zigzag I should put her on after the new course was set.

'Don't carry out any set zigzag.' he said. 'Never mind that book, just zigzag, and if you don't know what you are doing, how is any submarine commander going to find out.'

I consider that was the best common-sense advice I have ever heard. I kept it in mind and used it many times during the Second World War. He considered every German submarine commander would have the Allied Signal Manual in front of him, and know exactly what a British ship was instructed to do if attacked. If there were enemy submarines around we didn't see them and in due course arrived in Dakar. Our stay lasted only a few hours. The heat, after being used to the cold in the UK, was unbearable and it was a relief to get out to sea again.

When Captain Hunter opened his second envelope the orders were to proceed to

Cape Town – apparently nothing more. We arrived one morning in Table Bay and anchored. Eventually a launch came out and took Captain Hunter ashore. During the afternoon he returned, but it seemed nobody knew anything about us.

'As you are a naval store ship you had better proceed to Simonstown, that's a naval base,' he was told.

So round to Simonstown we went that night and arrived off the port around daylight. After waiting awhile a launch came off to enquire what we wanted. Not knowing what else to do with us, the young sub-lieutenant in charge said, 'Follow me, and anchor when I give the signal.' He led us close in near the end of the breakwater, signalled us to anchor, then came alongside and took Captain Hunter ashore. Less than an hour later another launch tore out and up the ladder came a four-ringed captain in a towering rage.

'Where is the master of this vessel?' he demanded when I received him on board.

'Captain Hunter has gone ashore.' I informed him.

'I am Captain Evans in charge of Base. Who authorised this vessel to anchor here in the harbour entrance?' I explained that a sub-lieutenant in a launch had showed us where to anchor. 'I will put you in an anchorage,' he said and stalked up to the bridge. That was the fastest shifting of anchorage I have ever seen. As soon as the anchor was off the bottom it was FULL AHEAD then STOP then FULL ASTERN and let go again. Then he was back in his launch and away. Shortly after, Captain Hunter returned.

'We now have to proceed to Durban, we are not wanted here. I informed Control I hadn't enough coal to reach Durban and was told to burn cargo until we arrived there.' So to Durban we proceeded. In the Royal Navy, we now understood, you do not *go* anywhere you *proceed*.

At Durban Roads we were told by the signal station to anchor and await orders, so we lay for several days rolling about at anchor. Finally a pilot came out to us and we proceeded inside. This naval control didn't know what to do with us either. Durban, being a coal loading port could, and did, supply all the coal the navy in that part of the world required. Then one day we came to life, at last someone had decided what to do with us, we were to go up to German East Africa*.

First we were moved over to one of the coaling berths at the Bluff and filled up with bunker coals. All bunker spaces were filled including the bridge space which until now had been empty. A pyramid of coal was heaped up over the saddle hatch and engine-room skylight, which had to be closed, and also on deck both sides of the fiddley casing, blocking access to the donkey boiler which had to be allowed to go out. It was now practically impossible to get fore or aft on the ship. All protests by the chief engineer and mate were brushed aside. When the bunkering was finished

---

* now Tanzania.

we were already overloaded. Then we were moved to a berth at the general cargo wharf. The coal in Nos.1 and 5 holds was now trimmed down into the lower holds and flattened out, the space this created was filled with cases of army stores and army boots. Then somebody discovered that the poop was empty. This was packed with cases of rifles and small arms ammunition. All this would not have been too bad, as it did not add a great deal to the overload. The problem was that control also found out that the deep tank was empty. Fresh water was scarce in East Africa and any ship bound there with an empty deep tank, capable of holding some 500 tons of fresh water could not be let pass – the tank must be filled. A pump and hoses were installed on deck for transferring the water to vessels requiring it. There was nothing Captain Hunter or Mr McNeil could say, the vessel was a fleet auxiliary and had to do as she was ordered. Gangs with scrubbing brushes, ladders and mops were sent down and the tank thoroughly cleaned out, then cement washed. While this was being done a fleet of small trucks was brought down on to the wharf, for stowing on deck.

It could not be discerned just how much the loadline was submerged when the deep tank had been filled and the trucks were on deck. Even the uppermost draft figures were covered and from the wharf she looked like a plank laid in the water. Captain Hunter had gone up to control when the loading was finished and demanded a surveyor to inspect the ship for seaworthiness. This was refused. He then refused to take the ship to sea on the grounds that she was dangerously overloaded.

With the pilot on board and tugs made fast, we awaited Captain Hunter's return. We were treated to the sight of him being escorted back to the ship between a file of marines. An RNVR officer appeared and ordered the crew to be mustered. Then he checked us over from a copy of the crew list. That done the pilot was ordered to take the ship out. Captain Hunter had the boats swung out and ordered all hands to wear their lifebelts.

Moving that ship was like trying to push a log; the engines seemed to be going for some time before the ship began to move and answer her helm. The pilot kept the tugs on until we were out in the Roads.

When he left he said 'Good luck and safe passage, and I mean that.' The pilot boat lingered outside for some time as we steamed slowly away, perhaps they were expecting us to sink at any moment.

Fortunately we had calm seas and light winds on the passage. I was convinced, and so was everyone else, that if we ran into any weather and began to ship water, she would sink like a stone. We crept, it was the only word to describe it, up the coast to German East Africa. We couldn't get more than six and a half knots on the normal consumption of coal and we were not authorised to burn any more. We had not been given any destination, just to proceed and await orders by wireless. To add to our troubles a German raider had been reported in the area so a strict blackout was observed.

A wireless message came through and, when decoded, it read 'proceed to Kilwa Kisiwani'. No further information was offered. Then there was confusion – Kilwa Kisiwani couldn't be found as we had only a small-scale general chart of the coast. Our large-scale charts were only for British East African ports. Directions only mentioned it in passing as a deep-water inlet and gave no detailed information. Speed was adjusted to be off the position of the inlet by daylight. When I went up on the bridge at 8 a.m. we were lying a mile or two off an unbroken line of mangroves with no apparent opening anywhere. Suddenly a small trawler appeared on the shoreline and headed in our direction. A bearded character hailed us from the tiny bridge.

'Are you the MFA *Gryfevale?*,' he asked. We agreed that we were at which he replied, 'Follow me then.'

'Where is Kilwa Kisiwani?' the captain asked. The skipper waved his arm in the direction of the line of mangroves.

'Now is a good time to enter, it's half tide and the sand banks are showing, the channel is all deep water.' We followed him and soon saw the entrance. It was very narrow and winding, but inside was a fairly large inlet surrounded with mangroves to seaward and elephant grass landward. Several ships were lying there, most of them hospital ships. The trawler came alongside.

'How did you get like that, you're sinking?' He was told how we got that way. Captain Hunter wanted to know where to report. 'Base Headquarters are over there.' The trawler skipper pointed to a makeshift pier and beyond it a hut with a flagpole flying the Union Jack. 'If you want to go ashore you will have to use your own boat, we have no ferry service here.'

We had to discharge the trucks, but how was not yet apparent. On the second day an old tug, the *Garth*, appeared, towing a square wooden pontoon on which were a number of natives. The skipper of the *Garth* said we had to load the trucks on to this. It could only take three trucks and even with those it swayed dangerously from side to side, leaking like a sieve. Our crew had to do everything. There was nothing to lash the trucks on to, all that kept them from running off were the pieces of wood we put under the wheels. I was sure they would never reach the shore, but they did. That was how they were unloaded, three per day. One morning I was ashore earlier than usual and had a walk around. Parked in the elephant grass were rows of cars and trucks, ours were just being added to the collection.

When the trucks were off the ship we had orders to go to Dar-Es-Salaam to discharge the army stores, then Zanzibar. This was the naval base for the whole area and for six weeks we became merely colliers. I found myself in charge of the fresh water tank. Any ship making a request for water had to hand me a chit, stamped by Base, stating the amount of water they were allowed. I became, I believe, the most unpopular person attached to Zanzibar Base as fresh water was the most precious commodity on that coast. I was referred to by various names, Hydrolus, Pani Wallah or just 'that bastard on the *Gryfevale*'.

The ship's carpenter was a man with an ugly temper. One day in Zanzibar he came on board with a young female baboon he had bought for a pet. He fastened a leather belt round her, spliced a rope on to the belt and tied her to a bulwark stanchion outside his room, and then forgot about her. The only food she got was what the Chinese galley boy fed her. When he remembered, the carpenter would take her into his room at night and give her a beating. I knew the ordinary Indian monkey but this was the first baboon I had ever seen. She must have been full-grown, as she was nearly three feet in height, and had arms like wire ropes. It was, I realised, a very dangerous animal. She was intelligent and soon learned to unpick the eye splice holding the rope to the belt and was off around the ship. Next the carpenter obtained a light chain and small shackle which only lasted till Jinny (the name for a female monkey) learned to unscrew the shackle pin. When the carpenter went ashore he locked the baboon in his room and coming back would thrash the poor thing with a leather belt for making a mess. It was a situation that could not last.

One night I was on duty with Haslam the senior apprentice. Sometime around midnight the carpenter came back in his usual drunken state and, as usual, commenced to thrash the baboon. But this time things were different. The leather belt had been fastened at the back with a buckle and she had found she could work the belt round until the buckle was in a position where she could see it. During that evening she had unbuckled the belt and was now free. The only reason she was still in the room was because the door was closed. The carpenter switched on the light and shut the door and in his drunken state did not notice the baboon was loose. He got his leather belt and began to administer the usual thrashing.

I was lying on my settee reading when Haslam came in.

'You had better come to the carpenter's room, sir,' he said. 'Something is going on in there, it sounds as if the place is being wrecked.' When I opened the door the carpenter was on his back with the baboon on top of him and I am certain she was trying to tear his throat out with her teeth. If we had not arrived on the scene she would have succeeded, as he was too drunk to defend himself properly. I remember getting hold of the baboon to pull her away from the carpenter, and then there was a whirling mass of struggling figures trying to keep hold of something that grasped, bit and tore in four places at once – three men and a large baboon battling in a space less than four feet by six. The strength in that animal was unbelievable. Then she got clear and was gone. I had the sleeve of my jacket half-torn off and lost some of the buttons. Haslam's jacket was ripped up the back, and the carpenter's suit was in ribbons. He was now cold sober and shaking with fright, but I had no sympathy for him.

'You had that coming to you,' I told him, 'perhaps you will leave that poor animal alone in future.' He did, for the good reason that Jinny was never in captivity again, that night made her the enemy of everyone. She had gone wild and thereafter lived by her wits.

We quite expected to be put on the coal run between Durban and Zanzibar, but were told we were surplus to requirements and were now needed in Mauritius to load a cargo of sugar, in bags, for London. Whether we were still a Fleet Auxiliary no one knew.

It was fine, quiet weather and it gave Mr McNeil a chance to get the ship cleaned up. The speed was down as, having been so long in salt water, we had collected a dense coating of weed and barnacles. The boilers had been heavily worked and were now badly in need of cleaning but the appropriate request had been refused.

All attempts to recapture Jinny were unsuccessful and now she roamed the ship at night and if a door was left open she would go in. Although she was only looking for food, people became scared. So many complaints reached the captain that he had the carpenter up and ordered him to get rid of her in Mauritius. That was easier said than done.

We did not remain long in Mauritius. We had hardly moored up the buoys before the ship was surrounded with sugar lighters. They way they worked was a pleasure to see after what we had been used to in East Africa. The trade wind kept the heat down and made everything fresh and cool. However we were a little longer there than the speed of loading led us to expect. This was because no one worked on Sunday or at nights and the three days following the Sunday were devoted to the annual Mauritius Races which everyone on the island attended. This was eagerly anticipated all the year and on these days any work, beyond the essential, was unheard of.

On arrival Captain Hunter was asked if he would take four jockeys as passengers to Durban. As we were still, as far as we knew, a naval auxiliary, he had to obtain permission from the naval authorities, of which there were none in Mauritius. The ship's agents were agreeable, indeed anxious, to get them on this ship as it was the only one calling in South Africa. On the Sunday the four jockeys came on board with the bulk of their luggage and stayed to lunch. They boasted that, as they were riding all the horses, they would decide who was going to win or lose and they proceeded to fix each race there and then. Afterwards we were given a list of the winners for each race, but warned not to bet heavily, and lose small amounts occasionally.

The next day was Monday and the first day of the races. The whole harbour was quiet, no work was done anywhere and Captain Hunter had given all hands the day off. The racecourse was practically in the town so it was easy to reach. By noon everyone – mates, engineers, apprentices and those of the crew interested in horse racing – were dressed and ready. After dinner off they went clutching their money and list of winners, intent on making their fortune. Being third mate I had to remain on board to look after the ship, but some time later Captain Hunter came on the lower bridge and called me up.

'I am remaining on board so there is no need for you to be here, go any try your luck at the races.' He handed me a 10 rupee note and said 'put that on for me.' I thanked him and lost no time in getting ashore. As luck would have it the horses given to us as winners seemed to have been picked by the majority of the racing crowd and, in consequence, the odds were short. Though we made quite a bit of money it was nothing like we had expected. I managed to make 25 rupees for Captain Hunter, plus his ten back. When I told the others he had given me money to put on a horse for him, no one would believe such a thing was possible. He was quite surprised when I handed him his 10 rupees back plus 25 more.

The cargo of sugar was loaded, the jockeys installed, and we were on our way to Cape Town. We arrived at Table Bay early one morning and boarded the pilot. It was warm and the pilot and Captain Hunter were clad in white suits. We were proceeding down the outer harbour at half speed when suddenly Jinny, the baboon, appeared on the awning spar above the pilot. She must have been in the bunkers as she was coal black. She dropped on to the pilot's shoulders and grasped him round the neck – perhaps it was the white suit that attracted her. Captain Hunter went to the pilot's assistance in the wing of the bridge. There was no room for a third person so I stayed where I was at the engine-room telegraph. Shouting and cursing accompanied the struggle and they were oblivious to anything but getting the baboon away from the pilot. Suddenly there was a shout from the forecastle head.

'FULL ASTERN for God's sake or we will be in the quay wall.' This was followed by the roar of both anchors being let go. No heed was paid by the battling figures in the bridge wing, so I gave a double ring astern on the telegraph. We managed, with braking hard on the anchor cables to bring up, and according to Mr McNeil our stem was only a few feet from the quay wall. Perhaps it was the sudden noise of the anchors being dropped, or simply that she had had enough, but Jinny disentangled herself and vanished as suddenly as she had come. The pilot was in a state of hysteria and it was some time before he recovered sufficiently to take control of the ship again. Both he and the captain were covered with coal dust and filth, the pilot's shoulder straps had been torn loose and his jacket was in ribbons, his cap had fallen on the deck and been trodden into a shapeless mass, and his face had been scratched. Captain Hunter was in better shape, his clothes were not torn, but he too looked as if he had been rolled on a coal heap. The pilot was besides himself.

'What kind of a ship is this when a wild animal can run loose. I will report that I was attacked while docking the ship and that there could have been a bad accident.' And so he kept on. I could sympathise with him as I too had been in a struggle with Jinny and knew what it was like. We eventually got into the berth and moored up. The last I saw of the pilot he was standing on the quayside shaking his fist at the ship and crying, 'God damn that ship, I hope she gets sunk.'

After the Cape Town incident Captain Hunter gave orders for the baboon to be destroyed, she was now too dangerous to be roaming loose around the ship. Among the armaments which came on board at Cape Town were six rifles of the old

Martini Henry type. These, we were informed, were for sinking mines. One of these loaded rifles was now placed on the bridge, the orders being that if a clear view could be obtained, Jinny was to be shot. Somehow that animal realised what was in store for her and before the rifle could be lifted to the shoulder she had vanished out of sight. She was still free and unharmed when we arrived in Dakar.

We were only one day coaling; we arrived in the early morning and sailed that night. To be included in the convoy leaving Dakar, we had to sustain a speed of nine knots. We could only guarantee, with safety, seven and so were ordered to Gibraltar to join the seven-knot convoy.

We were now in Spanish territory some 360 miles from Dakar on a stretch of coast called the Rio del Oro, and it was a warm day with a heat haze cutting visibility down to seven miles. As we were in the submarine area a lookout was posted on the forecastle head, after lookout being kept by the gun watch. I was alone on the bridge. At 11.20 a.m., I must have noted the time from habit, I heard the whistle of a shell passing over the bridge and saw a column of water rise up off the starboard bow. I looked round on the port quarter and could just make out through the haze the outline of a submarine lying on the surface. I blew the alarm signal, the gunner and apprentice on watch had also located the submarine and fired. I didn't have a chance to see where our shot fell as Captain Hunter arrived on the bridge and took over.

We were standing side by side looking at the submarine when he fired again. This shell landed close alongside to port and exploded, a piece of the shell casing passed between Captain Hunter and myself and lodged in the wooden awning spar stanchion behind me. Without thinking I pulled it out, it was still very hot, and dropped it into my pocket. Captain Hunter swung the ship's head hard round to starboard to avoid the next one. This missed as well but we were now heading for the shore. Keeping the helm on he brought the ship round in a circle and headed for the submarine, doing everything wrong as he said he would. Just then Templeton and McNeil came on the bridge. Templeton, in charge of the gun, had come to collect me for spotting. I got to the main cross-trees with my binoculars. I could now see the submarine was a very large one with two guns. We now presented the smallest possible target to the submarine who had to decide which way to open out. If he went to starboard he would be heading for the shore, so he opened out to port, expecting us to swing to starboard again to get our gun to bear, but instead we went hard round to port. The two vessels, when the first shot was fired, would have been about four miles apart, now the range was closing. She was missing us with every shot, it was very poor shooting. As the submarine came on the starboard beam the helm was steadied, I gave the range as 5000 yards, and our shot went over. Down 500, and the next fell just short, this was too close for Jerry and he suddenly disappeared, he must have crash dived. I had gone up 100 for the next shot, I didn't see where it landed but it must have been close. The gun crew claimed we had hit and sunk her, but I didn't think so. Captain Hunter headed for where he had last sighted her, but she was nowhere to be seen and so we resumed our course.

The German commander had not given up. How long an interval he gave us, I cannot say, but suddenly the whistle and splash of a shell started the battle again. In the meantime the sun had cleared the haze and the visibility was perfect. There was the submarine in the same position as before, on the port quarter, but considerably further away. We put the gun at extreme elevation and fired but our shot fell short, only half way to the target. Captain Hunter tried heading towards him again, but now he had the answer to that, he just increased speed and kept his distance, neither of us was getting anywhere. He submerged and re-appeared on the port quarter. His object, it could be seen, was to drive us inshore, where we had no room to manoeuvre, and would give him a steady target. As we could not get within range again the captain tried the *Warspite* routine, so we went round in circles, some small, some large, some at full speed, half speed and slow, once going astern. We put out smoke floats and instead of trying to get away behind them sat in the middle to try and entice him within range, as our shooting was good enough to land one on him if he came near enough. He knew this and kept outside our range. In circling we had been spiralling down the coast and were now only a mile or so off the land. The captain's object was to try and reach Cape Blanc and round into Leverier Bay to anchor. (All this was now taking place inside the Spanish three mile limit.) He asked the chief engineer for everything he had. Mr Simpson said he could shut down the safety valve and get about 12 knots but this could wreck the engine. The safety valve was shut and a flame, about six feet high, appeared above the funnel. No one had been told to slack off the funnel guys and, as the funnel expanded with the heat, it became corrugated like a concertina and stayed that way. All we could do was keep a steady course and make him stay out of our range and trust he kept on missing us. It was now past 3 p.m. and, with the sun to the westward, we were not a good target. The firing on both sides was now continuous – he was using both guns and seemed able to drop shells all around but not on us. Some were so near that the decks were covered with shell splinters. This lasted for some time and there seemed a chance we might get away with it. Then the gun crew reported all shells expended. In the excitement of firing no one thought to keep track of the shells being used. They must have sensed our ammunition was finished and began to close in. I watched a gun flash and counted the seconds till the shell arrived, thirty, six miles. There was a tremendous blow on the starboard side and the ship shuddered all over, but there was no explosion. From the wing of the bridge nothing could be seen, so Captain Hunter assumed the shell must have struck below the waterline and gone into the engine-room without exploding. Convinced the ship had been holed, he decided to get as close to the beach as possible and anchor with only few feet of water under the ship. The intention was then to take to the boats and get on the beach, till the submarine went away, as he expected the submarine to shell the ship to pieces.

When he got into the position he wanted, FULL ASTERN was rung on the telegraph, but there was no response from the engine-room, and the ship still carried on her way. As we had been heading inshore the helm was put hard to starboard, but enough way had been lost to make the helm ineffective, and she would not answer. She was going ashore and nothing could be done about it. He signalled to Mr McNeil to let go both anchors and let them run. Then I was told to blow the ABANDON SHIP signal; the time was 3.52 p.m. I have always remembered the crunching, grinding sound as the *Gryfevale* drove on to the rocks and then the jerk as she brought up.

Boat drill had been held every week in port, as well as at sea, so the abandon ship routine should have gone without a hitch; *should*, but did not. My boat was the dinghy on the port side of the lower bridge, complement six, seven with myself. The drill was to transfer to the mate's lifeboat if we got away safely, consequently there were no stores or water in the boat only the oars, mast and sail. After blowing the signal I rang FINISHED WITH ENGINES, as if that mattered, but it was part of the routine.

By the time I got down to my boat five of the complement were there. I put three in the boat, the big Malay sailor, the cook and myself lowered away. The fourth engineer should have been the seventh man but he did not appear. I could wait no longer so I slid down the lifeline into the boat and ordered the oars to be shipped. Then I looked up and saw a pair of legs topped by a lifebelt coming over the edge of the deck, and the fourth engineer slid down the line.

The submarine was so close I could see the men grouped round the guns and her number was quite plain, white letters on grey – U253. She had apparently stood in for a good look at the ship and was satisfied that she was well and truly aground. The submarine turned and went out to sea again. I found the lifeboat and the mate signalled me over. As I got near the lifeboat disappeared, came up again, then went down. The next time she appeared it was bottom up and the men were swimming and clinging to the keel and beckets. I realised then there was a heavy surf breaking on the rocks. The only possible landing place was a section of flat rocks, facing the sand, that were inundated by breakers. I turned the boat round heading seawards and let the breakers take her in. We were lifted over the rocks and on to the sand by a large wave, without any damage. Mr McNeil and all his crew had got ashore and the lifeboat wallowed in the breakers alongside the rocks. He brought his men over to my boat. 'We'll make sure of this one anyway,' he said, and all hands dragged her high up on the sand. Then a shell exploded not far away. Without being told everyone left the boat and made for the nearest sand dune. We had just got behind the dune when another shell made a direct hit on my boat. When the smoke of the explosion cleared away it had vanished.

The other lifeboat and the gig had gone round the bows of the ship and landed, without mishap, in a bay with a tiny beach, the only one along that stretch of coast as we discovered later. We joined up with them and lay behind the dunes until the submarine had ceased shelling. Captain Hunter decided it was not practicable to return to the ship before daylight, as we did not know whether the Germans would board and plant a time bomb, or clear out the storeroom, as we had heard they had done with other ships.

We would, it was decided, go to Port Etienne for the night. It was five miles away and dark long before we arrived. We were an odd collection, some dressed, some half dressed, some only in pyjamas, quite a number barefoot having lost their boots or shoes when the mate's lifeboat capsized. That was some walk. The desert was not level, but undulating sand ridges with frequent steep gullies covered with small stones, which did the barefoot section no good. At one time a cry was raised that wild dogs were following us, but it turned out to be Jinny. How she got ashore I just have no idea.

At Port Etienne, in addition to the wireless station, there was a fort and a few houses. They were expecting us, we later learned, as the battle had been watched from the top of the wireless mast, and they had seen us set off across the desert. I am unable to describe what happened after our arrival as someone gave me a mug, half full of what I thought was coffee but which was, in fact, neat rum. That, on an empty stomach, put me out like a light. The next thing I remembered was gazing at a gate under an archway. It was bright moonlight and I was held up by two people, one on either side. The top of the wall was crenellated and in each opening was a round, brown face topped by a red fez, then the whole scene faded out. I came to in broad daylight with a splitting headache and found myself lying on a mattress on the floor of a small room. A young man in an army officer's uniform was sitting on a chair. When I sat up he spoke to me in French. I didn't understand at first what he said but then my mind began to translate, he was asking me if I had recovered. Someone brought coffee and this did me the world of good. He told me the captain and crew, with the exception of the chief engineer and the Chinese firemen, had gone back to the ship. The wireless station staff and the garrison of the fort, being on rations for food and water, could not do anything for them. He gave me a note from the captain, which said I was to remain in charge of the firemen and look after the chief engineer, who had a nasty gash along his forehead.

The fort, from what I could see of it, was built exactly like a child's toy fort. It was a square shape with what looked like small towers at two of the corners, and was garrisoned by 200 Senegalese soldiers with white officers. The fort guarded the border between French and Spanish territory which ran down the middle of the small peninsular which terminated at Cape Blanc.

Mr Simpson had been attended to by the army doctor and was now in the lighthouse basement which had been allocated to the ships' crew. It had dawned on the firemen that they were not going to get anything to eat here so, after a conference amongst themselves, they set off to walk back to the ship. I spoke to the lieutenant and he arranged for two camels to transport us. I nearly fell out of the chair attached to the front of the hump when the beast rose to its feet, and the swaying motion when it was trotting had me clinging terrified to the sides. I was glad when the journey was over although it lasted only just under an hour.

65

We could see the ship from the top of each sand ridge long before we got to her but I had my whistle so I wasn't long in attracting attention. The gig came off and took us on board. We found everyone had been organised into a gang hauling up buckets of seawater to fill the donkey boiler. We needed it to raise steam to pump up the main boilers and for heaving on the anchors, when required. It was now seen that she was across a reef at No.2 hold. She hadn't been holed by the shell at all. Because the shell had been fired at long range, it had lost its spinning motion and landed bodily against the ship's side instead of head on. There was a deep dent on the plate and the force of impact had loosened the rivets causing a slight leak. The next day at high water an attempt was made to refloat, but she was hard and fast. The anchor cables were tightened and the wire on the stream anchor aft to try and keep her from being driven further in by the heavy swell. As the dynamo could be run we were in touch with the wireless station and through them received orders to remain by the ship for salvage. There was nothing to do but wait. The only people to carry on working were the cooks and catering staff. We were put on ration for food and water. Tarpaulins and awnings were kept handy to catch rainwater, if ever it rained here, which did not seem likely with all that desert around.

This part of the coast, I found out later, was one of the best fishing grounds in the world. Fleets of fishing boats from the Canary Islands worked here all year round and within a few days we could count a dozen or more lying near us or just drifting. Line fishing was the method used, the fish being salted down in the hold. The reef over which the ship lay swarmed with fish, especially at half tide and was a welcome addition to tinned and salt beef and, when the meat ran out, was the main food supply.

A week after the ship had grounded there was a spell of heavy weather and for a day and a night the decks were awash from end to end, and all the accommodation flooded. Abandoning ship and camping ashore was considered. Finally it was agreed everyone would pack up their effects except what they were wearing and needed, like blankets and pillows, and the baggage would be landed on the beach with a guard. This was in case the ship began to break up. She was working heavily during the gales and when the weather improved she was found to have broken her back. The crack widened as time went on.

The first trip by the lifeboat which landed at the small beach was successful, as was the second. The third time the boat overturned and all the baggage in it was lost. The boat was righted without damage and fortunately the oars had been lashed to the boat. Some lost nothing, some lost all they had, and others, like me, part of their effects.

I was to command the guard party consisting of the four apprentices, two gunners and the Chinese mess boy who would cook for us. I demanded, and was given, two of the rifles and some ammunition. We built a house out of the seabags, sea chests and suitcases with oars and boat hooks for rafters and a hatch tarpaulin for a roof. It kept the sun off during the blistering heat of the day and was warm during the bitter cold at night. A boat ensign was hoisted on a boathook and we were settled in. The trouble was we had nothing to do. We had two or three packs of cards, but during the day couldn't remain out in the sun; there was no shade anywhere and the bag house, as it was called, was too hot. After sunset we were in darkness. We had boat lamps but the smell and risk of fire made it safer not to use them. The fresh water was only for drinking and cooking not for washing. When the sun had warmed things up we stripped off and went into the sea using sand to scrub ourselves. We all grew beards.

There were plenty of mussels and whelks on the rocks at low water and the mess boy made a good job of cooking them. The only vegetation to be seen was some kind of thorn bush which didn't appear to have any leaves. Then after a few days came the flies, which remained with us until the camp was broken up and we returned to the ship.

There was a belief, prevalent amongst the crew, that the desert was full of wild dogs. One day the mess boy reported that someone, or some animal, had been stealing biscuits during the night. We set a trap, leaving a couple of biscuits lying just inside the baghouse, then two of us kept watch. The following night Haslam and I were on watch again. Sometime after midnight we heard a noise and a dark shape crept quietly into the doorway. I dropped a sailcloth over it and there was a violent struggle, we had captured Jinny. She was completely wild and Captain Hunter's orders were to destroy her if the opportunity arose. The question was how. It was finally agreed that she should be drowned. Why it wasn't done I don't know, I was not in the execution party. The four apprentices and the two gunners took her down to the beach and tried to hold her under. Even six of them could not hold her. She bit and tore and struggled so violently that she finally broke free and fled for her life. The youngest apprentice had been pushed beneath the water and could not get up to the surface. He was unconscious when he was fished out and I thought he was gone, but after artificial respiration I managed to get him breathing again, but it was a near thing. We saw no more of Jinny while we on the beach, but that was not the last of her.

One day a large party of Moors, complete with tents, camels, women and children arrived and made camp a short distance inland from the beach. They expected the ship to break up soon in the autumn gales and when the cargo washed ashore they were going to collect it. If they had known the cargo was sugar, which would dissolve in the sea, I don't think they would have bothered. The Spanish fishing fleet seemed to have similar ideas.

For something to do we taught the Sheikh to play whist and that was how we passed the time in the shade of the baghouse. It was a weird situation, we couldn't understand a word the Sheikh said, and vice versa, but he learned to play and, in time, became a formidable opponent.

Then a prolonged spell of bad weather set in. The boat was unable to bring us food or water and finally we were down to one ship's biscuit and a quarter of a cup of water each per day. One morning I signalled we were right out of food and, if no further supplies could be sent, we would have to proceed to Port Etienne. On board the ship food and water had become acute problem, as even in the gales it never rained. The result was that volunteers from the Spanish fishing boats manned our lifeboat and landed a supply of food and water that afternoon. It was a wonderful display of boatmanship. The two halves of the boat's crew faced in opposite directions, with a steering oar at each end. One half kept the boat end on to the breakers while the other rowed her in. They gave me a letter from the captain to say he had arranged, when the weather calmed down, to have all the baggage transferred to a fishing brig to be taken to Port Etienne and stored there. I was to superintend this operation, which would be carried out with the brig's boat. The baggage was to be stowed in the lighthouse basement which had been offered as a storeroom, then we would return by land.

The heavy swell during the spells of bad weather had caused the ship to move so much that the bottom under No.2 hold had opened up. It was now open to the sea, and all the sugar in the lower hold had dissolved away. As the bottom and tank top opened up still further the now empty bags were washed out and thrown on the rocks. As well as fishing the Spanish fishermen were now busy collecting the bags and laying them out on the sand dunes to dry, then stowing them on board their schooners to be sold in Las Palmas. The Moors' camel patrol had also found them and were busy collecting. There were knife fights but so far no one had been killed.

The food and water position was now becoming desperate. No rain had fallen. An attempt was made to distil fresh water but only an inch or so could be made in a day, and that tasted of copper and was only fit for washing. Fish were plentiful but such things as salt, fat, tea and coffee were nearly finished. It was now six weeks since leaving Dakar, where we only took sufficient stores to reach London, and there was no indication of how much longer we would be here.

It became my job with the four apprentices to take the gig, stow bags of coal in the boat, and visit the fishing schooners trading the coal for water, salt and anything edible I could get. This had to be done every day no matter what the weather, and it was then I learnt to handle a boat in all sea conditions. Overturning in the gig was now so common an occurrence that a righting routine came into being. The oars were a precious commodity and were lashed to the rowers' wrists. It mattered not whether you surfaced again as long as your oar came up!

It became necessary to learn Spanish to be able to bargain as none of the fishermen spoke English. A lump of coal for a dipperful of water was the usual exchange. This involved visiting several boats a day in order to get even one keg full. In addition I was sometimes able to obtain a quantity of yellow meal, some of the salt they used for the fish and occasionally some bottles of Madeira wine, but this last had to be paid for with sugar.

One day I boarded a schooner that had completed filling his hold and was preparing to leave for Las Palmas. I finally managed to convince the skipper that, if he brought back a stock of wine, extra water, fruit, flour and various other items, he could make a good profit either in coal, sugar, or the captain would give him a paper for the British Consul to pay him in money. From then each schooner which went back to Las Palmas returned with food, wine and vegetables, including potatoes, tobacco and in one case fowl and pigs. Now they wanted to be paid in bags of sugar instead of coal. I think Captain Hunter must have obtained permission from Dakar to do this. The schooner's large boats brought the goods to the ship and the bargaining was carried on at a higher level. We were getting more to eat but the problem of fresh water remained.

Early one morning we sighted a vessel standing in from the sea which finally anchored two miles outside of us. We were informed by Morse lamp that she was a salvage vessel from Las Palmas and would we send off a boat to put the salvage master on board our ship. He was on board for just one hour and I could see he considered salvage was hopeless.

'This,' he said, 'is not a ship anymore it's a wreck, even if the impossible happened and we got her off the reef she would simply sink. I will report salvage impossible and try and find the damned fool who sent me here.' We took him back to his ship and before noon he was gone.

Before long dysentery struck probably due to the water, but in addition we suffered a low fever that became rampant throughout the ship. Living conditions were damp, cold and wretched, but the salt water and salt air could not cause fever. Temperatures never rose beyond 100°F, and no one was actually laid up, but crawled around in a tired, sick and miserable condition which persisted until we finally left the ship. Someone suggested the stink of melting sugar was the cause, and certainly everyone made a rapid recovery after leaving the ship.

Instructions came through a day or two later that all cargo possible was to be discharged. Then the vessel was to be stripped of all stores and anything that could be put to further use. When word got round that the ship was to be abandoned the fishing fleet were more interested in us than fishing. More boats than ever arrived, like vultures around a corpse.

An Admiralty tug from Las Palmas appeared towing a lighter to take the gun and mounting, rifles and all Admiralty stores off the ship. I understood that the 4.72-inch gun and mounting weighed around seven tons, but it was certainly a very heavy weight for an improvised sheerlegs to lift.

Then came the *Ethelric*. She had been discharging coal in Dakar when she was suddenly ordered to the wreck of the *Gryfevale*, to load all cargo that could be salvaged. With the help of the fishing schooners the work went quickly; it was surprising the number of sugar bags those boats could carry. In a few days all that was worth salvaging had been removed. We spent two days stripping down the ship and when we were finished there wasn't even a derrick shackle left on board. The weather held up even though it was well on in December.

Jinny was back on board, no one knew how, she just appeared. Captain Hunter mustered the crew and then, with instructions to search the lifeboat and gig to make sure they were empty, we pulled away from the *Gryfevale* for the last time. It was only a short run to Leverier Bay and we anchored there before noon. The next morning I heard someone reporting that a monkey had bitten the bosun. Jinny was now onboard the *Ethelric*!

In Dakar, Tom Templeton, the four engineers and myself were transferred to one of the Lamport & Holt ships, the *Raphael*, bound from Buenos Aires to Liverpool. Captain Hunter, Mr McNeil and the remainder of the crew went on board the naval escort. We understood we were consular passengers but later found we had been entered in the ship's articles as distressed British seamen. Only one incident marred a peaceful passage, when we heard the whistle of a shell passing over the bridge – I knew that sound only too well. The ship on our starboard side sighted the periscope of a submarine and fired. The whole convoy opened out like a flock of ducks taking fright. If he had fired a torpedo at either of us the explosion would have taken care of him as well, so he dived out of it. The escort, after the convoy had formed up again, went up and down between the columns and gave each ship in turn his personal opinion of them for acting without orders.

We docked in Liverpool and, after breakfast, waited on deck with our luggage. I had only the clothes that I had worn continuously since the *Gryfevale* went aground, and I felt like a tramp. We were expecting to be taken ashore by the captain, but after a while we realised that everyone had disappeared and the ship was now deserted. Just after 3 p.m. he returned in a great fluster and we all went to the immigration department. Then the trouble started. We were asked to identify ourselves. Mr Simpson, the chief engineer, who was our spokesman, stated we were the mates and engineers from the British steamer *Gryfevale* lost by enemy action and placed by the British Consul on the *Raphael* for passage to the UK. Glasgow was our port of signing on and we had to be sent back there. The immigration officer was not satisfied.

'You still have to identify yourselves, where are your papers?' he persisted. We replied they were with Captain Hunter on another ship. We produced our certificates and the officer agreed we might be British subjects. Finally Mr Simpson had an idea and suggested he telephone Crawford, Barr & Co., in Glasgow. This was done and the officer had to be satisfied when our names and ranks were read out to him, but he still regarded us with deep suspicion.

Eventually after a great deal of negotiation we managed to get a meal and train tickets to Glasgow. We did get seats but were packed as tightly as sardines. It was a miserable journey but we reached St. Enoch's station some time around 6 a.m. I had breakfast and just after 9 a.m. arrived at the owner's office. I received my account of wages and found they had gone up to £14 per month, due to a war bonus. I now had considerably more money than I had expected. I went back to the office to pick up my mail, which had not been sent on. The Admiralty gave the company no information at all except that the ship had been lost by enemy action but all crew were safe. In the train going home I sat with a large pile of letters on my knee, an object of curiosity to the other passengers. There was no point in reading them now. The family had been told by the owners that the ship had been lost and they had no idea when I would come home, so my unannounced arrival caused consternation. I was shown one of my letters, and it was little surprise that they never knew where I was – after the censor had finished the only information remaining was that I was still alive.

I was told by the office they could not offer me further employment as the firm was now out of business. Well that was the end of that. In any case I was going up for the first mate's examination.

Mr McNeil told me, when I met him in the office, that a salvage claim had been put in on behalf of the ship's crew. Years passed and I forgot all about it. In 1930, when I arrived home on leave, a money order for £60 was waiting for me signed by some government office. All it stated was 'For services rendered'.

Chapter 8

Back to the Academy

I had not done any studying at all while on the *Gryfevale* so, when I enrolled again at Captain Tait's Academy, I had to start at the beginning.

A new examination system operated where marks were allotted for each subject. This was better as, if you did not do so well in one subject you had a chance of pulling up in another. Under the old examinations the principal subject had been seamanship and the handling of a sailing ship was more important than navigation, or any other subject. The examiner had to be satisfied that you were a capable sailor. The seamanship for a steam certificate was nothing compared with that for sail, so the gap this left in the examination had to be filled with other subjects, such as trigonometry, meteorology, ship construction and stability. All this kept me at school for about six weeks. There seemed to be more candidates than ever.

One evening I had just boarded the train on my way home when a figure rushed along the platform and scrambled in. It was plastered in mud under which a khaki uniform could be faintly discerned. When he said 'Hullo Wully.' I nearly jumped out of my skin, the voice was that of my old friend Matt Latta.

'Good God where have you come from?' I said.

'Out of the trenches on 72 hours leave.'

'But I thought you were in the Army Medical Corp.'

'I was until there was a shortage of men, then all the able bodied were pulled out of the non-combat services and put into fighting units. I landed in the Scottish Borderers; they were wiped out, and then I went into the Highland Light Infantry where I am now.' I didn't see him again until after the war.

I had recently been called before the local tribunal in Hamilton to explain why I was not in the services. The army was very short of men and those who had previously been rejected as medically unfit were being accepted. Anyone not in a reserved trade or over 45 was hauled before the tribunal. Previously a seaman could not be acalled up but the navy now had plenty of men; many merchant ships had been sunk and there was a surplus of seamen. Strict new rules allowed one week ashore for each month at sea, and that applied to the last voyage only. I had been at sea for nine months, so I had over two months to obtain a first mate's certificate and another ship. The first examinations were to take place in Greenock.

The routine was the same as when I went up for second mate. All went well and there was only the final oral seamanship to go. When my turn came the examiner had my discharge book lying open in front of him.

'What happened on your last voyage? The date and place of discharge is 17th December 1917 Cape Blanc, but the report of character entry is dated 14th January 1918 at Glasgow.'

I explained what had happened and, by dint of continuous questions, he got the whole story in detail. The fight with the submarine, how the ship got ashore, efforts to get her off again, laying out stream anchor, living conditions on board in bad weather, how we lived on the beach, boat sailing and handling in surf, dismantling and discharging the gun, transferring cargo to another ship and stripping the ship down.

'Well,' he said when I had finished, 'You seem to have kept your eyes open and appear to have learnt a great deal.' I realised that, without my knowing, he had put me through a thorough seamanship examination which I seemed to have passed. He handed me my blue paper and shook hands. 'Try and keep clear of German submarines in future and good luck.' I was now competent to carry out the duties as first mate of a foreign going steam vessel.

During this period the German breakthrough had taken place and the news was getting worse each day. One morning I turned to the back page of the paper for the local news, and found page after page of photographs of local boys killed and missing in action. All, with very few exceptions, were my old school mates and I knew a great many others. It seemed my generation in Uddingston had been practically wiped out.

During the week following the examination I received a letter marked OHMS requesting me to report at the office of the Merchant Fleet Auxiliaries in Glasgow. I remarked to my father 'These people have nothing more to do with me now the *Gryfevale* has gone.'

'When you see OHMS on a letter it is wise to do what it tells you to do, that is an official order.' he said.

I called in and enquired what they wanted as, now the *Gryfevale* was lost, I had no longer anything to do with them. The clerk behind the counter reached up to a shelf and brought down what looked like a set of ship's articles. I recognised them from the red printing. He opened them up.

'Is that your signature?' I had to admit it was.

'You evidently didn't read this document before you signed, if you had you would have known it was a contract to serve in the Merchant Fleet Auxiliaries for the duration of the hostilities.'

I told him I had just passed for first mate and was intending to join the RNR. 'You are under contract,' he said, 'and as your time ashore is now up, we require you to report on board the *Carston*, at present in Greenock, to sign on as second mate. She is a fleet collier and is due to leave for a loading port.'

'Can I refuse?' I asked.

'You can try but I wouldn't advise it. Report on board tomorrow evening.' I went round to the Merchant Service Guild and asked their advice.

I was told, 'If you have signed that contract you will have to go where you are sent.'

It seemed I had no choice.

Chapter 9

S.S.Carston

and a brush with death

The *Carston* was in the James Watt Dock. Where she had come from or what she had just discharged I didn't know. There was no information about the previous voyage which was very curious; everyone including the master had just joined the ship.

'Are you a good navigator?' asked the captain.

'Well,' I said, 'I hope so, I have just passed for first mate.'

'The second mate here has to navigate the ship as I have my hands full with other things,' continued the captain. I wondered what kind of a ship I had joined, where the master had more important things to do than navigate.

Captain Dawson had spent most of his time on the Baltic trade so this was his first deep-sea command. He turned out to be of a very excitable nature and an awkward man to work with. The following forenoon he came back with the orders – Barry Dock to load – and an envelope with route orders and instructions which he handed to me. After we were under way I laid off the route. It took us through the Largs Channel between Ailsa Craig and the mainland. I asked Captain Dawson to have a look at the chart.

'Why?' he said, 'can't you lay courses off?'

'I have done so,' I informed him, 'and as they are a bit unusual, I would like you to have a look.'

'You are the second mate, your job is to navigate the ship, you have the route instructions.' He wouldn't go near the chartroom so I asked the third mate to check the courses. Towards the end of the watch, we were coming down into the Largs channel and getting close to Ailsa Craig, when the captain came rushing up on the bridge.

'Where are you taking the ship?' he demanded.

'Down through the Largs channel sir, that is the route.'

S.S. Carston

'Keep outside that island, there is no need to pass inside.'

'If you look on the chart, sir, you will find the course laid off.'

'Never mind that, we are not going inside that island,' he was now getting frantic.

'In that case I will have nothing further to do with setting the courses,' I said. 'If you want to pass outside Ailsa Craig you will have to alter course yourself, there may be a minefield between there and Arran.'

Just then Mr Morton came up to take over his watch. 'Do you think it is safe to pass inside that island Mr Morton?' Captain Dawson asked him.

'Of course, as many ships pass inside as outside, there is deep water and plenty of room.' Without saying another word the captain went down below again.

'I don't know what to make of him,' I said. 'He will not check a course or even look at a chart, he just handed me the route instructions without opening them.'

The weather had been fine and clear with light winds and slight sea, but even in that kind of weather the *Carston* could make no more than nine knots. We anchored in Barry Roads around midnight.

Coming on watch after dinner the following day I noticed a long canvas-wrapped bundle lying on No. 2 hatch.

'What's that?' I asked the third mate, Mr Cameron.

'That,' he said, 'is the bosun.'

'The what?'

'The bosun,' he repeated, 'he dropped dead about ten o'clock this morning.'

'What was wrong with him?'

'Nobody knows, he was dead when he was picked up.' I couldn't even visualise what he had looked like. A nice start to the voyage, I thought.

We loaded a cargo of Welsh coal and went down from Barry to Milford Haven and arrived just as the convoy was leaving. A launch came alongside and tossed an envelope marked M.F.C. *Carston* on board and, as at Greenock, I was handed the envelope. There were the usual contents, convoy diagram, in which we were not included, an envelope to be opened when the convoy dispersed, one if we dropped out of the convoy and so on. There was nothing to state where we were bound, unless it was in the envelope to be opened on dispersal. Outside, the convoy was forming up. As we had no position, we just tagged on at the back until a destroyer came alongside for our particulars, then the escort allotted us a station – rear ship of the port column. The convoy headed south.

One of the merchant ships was chosen as guide to the convoy. Stationed at the head of the centre column he steered the courses passed to him by the escort and maintained the convoy speed and the ships kept station on him. The organisation and running of the convoy was in the hands of the escort, who made all signals; for this type of slow convoy it was usually an armed merchant cruiser. It was fortunate we were a rear ship. The distance between the ships was two cables fore and aft, 1220 feet, which is ample room, but whenever we got up into station, Captain Dawson would come rushing on to the bridge.

'Slow her down, you are too close to that ship ahead.' It was no use pointing out that the distance to the ship ahead was the regulation two cables. Down the revolutions would have to go until we were several cables astern of station, not till then was he satisfied. During daylight this would bring the destroyer on station astern up alongside ordering us to regain station at once. By this time the navy had given up the hopeless task of trying to make a collection of ships of all nationalities, sizes, types and speeds do what they were told. They had to be content if the vessels were actually in sight. I once heard someone describe a convoy of merchant ships as a collection of individualists held together by fear – an accurate description.

We had been warned by signal, during the forenoon, that the convoy would disperse at a certain time during the afternoon; all ships were to open sealed route orders. We were for Sierre Leone and had to report to the naval base on arrival.

It may have been the owner's instructions, or Captain Dawson's idea, but this ship was run on Board of Trade scale, pound and pint, for mates and engineers as well as sailors and firemen. I am inclined to think it was the owner's as this would account for everyone, including the master, getting out of the ship when she paid off in Greenock. The first indication was the cabin boy putting a tin of condensed milk, a quantity of tea and sugar, and a tin of jam in each room. This I was told was Board of Trade allowance for three weeks!

'Captain's orders, Board of Trade scale for everyone.' said the steward.

When I mentioned this to Mr Morton he said, 'I have been on some hard living ships but never been put on pound and pint before.' The food served out at meals was not good but did not warrant a complaint until we left Barry.

The first battle took place on the day we left Greenock. I expected, as had been the custom in my previous ships, tea and toast about 3 p.m. Half past came and went and no tea. The chief engineer and the mate had also been to the steward about the tea and, getting no satisfaction, had taken the matter to the captain. At the same time the chief had demanded why the mates and engineers had been put on Board of Trade scale, adding if that was the way the ship was going to be run he could find another chief engineer when the ship got to Barry. Mr Morton said the same went for him and he had no doubt for the other mates as well. Afternoon tea was allowed from then onwards, but had to be taken out of our allowance. The next struggle was to obtain sandwiches on night watches. This was obtained, but still the milk and sugar had to come out of what had been placed in our rooms. The *Carston* was already, not a week on articles, an unhappy ship.

When we got to sea the food situation became the worst I have ever known. We didn't live in the lap of luxury on the *Gryfevale* but we got sufficient, well cooked and edible food. Here it was neither sufficient nor well cooked and quite often uneatable. After the fresh meat was finished it was salt meat one day, salt pork the next, heated up for dinner, served cold for tea. There was butter and soft bread three times a week, and ship's biscuits the rest of the time. Tinned meat was made up into wet or dry hash, for breakfast and tea, with salt fish an alternative for breakfast. If you had porridge you didn't get the hash. We never saw an egg. We demanded bread every day, and in the end we won, if bread it could be called. One day a deputation from the crew dumped their breakfast on the deck in front of the captain's door. That was the situation on board the *Carston,* fleet collier, when she arrived in Sierra Leone.

We were eight weeks in that place. It couldn't be called a harbour, just an open anchorage bounded by mud banks to the north. The heat during the day was terrific and there was a peculiar sweet, sickly smell which I recognised as the mangroves, but it was more pronounced than in East Africa.

After our arrival we laid for a fortnight doing nothing; we were collier in reserve. We were, we gathered, primarily the collier for H.M.S. *Kent*, an armoured cruiser, but she was out on patrol. When she returned a signal went up 'Collier No... proceed alongside', followed by a time. We had to keep watch for signals as one bearing our number was liable to be hoisted by any one of the warships. It was unusual calling the collier alongside the evening before. Naval ships, except in an emergency, never coaled at night. It was, however, the custom with H.M.S. *Kent* to have a concert the evening of arrival back at Base after a cruise, the collier being brought alongside so that her crew could enjoy themselves as well. It was a very kindly gesture. I never enjoyed anything as much as I did that concert. It was surprising what talent could be found among the most unlikely people. It was staged on an open space amidships and we had a grandstand view from our bridge deck. The marine band supplied the music, and there was singing, community, in groups or solo, a short sketch, accordion and violin playing. The best of all, in my opinion, were two stokers. They gave the best rendering I have heard of *I wonder what it feels like to be poor, Burlington Bertie, My Old Dutch* and other songs of that kind. Another good turn was a foo foo band with wash tubs, bottles, marline spikes, whistles, mouth organs and a saw. The concert lasted two hours. Next day we coaled her and were back at anchor in the evening.

West Africa has the name 'White Man's Grave' due to the incidence of malaria and blackwater fever. Lying out at anchor we were beyond the reach of the mosquitoes, so while in Sierra Leone we had no cases of fever. About four weeks after arrival Mr Morton was laid up and it was at first thought that he had contracted malaria, but his temperature would not go down, and he had a cough as well. The captain went ashore and brought back a doctor; his diagnosis was consumption in an advanced state, and Mr Morton was taken ashore to hospital that afternoon.

Captain Dawson called me into his room and said 'You are now acting mate until Mr Morton comes back, Mr Cameron acts as second.'

We had now been here a month and no fresh provisions had come on board, each day it was the same salt meat, dried beans and peas. The captain said fresh provisions were unobtainable in Freetown, and this could not be checked as he was the only person who went ashore.

One morning after I had taken over as acting mate I, along with the second engineer, went forward to find out why the men hadn't turned to. They were all, both sailors and firemen, sitting on No.1 hatch. I asked the bosun why they were not working.

'We are on strike.' he said.

'Why?' I asked.

'We are no longer strong enough, through lack of food, to do any work.' I informed the captain.

'Send them along here at once,' he shouted, 'I'll log the whole pack of them.'

'You tell the old bastard mister, that we are sick and tired of going to him, now he can come to us.' He actually did go forward, raved and threatened, while they remained quiet and stated they would only resume work when they were properly fed.

'I am going to report to the Base Commander,' he said finally, 'and call for a naval court.' Then he went off ashore. Sometime later a naval launch arrived alongside with several ratings in charge of a lieutenant RNR. He introduced himself to me.

'I am instructed to inquire into the trouble on this ship,' he said. We went forward and talked to the men. He was shocked at what they told him. Then he ordered one of the ratings to make a list of the contents of the storeroom. 'I am surprised,' the lieutenant said, 'that scurvy has not broken out here. I suppose only the lime juice issue has prevented that.' When the list was compiled he ordered the steward to make out a list of fresh provisions for one week, and not Board of Trade either. When he had this he departed ashore in his launch. Around noon a motorboat came alongside loaded with fresh meat, vegetables, fruit, eggs, bread, things we had forgotten existed. The crew resumed work.

When the captain returned he never spoke a word, he was a very chastened man from then onwards. We did not fare so well later but had fresh provisions in port and all the time we were on the coast.

The heavy rain squalls now became frequent, and these were our only means of obtaining fresh water, which had become a problem. I found what could be called a 'water sail', a triangular shaped affair made of canvas. When the peak was hauled up the mainmast and the wings to each corner of the bridge deck, it gave quite a large spread. In the centre where the rain collected, a canvas hose was attached which could be led to either water tank. This water sail was well designed, well made and the only one I have ever seen.

The ship used salt water in the main boilers and they had to be cleaned out at frequent intervals. Blowing down, cleaning and raising steam took about two days. We had permission to do this and were in the middle of it when the *Kent* came in. In response to her signal we replied 'engaged boiler cleaning'. She replied 'endeavour to come alongside, imperative coaling commences daylight tomorrow'. I then saw Captain Dawson do something I have never seen done before or since.

Both ships were lying to the ebb tide, which ran strongly at all times in the anchorage. We were upstream from the *Kent*. The captain told me to signal 'we are going to dredge down alongside,' and I was sent forward to heave short. What I saw done then I have always remembered. This was how the sailing vessels in olden days got up and down rivers, by 'dropping down with the tide'. When the anchor was just touching bottom he let her shear across the tide and down we drifted; at the same time we were closing in on the *Kent*. I noticed the whole ship's company were lined along the side watching us. By paying out on the cable, or heaving in again, he worked her into position the required distance off the cruiser's starboard side. Then enough cable was slacked out to bring her head to tide again and hold her, then the crew of the cruiser took over. The commander was watching from the bridge and, using a loud hailer, congratulated Captain Dawson on the finest feat of seamanship he had ever seen.

After we had been there eight weeks we were turned over to the firm of Elder Dempster to load in Lagos for home. They put 50 Kroo boys on board to work cargo and anything else we wanted them to do. They were familiar figures on the West African trade, but I only had them on board that one time. The head man was an old gentleman called Tom Kroo, I believe every head man was given that name. All orders and complaints had to go through him. They brought their own food and cooked it themselves in a kind of galley rigged up on deck. Fortunately the poop was empty and they used that as their house.

When I set them to clean holds I found that each gang had its own hold and would not work in any other. They could be put to any job when not working cargo, but each gang only worked over the top, or side, of their hold. This was very complicated but all I had to do was tell Tom Kroo what I wanted done and he sorted it out. They were a cheerful, happy lot, just like children, and how they worked! Each had his own part-time job as well. The cook found he had assistants in the galley. The steward did well, he had pantrymen and saloon stewards, and they knew their work. Some kept the crew quarters clean, and I found Mr Cameron and I had a steward of our own, as did the engineers. In fact every position in the ship was double or treble banked. Of course this had to be paid for in cash, old clothes or food, but it didn't cost much. It was just as well later on that we had them aboard or the ship would have come to a standstill.

While it was decided what to do with the ship we lay at the buoys and then moved to the Iddo wharf. Everywhere there was a stink of garbage, bodies of dead animals, rotten vegetation and nameless other things. At first it seemed it wouldn't be long before we were loaded and out of this stink hole, but we laid there week after week. When the rain permitted, we loaded what could be scraped up from round about or brought in by the small coastal ships. Everything was damp and clothes became covered in mildew. The heat was unbearable. If one didn't get soaked by rain, one got soaked in sweat. This continued for over a week, then came breaks which gradually became longer and more frequent. Everything steamed in the baking sun and the stink at low water was horrendous, but there was also the mosquito. Many went down with the fever without realising they had been bitten. Not having contracted malaria since the bout in Calcutta I considered I was safe, but I wasn't. During this time, Captain Dawson disappeared ashore, and I only saw him occasionally.

Quinine was not issued in tablet form at that time, all we had was powder. Inevitably it fell to me to make up the doses for the whole crew and, as it had a nasty taste, it was not easy to make them take it. I had to run 50 Kroo boys, in addition to my own men, and supervise loading, so I did not have time to dispense the medicine. The wireless operator was doing nothing so I gave him the job. First one and then another went down with malaria, and succumbed again after a brief respite. We looked like a crew of scarecrows. At one time only the fourth engineer and myself were able to get around, and I had a temperature of over 102 ° most of the time. The Kroo boys ran everything, if they had not been on board the ship would indeed have come to a standstill.

Dr Gray attended the ship twice a day. One day he took my temperature. 'You should be laid up,' he said, 'you have malaria and a bad attack of it.' I told him I hadn't time to be ill. In all, out of a crew of 31 people, seven died.

The person who attended to everything that the captain should have done was

Elder Dempster's cargo superintendent. He arranged the removal of the bodies, the burials and notified the authorities. To cover myself I wrote in the mate's logbook a detailed account of each illness which ended in death, and noted each day the number of persons down with the fever and their condition. It was from these accounts that Captain Dawson wrote up his official logbook when we got to sea.

One afternoon, when we had some cargo to load, one of the winches broke down. All work had to cease until it was repaired. I went to find an engineer. I had a high fever and was very weak and the only way to move about was on hands and knees. The fourth engineer came along, also on hands and knees and under his direction the Kroo boys managed to get the winch working again. I remember, during the afternoon, laying down on my bunk with a raging fever. I woke up feeling as cool as ice, went out into the alleyway and promptly fell flat on my face. Mr Cameron, who was just coming out of the saloon alleyway, picked me up. I asked him what time it was.

'Half past eight; can you eat anything?'

I felt hungry and did manage to eat something. I asked what day it was – it had been three days since I had taken to my bunk.

'No one could get you to wake up, you were unconscious all the time,' said Mr Cameron. 'The doctor said to leave you alone, you would die without waking up.' I had lain there without food or drink for three days and nights. When the doctor arrived he was astonished to see me up and about.

'You're a mystery,' he declared, 'there is no medical reason as to why you are still alive.' The fever had left me and my temperature was normal. I never had another attack of malaria.

I think someone must have remarked to Captain Dawson it was time he had a look at his ship as everyone onboard seemed to be dying of malaria fever. One morning he came on board in a great fluster and demanded to know what was going on. I told him.

'Why was I not informed of this?'

'For the good reason,' I told him, 'that I did not know where you were.' He didn't stay long. What really bothered him were the gangways, they had not been painted. I told him the paint was finished

'Surely you can find something to cover them up,' he cried.

I did. The bosun dug out some rusty tins of funnel black, red hold paint and a stone colour. He had difficulty in mixing them as they were in powder form and very old. However he managed and I made up a tartan pattern with the three colours on each gangway. We were an odd sight when it was finished.

'That will give the old bugger something to shout about.' said the bosun with great satisfaction.

Eventually we completed loading as much cargo as was obtainable, and were ordered to a place called Lome, the capital of what had been German Togoland*. We were there only about two days then back to Sierra Leone where we discharged the Kroo men, then loaded for Dakar where we anchored in the harbour to await the convoy.

After leaving Lagos everyone recovered from the malaria, but then an epidemic of dysentery went through the ship. I caught a bad dose and it pulled me down until I looked like a walking skeleton. I never laid up but was not much use on watch.

We were instructed after leaving the convoy (which was bound for Liverpool and Glasgow) to call at Portland in Dorset for coastal escort. This was a nine-knot convoy, but Captain Dawson knew that we would be lucky to achieve seven. The firemen were in poor condition and the vessel had weed on the bottom. We didn't stay in the convoy long and by mid-afternoon they were out of sight. It was just as well we dropped back, as it appeared from information the wireless operator picked up that a submarine wolf pack had found the convoy and were having a wonderful time for themselves.

Our call at Portland was not for coastal escort as we discovered upon arrival. So many deaths had occurred from malaria on board colliers and store ships in West Africa, an Admiralty order had come out stating that all vessels on Admiralty service had to have their crews medically examined on arriving from the West African ports. In my case I was pronounced medically unfit for further service in the Merchant Fleet Auxiliaries, and given a certificate to that effect. The doctor advised me to remain at home for three months; the certificate would prevent the tribunal from interfering with me. I had an idea the doctor considered I would not live that long. My weight was now under six stones, but I was recovering from the dysentery.

When I arrived home on 6th September 1918, the first thing I did was call in at the Merchant Fleet Auxiliaries office and produce my medical certificate. I was signed off their list and became a free man again.

I now found I had to take the submarine menace course. There was one commencing on 24th September lasting for four days, and it was to be held in a building which faced on to Sauchiehall Street and Scott Street, the old Hengler's Circus. I went in with my papers and was interviewed by a lieutenant commander RN. He told me the course was only for masters and first mates but he would accept second mates, as they usually seemed to be the ship's gunnery officers. The pay was 15s 6d per day for living and travelling expenses. Three of the four days were spent in the old circus building. We were divided up into sections of ten with an elderly chief petty officer assigned to each section. During the morning we had gun drill, then a lecture on the construction of a 6-inch gun. The petty officer dismantled the gun, instructed us how to put it together again, and then went away. We made

---

* now Togo.

some kind of attempt but there were too many bits and pieces and it was hopeless, so we gave up. One of the captains suggested we bribe the petty officer to put it together again, which he did, and we all duly rated as having passed the gun maintenance test.

There were lectures on forming gun crews, fire parties, first aid parties, lookouts and gun drills and talks on types of shells and propellants, cartridges and cordite bags, and the markings and colours of the various sizes of shells. Most of this went in one ear and out of the other; we had already had nearly four years of gun drills, submarine lookouts and all the rest of it.

Thursday was the big day when we had to report to the James Watt Dock in Greenock. A large trawler was lying at the outer wall of the dock armed with two 12-pounder guns, also smoke canisters, bomb throwers and depth charges. In the dock was a submarine, one of the E class, which meant nothing to us at that stage, and each section was shown over it in turn. We were then taken on board the trawler and proceeded down the Clyde to somewhere off the island of Arran, where we met up with another trawler towing a target. We were now to practise controlling a gun in action, and I found I was credited with at least two hits, which was considered the best one could obtain.

The submarine was now to stalk and torpedo the trawler, which in turn had to try and evade the torpedoes and sink the submarine. In the end a draw was conceded, neither vessel being able to sink the other. On the way back to Greenock I received a certificate stating I had passed as a seaman gunner, a sheet of paper on which had been plotted the six shots, and a certificate which said I had attended the submarine menace course.

I had arranged to meet Duncan Cameron one Saturday morning at the Guild Rooms and we were going to spend the day together. I arrived early and while I was waiting a very large man in a bridge coat and sea boots came in. I took no further interest in him until the clerk called me over and introduced me.

'This is Captain Basset of the *Dunbar*. He is looking for a second mate with a first mate's certificate. I have none on the books, men are scarce now.'

'I haven't put my name down for a berth,' I said, 'I only came home less than a month ago and am supposed to be on the sick list.'

'The ship is in the Govan dry dock under repair,' said Captain Basset. 'Apparently she tried to get into the Rothesay Dock through the dock wall instead of through the lock, and it will be some time before she is ready for sea. Come down with me and have a look her.' Standing by this ship would be something to do and if I didn't like her I need not sign on when she was ready for sea.

I stayed for dinner and got a surprise. After the *Gryfevale* and *Carston* I was not expecting anything much as this was just an ordinary tramp. But the food that came to the table was better than that served on the *Bengali*. I told Captain Bassett I

SUBMARINE MENACE COURSE.

(Not to be taken to Sea.)

This is to certify that *William Donald* ~~Master or Chief~~ Officer
of the S.S. *late Carston* Owners *S. Christie & Co* has attended
Submarine Menace Course at *Glasgow* commencing *24th Sept 1918*;
Date. *28th Sept 1918.*

J. H. Law *Lt Comdr R.N.*

Officer in Charge.

Requalified at............................ Date............................

....

Officer in Charge.

N.B.—This certificate must be produced, if required, for the information of the Naval Authorities or Board of Trade.

O (33) AS 4980 Pk 2990 10,000 3/18 E & S

'...and a certificate which said I had attended the submarine menace course.'

would take the berth on condition I could leave at any time if a better offer came along. I discovered the ship was owned by the Britain Steamship Co., of London, Managers, Messrs. Watts Watts & Co. Ltd., London. I had never heard of them until then. This was how I came into their employ, on 2nd October 1918. Though I could not know it then I was to spend the rest of my time at sea with them.

Chapter 10

A riotous armistice

*W*atts Watts & Co. had bought the ship earlier that year. While repairs were being carried out the name *Dunbar* was painted out and replaced by *Chertsey*. Mr Woodcock, the first mate, explained that all the firm's ships were named after places in and around London. This was *Chertsey* No.2, the previous one had been lost to enemy action off Algiers not long after they had bought her. She was a fast ship capable of maintaining an average speed of 12 knots, but the coal consumption, 28 to 30 tons a day at that speed, was high for a ship with a dead-weight of barely 6000 tons.

Captain W. F. Bassett was one of the largest human beings I have ever known; he possessed enormous strength and a great sense of humour, there was no swank about him. He was a man you could talk to and he would listen. I felt she was a happy ship, and that was precisely how it turned out to be.

After completion of the repairs we moved into the Queen's Dock to load a cargo of coal for Genoa. On the strength of my certificate as a seaman gunner and the submarine menace course, I was now appointed ship's gunnery officer in charge of all armaments aboard. While under repair there had been fitted aft, on the poop, a runway for dropping depth charges and a supply of them now came on board and were secured to the rails on both sides.

We left Glasgow on October 18th and laid in Lamlash Bay. When the convoy was assembled, some eight or nine vessels, we proceeded to Milford Haven where quite a concourse of ships of all nationalities were gathered. When we left we were the largest convoy I had yet been in, and what a collection – Italian, Greek, Dutch, French, Spanish, Norwegian and Danish as well as British. We streamed out during the forenoon, nobody in the order given in the instructions. The chaos caused by trying to form up went on most of the day. The foreign ships either could not, or would not, understand the convoy diagram. The escorting destroyers raced around trying to shepherd them into station, the task being made more difficult by their shouted orders not being understood. Fortunately the column leaders were British;

they got into position and kept station and speed, while behind them the mass of ships swirled around, chased here and there by the destroyers. Station keeping was a nerve-wracking affair. The escorts gave up the impossible task of keeping order and just steamed along in sullen silence at the head of the shambling mass of vessels, leaving them to their own devices. There was an air of discontent and lethargy about the convoy, if indeed it could be called a convoy. The war had lasted too long and everyone had ceased to care what happened.

The ships which were heading south disentangled themselves from the mass and formed a convoy of their own. Under the wing of the other escorts we struggled towards Gibraltar. One morning at daylight, in sight of Cape Spartel, the signal went up to FORM SINGLE LINE AHEAD to enter Gibraltar and pick up anchorage. That was a memorable day. We were in six columns. The exercise, as the Navy called it, was simple enough: centre column increases to full speed; remainder decrease speed; starboard inside column falls in astern, then port column, and so on, the wing columns last. As we were second to last in the port wing column it was afternoon before we were in line. We were lucky at that, as before long complete chaos reigned. Signals and expostulations from the escorts went unheeded and instead of arriving in the orderly procession envisaged by the naval authorities, the convoy arrived in the Bay like a football crowd coming out after a match, it was every ship for itself.

That night the whole Rock was lit up and sounds of rejoicing floated out to us. A passing patrol boat informed us that an armistice had been signed but then all went quiet again. We heard next morning that there had been a misunderstanding, there was no armistice yet. Still everyone had the feeling the war was over.

We had come here to join the Mediterranean convoy for Italian ports. This convoy was also multi-national both in the merchant and escort fleets. In addition to British there were French, Italian and American escorts, but which nationality was in charge I don't know. Somehow we formed up in two columns in Gibraltar Bay. Being November the days were short and, though this convoy was much smaller than the previous one, it was quite dark by the time we were all round Europa Point.

A vessel in station on our starboard beam continually kept crowding us and signalling him to keep his proper distance had no effect whatsoever. After a session with him one morning Captain Bassett said, 'I'll fix that fellow, hoist the signal, MY STEERING GEAR IS UNRELIABLE.' That fixed him all right. What Captain Bassett considered a good joke had consequences he had not foreseen. The other ships had read the signal as well and kept away, so we had a wide-open space all round us. The escort had taken the signal to mean what it said, and we were told to take up station as rear ship of the column. In the event it was fortunate we had been demoted to the rear.

It was sometime the following morning that the alarm sounded – the steering gear had jammed with the starboard helm on. Captain Bassett immediately rang the engines to STOP and FULL ASTERN to keep clear of our next abeam, also hoisting

S.S. Chertsey at the buoys.

the signal, STEERING GEAR OUT OF ORDER. In the meantime Mr Woodcock and I tried to locate the trouble. The steering gear in this ship was the rod and chain system. The rods which ran along the bridge deck terminated in a gear box under the engineers' mess-room settee, and part of the carpenter's duties was to oil the steering gear, which had a wooden cover over it. On this occasion he had omitted to replace the cover, and it was unfortunate that the mess-room steward had been in the habit of throwing the dirty tablecloths under the settee. He had tossed one under that morning and, the lid being off, it got pulled into the gears and which became jammed. The whole incident lasted less than half an hour but if we had been in our previous station a collision would have been unavoidable. It brought to mind the saying 'talk of the devil'.

With the arrival of the convoy the harbour at Genoa was full. At that time it was only a shallow bay enclosed by two breakwaters. With British troops down from the front for a rest camped just outside the city, and convoy crews of many nationalities in the harbour, the place was liable to boil over at any time.

We had been discharging our coal for two days and during that time the whole place was buzzing with rumours about an armistice. At 11 a.m. on 11th November 1918, all the church bells commenced tolling and ships blowing their whistles. The news came, authentic this time, that an armistice had been signed and the war was over. The cargomen dropped shovels and raced ashore, the crane men tied down the lanyards of the crane whistles and cleared off. The third mate tied our whistle lanyard down and let it blow till the steam died down, and no work was done by anyone. Captain Bassett was not on board, in fact he was not seen for two days. Shouting and singing could be heard from all parts of the city.

That evening Mr Woodcock and I went ashore to have dinner and see what was going on. Up till then things had been noisy but orderly enough. Now the leave parties were ashore and getting drunk as fast as they could. On this particular night it meant everybody from the naval craft and also the crews of the merchant ships were ashore at the same time.

Mr Woodcock and I got into the Cafe Verdi, near the main piazza, which was one of the posh places at that time. The dining room had been practically taken over by British naval officers who had arrived at that stage of drunkenness when the desire is to fight or break something. We had not been sat down for many minutes, and were still waiting to order, when a number of officers started breaking up the tables and chairs and heaping them in the centre of the floor. Using paper napkins and anything else that would burn they set the bonfire alight and, joining hands, danced round it roaring and singing. The waiters, led I presume by the manager, tried to break through and put the fire out, but the ring of dancing figures kept them away. Fighting and scuffling broke out and it looked like the whole place would go up as the fire was continually being fed with bottles of spirits. We got out fast.

The piazza was packed with a shouting and singing mob. The statue of Garibaldi on horseback had a British bluejacket standing on the horse and waving a blue flare. Just how he managed to get up there I do not know. Whether we did get a meal that night I can't remember. What I do remember clearly was sitting in a small cafe when a party of Tommies poured in, all well oiled. They asked if we were British. They were, they said, down from the front for rest and camped outside the city.

'Come along with us,' they yelled, and tried to pull us out of the door.

'What are you going to do,' I asked. 'Do they roared, 'hit everybody who's not British.' So four years of war did not provide enough fighting. We were all supposed to be rejoicing that the war was over, but for some it was 'hit everybody who's not British.' We managed to break loose from them and stayed where we were, neither of us wished to hit anybody.

We got back to the ship sometime in the early morning to find it deserted, not a soul anywhere. During the day the ships' company gradually trickled back, some showing scars of battle but nothing serious. Mr Woodcock and I ran a first aid station patching people up with sticking plaster and bandages. To make things more difficult nearly everyone was still drunk. The third mate had two beautiful black eyes and looked as if he had been rolled in a rubbish tip.

Sometime during the following forenoon someone kept hailing the ship from a boat alongside. In it was Captain Bassett demanding that the accommodation ladder be lowered down to enable him to come aboard. With some difficulty I managed to convince him that we were moored to a quay, not at anchor in the harbour, and got the boat to the quay astern of the ship. He was a sight with his clothes all torn and rumpled, his face looked as if it had been trodden on, besides being unshaven and filthy. He was still half drunk and, when I got him to his room, he insisted that all the mates and engineers come along and celebrate the armistice. It ended up with everyone getting drunk again. He also sent bottles of whisky forward, roaring and singing went on there for hours, but mercifully no fighting started.

Discharging resumed and some days later we left Genoa for Gibraltar to coal on our way, in ballast, to the River Plate, South America. By the time we left, everyone had forgotten about the war and navigation lights were on as there was no blackout. I have no memory of the war ever being discussed again.

Now the war was over, and there were no more lookouts and gun watches, the mate put his deckhands and apprentices on to the task of getting the ship back into condition. When the rust was chipped away the state of the vessel could be plainly seen. On reaching the tropics all the awnings were brought out on deck for overhaul and, when everything was set up, she was as well fitted as any Brocklebank ship. Everything was in good condition.

We made a fast run to Montevideo then up to Rosario for bulk wheat where we berthed in what was called a cliff berth. The grain sheds were on top of a bank about a hundred feet high, although not exactly a cliff. Long wooden shutes led from the sheds to each hatch; the bags of grain slid down, were slit open and the contents emptied into the hold – a surprisingly fast method. This was just as well as this berth was next to a bone yard. Because meat still adhered to the bones the place stank to high heaven and was the happy hunting ground for millions of flies. What with flies during the day and mosquitoes at night it was a typical Argentine summer.

We completed loading with bagged wheat in Buenos Aires. Our berth was in one of the row of small docks along the front of the city, which went out of use when the New Port was built. Between the inner side of these docks and the front of the city was an area of waste ground where the beachcombers lived in shacks built out of empty tin cans, boxes and corrugated tin sheets. At that time in Buenos Aires it was not advisable for anyone to return alone from the city at night. Quite often bodies were seen floating in the docks, and we had to go ashore in groups of not less than half a dozen – it could be a very dangerous place.

We called in to St. Vincent, Cape Verde Islands for coal and received orders to discharge at Avonmouth.

Barry dock was full of laid up ships and the *Chertsey* joined them. While the war was on there were too few ships, now there were too many, so there we stayed with a skeleton crew and waited for better times. It was here we acquired Mr Jackson as mate. A barrel-shaped man with the smallest feet I have ever seen on a man, so small that he minced along like a lady in high heels. The period he had spent in the navy appeared to have had a profound effect on him and he was full of navy jargon which no one understood. It was 'dear boy' this and 'old chap' that, he never sat down anywhere he 'came to an anchor, breezed or drifted in,' and such talk. He had also acquired a taste for whisky and gin and was, as we found out, well on his way to becoming an alcoholic.

Orders came at last to load a cargo of coals for Venice, what we were to do after that was not yet known. It transpired that we were to go to New York, Rotterdam and finally the Tyne for survey.

Standing on the poop on a dreary, wet afternoon I had my first sight of the River Tyne and what lay along its banks. A more depressing picture I had never seen, everything looked dirty and dilapidated and most of it seemed to be falling to pieces. We had arrived on a Saturday afternoon and had to wait until Monday morning for paying off. It was then I found out I had been selected to standby during the survey as officer in charge. Mr Lang, head superintendent of Watts Watts & Co. Ltd., arrived on board.

'So you are the officer in charge.' He looked me over without further comment. 'This is a list of the repairs I will put in hand. I wish you to keep a record of what work is done each week and send it to me at the London office. Also include your opinion of the work, good or bad; it will be a guide for me when I come up to make an inspection. Do not mince matters, remember you are in charge.' The chief engineer received similar instructions.

While we were lying at the dry dock quay I received a postcard from my sister. She had just been demobilised from her wartime job and was on her way home. She would stop, she said, in South Shields and pay me a visit over the weekend. There was no habitable room on the ship so I had to put her into the Neptune Hotel. That weekend cost me something apart from the money she borrowed; that I assume was the real reason for the visit rather than sisterly affection.

The extent of the repairs that had to be carried out astonished me and in all we were there two months and 22 days. We were now painted out in the company's colour scheme and after the all grey of the war years she looked very smart indeed.

Mr Jackson returned as mate and a Captain Thomas Mitchell arrived to take command. He appeared to be teetotal but soon fell under the alcoholic influence of Mr Jackson and that ultimately the downfall of them both.

Mr Jacques, the chief engineer was a very peculiar man. He wrote up his log in copperplate handwriting and as far as I knew that was all he did – according to the engineers he never went below. When I was promoted to mate I became his deadly enemy, first mates were his natural foes. Later still, when I took over command, we became friends again.

The passage down to the River Plate was uneventful. From there it was to Dakar then Le Havre where we arrived just after Christmas. We were there nearly a month as constant rain made discharge almost impossible. However, the third mate, wireless operator and myself had a good time. The place was boiling over with displaced persons and the value of the franc had dropped against the pound so everything was cheap. We discovered, along the coast, a roller skating rink cum dance hall, nightclub and cafe all under one roof, and spent most of our time there.

We were joined by Mrs Mitchell and Mrs Jackson. One day Mrs Mitchell returned from a visit ashore with a roulette wheel, only a small one, which was intended as a present for their children. She brought it out after dinner to see if it would work. Suffice to say it did. By four in the afternoon she had cleaned us all out – that wheel was no toy. Offers to come along for a game of an evening were subsequently declined.

This coming passage would be my first winter crossing of the North Atlantic in ballast, as we had no cargo. Captain Mitchell had insisted on taking 600 tons of sand ballast, some in the lower holds and the remainder on deck. This caused two or three days delay as it had to be properly secured. The first time we attempted to sail something broke in the engines and we were towed back to a berth near the locks. A day or two later we tried again and actually got through the locks when the boiler tubes began leaking, so it was back to berth again. In pouring rain and strong winds we managed to get away at the third attempt, but when unmooring our stern ropes were found to have been overlaid by the head ropes of the ship astern. No amount of shouting could rouse anyone on board to slacken them, so finally they had to be cut adrift.

The rolling was sickening and, with the racing of the propeller, I thought the whole fabric of the ship would come apart. Gale followed gale and by heading up to the seas we were making no headway. Because of the constant racing there was also the risk of the propeller coming loose and dropping off. That was no uncommon happening in the North Atlantic. So when the south-westerly gales came on we just laid beam on and rolled it out. Eating under those conditions was almost impossible. Food arrived in a basin, which had to be clutched in one hand, with the fork or spoon in the other, and your legs firmly braced around the chair pedestal.

The weather on the passage back was good, for the time of year, until we got just over half way and then we caught a full western ocean gale. During the forenoon the wind had freshened and, with a rising sea and falling barometer, it showed all the signs of a really hard blow. The wind and sea were dead astern and we were making good time but, when I took over my watch, the wind was reaching up to gale force with a heavy breaking sea. As long as I kept the seas astern she was not taking much water but, if she fell off, even a point, the after well deck filled up. I sent down to Captain Mitchell and said that, in my opinion, the ship should be hove to now while there was time, as before long she would be pooping (taking heavy weather over the poop). The only reply I received was to the effect that we were doing 14 knots and going along fine. The man I sent down reported the captain was in his bunk and had a bottle with him. Mr Jackson came up for his watch and got a fright.

'My God,' he said, 'why aren't we hove to?' By then we were driving along before a full gale with towering seas roaring up astern. 'What course are you on?' he asked.

'I'm not steering a course,' I told him, ' just keeping the seas astern.' Just then one caught the bridge on the port side and took away part of the overhang.

'I shall have to go down and see if I can get him out, she can't stand this much longer.' When he came back he said, 'He's as drunk as a lord, I can't get any sense out of him.' I tried to persuade him to heave her to himself while there was still daylight, but he was too afraid he would be blamed if things got badly damaged.

I went below and some time later a tremendous crash woke me. Apparently a huge sea had smashed in the captain's alleyway door and flooded his cabin. Both lifeboats had been carried away. That sobered up the captain. He tried to heave to but she lay in the trough and would not come up. There was only one thing to do, run her off again and keep the seas astern. All hands were called out – it was now a case of saving the ship. I was sent to collect drums of oil from the engine-room and these were put in the after heads (lavatories) with holes pierced in them to let the oil seep slowly out. In the course of time this had some effect and smoothed out the breaking crests. At some time during the night the barometer started to rise, the wind hauled to the north-west, and the seas began to moderate. The ship was a wreck, everything that was not part of the built-in structure had gone. Worst of all was the galley, it had been completely gutted. A kind of stove was contrived out of an empty forty-gallon oil drum and we did manage to get some hot food. We were lucky to find most of the pots and pans. Fortunately we had fine weather long enough to reach Cherbourg.

When the discharge was completed we left for the Tyne, and I went home to study and sit the examination for master.

Chapter 11

Glasgow Technical College

*T*he new additions to the master's examination syllabus had made Tait's Academy out of date so I enrolled at the Technical College. The navigation department was full to the brim; even candidates for master were there by the score, partly due to men from the naval reserve coming back after the war. I was still only 22 and new regulations stated the exam for second mate could not be taken until the age of 21, so one would have to be nearly 24 before the master's exams could be sat. The verdict was that, as I held a first mate's certificate before the new regulations came into force, and had my time in for master, I was entitled to sit the exam, so I carried on.

I was just over three months studying but, as I had some £200 saved, I was in no hurry. I hadn't had a decent spell at home since the *Bengali* was under repair after the fire. I found working at home was impossible with two brothers, and the friends of Jenny and my mother, so the only time I spent studying was in the train.

The master in charge of mates and masters was a Captain McDonald, a superb teacher when you gave him a chance to teach; actually there were far too many for him to handle. Smoking was not allowed in class or in the corridors and this became a sore point. From eleven in the morning an interval of ten minutes was given for a smoke, but for most of the class it was noon before they came back into the classroom, then it was time for dinner. The washroom of a morning would be packed full and covered with a dense haze of cigarette smoke. On one occasion Captain Brown was to deliver a lecture on tides. Finding only a few in the classroom he appeared in the washroom armed with desk and blackboard.

'If the class will not come to the teacher, the teacher must go to the class,' he said and he proceeded to give his lecture right there in the washroom.

No classes were held on a Saturday, but as the college belonged to the Glasgow Corporation it was never closed. Anyone who was in possession of a ticket was free to go in and work. I, and one or two others, usually went in to get some practice on the deviascope, the model on which we were taught ship's magnetism, deviation of the compass by the earth's magnetic force and a ship's induced magnetism. For a long time I couldn't make head nor tail of this, it was as clear to me as Greek. I had it word-perfect but still could not understand it. Then one morning I woke up and the whole thing was crystal clear. I had heard of things like this happening but didn't believe it was possible, now I knew it was. Others got to know about our Saturday mornings and before long there were quite a number. By this time I was a crack hand at this subject and found myself at the blackboard, with the deviascope, conducting what was, in effect, a class of my own. We all seemed to learn a great deal more on those mornings than we ever did in class. We were not aware that anyone else knew about this and I was quite surprised one afternoon when, for some urgent reason, Captain McDonald was called away. He threw his chalk over to me with the remark 'I understand you take a class in this subject on Saturday mornings so you will be able to carry on in my place, I now hand over the class to you.'

Running round with my sister's friends was proving expensive and the day came when father warned me my money was getting low and I had better sit the exam while I still had some left.

I went to put in my papers for the examination and ran into trouble. During the war, regulations had come out to ensure no one but a British subject could command a British vessel, and a candidate for master had to produce his birth certificate as well as those of his father and mother. I hadn't got a birth certificate, only a certificate of baptism, which was accepted. Similarly, father and mother didn't have birth certificates so I got father to apply to Edinburgh House for copies. He got one for mother but, as he had been born before registration of births became compulsory, they had no record of him at all. He wrote to the minister in charge of the parish church in Alford, where he had been christened, and was told the old church had burnt down with all the records lost. There was only one thing left to do. In Scotland the family Bible had a number of pages in the front for recording births, deaths and marriages and an entry in the family Bible was allowed as proof. Uncle George had the family bible in Kildrummy and it was sent down to father. I took it to Sergeant Gordon, who was registrar in Uddingston, and he sent a certified copy to Edinburgh House. In due course they issued a birth certificate for father – he had now been officially born! When the Bible arrived he saw to his astonishment that he was two years younger than he thought. 'There's something wrong with that,' he said, 'otherwise I joined the Army when I was 15.'

I had no trouble with any of the papers until my seamanship, on the Thursday afternoon, with Captain Ellery who had been in command of Brocklebank's *Mahratta*. He commenced with the rule of the road and, as well as covering steamers, he introduced questions about sailing ships. He looked at my papers.

'I see you have an AB's discharge from the *Bengali,* that is one of Brocklebank's ships.'

'Yes sir, I served most of my apprenticeship in that ship.'

'Oh, so you should know something about sail.' He pulled the sailing ship model towards him and indicated the topsail. 'What is the name of that sail?' I told him. Then he went over each one. He began to get annoyed, things were not turning out as he thought they would. 'You have lost your propeller and no assistance at hand for a tow, put the ship under jury sail.' I survived that one as well, and the next few questions. Then it was back to the sailing ship. I could see he was determined to fail me if he could, but I was not going to let him catch me out in either steam or sail. Then I had to make all sail, take it in as the weather grew worse until I hove to under a reefed main lower topsail.

Looking at my papers again he remarked, 'I see you are still only 22, you are just a boy and have not got enough experience to be in possession of a master's certificate.' He persisted, 'You are lying with two anchors down in a river with a strong ebb tide running and blowing a gale down river. No main steam. Three mooring buoys in a line across your stern close to. The anchors start dragging, what are you going to do?'

'If the anchors are dragging, sir, it would be no use paying out more cable. With the buoys so close astern the anchors would be bound to foul at least one of the buoy moorings. I would heave them both off the bottom and let her drift down, if not able to sheer clear, the buoys would do no harm, just rub along the ship's side, when well clear of them try to re-anchor again.'

'You have no deck steam,' he said.

'In that case I would be unable to use the anchors for dredging or the rudder for sheering so she would just foul one of the buoy moorings but, by that time, the tugs would have hold of her as I would be flying the signal for tug assistance.' I could now see that this was one of those situations in which any answer I gave would be the wrong one. What he expected me to say I did not know.

'What would you do?' I asked him

'I am the examiner not the candidate. I am sorry but I am unable to pass you. In any case you should not be here as under the regulations the examination for second mate cannot be taken until the age of 21, you would have to be at least 24 to be able to sit for master. You can come again in three months, but I advise you to wait for a couple of years.'

So that was it. Why, I wondered, was I accepted for the examination when I put my papers in. Perhaps he had decided to fix that 'young know-all' good and proper. Anyway there it was. I would not now be able to boast that I passed for master at 22. I went back to the college to see Captain Brown and explain what had happened.

Chapter 12

S.S.Kandelfels

I now had to find myself a ship before all my money disappeared. I toured the tramp firms in Glasgow but there was nothing doing. Every Saturday I wrote to Watts Watts, but there were no vacancies. I was getting desperate when, early in the fourth week I received a letter from them. I was to join the *Kandelfels* in Cardiff, at a wage of £26 per month – my persistence had paid off. With just about enough money for train fares and expenses I arrived in Cardiff during the afternoon of July 3lst 1920.

Captain Henderson Gow came on board soon after I arrived and read the letter I had been given.

'Donald, that's a Scots name, where are you from?'

'Aberdeenshire, brought up in Uddingston, but my father came from Kildrummy.'

'Who was your mother?'

'Her maiden name was Jane Bain from Clynelish in Sutherland.'

'You may be wondering why I am asking all these questions. Well you somehow remind me of the master of my first ship, by the name of Gauld from Portsoy.'

'My grandmother's father.'

'So you're the spawn of that old villain. I ran away from that ship in New Zealand and lived with the Maoris. Your great-grandfather was a very peculiar man, very peculiar indeed.'

This was all very interesting. As great-grandfather William had died in 1871, in his eighties. How old was Captain Gow?

One afternoon when he came up on the bridge he seemed to be in a mood for talking. I took a chance and asked him about my great-grandfather. 'You said you made your first voyage to sea with him, what kind of a man was he, sir?'

'He was about your height, broad and powerful, with a long beard. He had religion and had it bad, but it was never allowed to interfere with business or the

The ex-German Hansa Line Kandelfels.

way he ran his ship. On a Sunday all hands, except the helmsman, had to assemble no matter what the weather, for Sunday service which he took himself, reading from a huge Bible. He dressed in a frock coat, black silk stock and a plug hat tied on with rope yarn if it was blowing hard. He also had a belaying pin in each pocket. If anyone was caught yawning they got it, he was a dead shot with a belaying pin. We didn't get much to eat and could never get any money out of him. He drove everyone so hard the crew jumped ship the first opportunity they got. I suppose that was the idea, a ship lying waiting for wool did not need a crew aboard. I cleared out when we got to New Zealand and went to live with the Maoris.' That was all I got out of him.

This proved to be the ship's last voyage with Watts Watts, she was not suitable for their type of cargo, and shortly afterwards she was put up for sale.

When I arrived back home I couldn't make up my mind whether to go back to the technical college, try to find another ship or give up seafaring altogether. I was completely fed up.

'What you need is something to do,' said father, 'I have plenty of work for you.' This I realised was another attempt to get me into his business, but I agreed, for a short while anyway.

I was given the outside work to do, collecting rents, insurance premiums and acting as investigating official for the labour exchange. My wages were £3 16s per week, of which 30*s* was to be handed over to mother. It was often a fruitless exercise, but I did manage to collect something now and then. This was the one and only time I tried working ashore, and the only time I got the sack, and that from my father. Mother kept pleading with me to go to the office again, but I had had enough. The conviction was growing in me that this was not the life for me at all. Perhaps if I had a girlfriend things might have been different, but there was none that I cared to bother with. In any case I had decided I would never marry.

My young brother James had now definitely made up his mind that he was going to sea. Since he was born he had always looked to me for everything, what Will said went, as far as he was concerned and that was that. When father realised there was no hope of him going into the business he lost interest. I had heard of a cadet's course that Captain Brown was planning to introduce and I went to talk with him. It would be for 12 months with an examination to decide if the course had been of any use. He was enrolled and I would pay all the expenses.

I wrote once again to Watts Watts and one afternoon received a telegram. JOIN MORTLAKE SECOND MATE 27TH JANUARY HULL. ACKNOWLEDGE. I was thinking this over when another telegram arrived. JOIN CHATHAM 27TH MIDDLESBOROUGH SECOND MATE CHINA VOYAGE. ACKNOWLEDGE. I acknowledged. JOINING CHATHAM 27TH SECOND MATE. DONALD.

It was a very cold winter and I didn't seem able to get warm no matter what I put on. I was cold and I didn't know where the *Mortlake* was bound, but the *Chatham* was going to China and that meant warm weather. I had been working ashore for just eight weeks.

Chapter 13

Slow boat to China

I arrived on board the vessel lying at Dent's Wharf, Middlesborough late on the afternoon of 27th January, and reported to Captain Robert Anderson, a Scot from Dundee. He was pleased to have one of his countrymen with him, but would rather have had one from his own area.

'A Glasgow man thinks he knows it all,' he said.

'Well, why not,' was my reply, 'he usually does.'

'What experience have you had east of Suez?' he asked. This seemed to be worrying him.

'I served my apprenticeship on the Calcutta run and have been in East Africa,' I said. That appeared to satisfy him. He had never been east and neither had the mate who was a Black Sea and River Plate man.

Our cargo was pitch and during loading the dust got on hands and faces causing itching and blisters. We were supplied with goggles, edged with fur to fit tightly, but they caused sweating round the eyes and became fogged up. Exposed skin had to be whitewashed, so we were a queer looking lot while loading went on.

Our port of discharge was to be Hongay which we couldn't find on our general coast chart of the Tongking Gulf, so we wrote to London for the latitude and longitude. This indicated a bay, seemingly chock-full of small islands. A pilot, on request to the pilot station at Haiphong, would proceed to Cleft Island to meet inbound vessels. There was no other Admiralty chart of that region.

As we had to proceed direct to Hongay from Suez it would be a long passage with such a slow vessel, and fresh water was going to be vital. A rigorous check had to be kept and the whole ship put on ration from the time of leaving Suez. Being the north-east monsoon season we could not hope for rain; we had no awnings and I was the only one with tropical kit and a sun helmet. Down below the stokehold became an inferno and first one fireman, then another, was brought up and laid

S.S.Chatham loading guano at the isalnd of Juan-de-Nova, January 1922.

out under the boat deck overhang to recover. The firemen and engineers were sweating so much they had to drink gallons of water and this put more strain on our small supply. We were allowed only one decanter of drinking water per day.

Slowly we crept our way towards Hongay, and in due course a radio message was sent to the pilot station at Haiphong. The pilot, we were told, was proceeding to Cleft Island. As the sailing directions gave no advice as to how to get to this island, I assumed it must be one of the outer islands and easy to approach. Sure enough we eventually saw a high cone shaped island which had a distinct gap splitting it into two peaks. We could see a white house and a flagstaff with a pilot flag flying. I have seen some pilotage in my time but nothing like that. It was pitch black when we started off, at full speed, steering straight for one of the islands which showed a tiny light to one side. When we seemed about to crash into it we went hard over round the light which turned out to be on the pilot's sampan. When we had rounded it the sampan cut across and was lying with his light at the next turn, and that was how it continued. Daylight revealed we were anchored in an open area surrounded by small islands. There was no sign of habitation, just some sheds and offices surrounded by a 12-foot-high fence, but I was told there was a town, about nine miles inland, near the coalfields. Two junks arrived and moored one either side of the ship and a stream of men, women and children poured onboard. The whole surface of the pitch was marked out into squares and each square was worked by a family using baskets. Every particle of that pitch, 5000 tons, was taken out, but it took six weeks to do it. The pitch was to be mixed with coal dust to form some kind of brickette.

My endeavours to obtain one of the ship's boats for a Sunday outing among the islands met with no success. We would get lost, run the boat on a rock, get it stolen, any mishap that could possibly happen was given as an excuse. So one Sunday morning I chartered one of the sampans for the day. Anyone who wished to come was welcome. Ships owned by Watts Watts had been coming here with cargoes of pitch for a long time. A number of years' ago a captain had drunk himself into such a state that he ran up on to the poop, jumped over the side and drowned. He was buried on one of the islands and it became tradition for each one of the Watts' ships that came here to send a party over to repaint the wooden cross and tidy up the grave. It was also a tradition for the name and date of each ship to be painted on the gallery of the big cave, one of many caves on the islands. Our first visit was to the captain's grave, which was just a mound with a decaying wooden cross, the name not now discernible. It was given a coat of paint. Next we went to the big cave, which was enormous. The gallery was a wide ledge which ran along the whole of one side and we added *Chatham* to the list of ships' names. Then we wandered from island to island and eventually arrived back at the ship after a very enjoyable day.

After a brief stop in Saigon we loaded rice in Hong Kong for Hamburg, a passage which was to take us 92 days! By the time we arrived, only the first few tiers of rice were in good condition, the rest was rice soup. Cleaning the bilges on the way back to Cardiff was a lovely job.

When I arrived home in March 1922, after a second voyage in the *Chatham*, I enrolled at the technical college. There would be no playing around this time, a master's certificate I intended to obtain and by the middle of June, Captain McDonald judged me ready for the examination. I put in my papers and was accepted for the week commencing June 15th. Everything went smoothly and by the Thursday morning we were through everything except the deviascope and seamanship. To my surprise I was told I was finished for the day and to return at 10 a.m. the following morning. I couldn't understand why.

'You're all right, you're through,' said the clerk, 'he will fix you up in a few minutes tomorrow.'

The next day I was asked to read the barometer, answer one question on master's business, and a question on the deviascope which was the toughest one in the whole subject. Then he got up, shook hands and vanished down the stairs.

'That was fast work,' I said .

'All you had to do was the written work,' said the clerk, 'the rest you had passed before. I'm not supposed to show you this but you are an unusual case.' He opened a large ledger at an entry marked with red ink. 'You passed the examination when you were up before. Somehow you got on the wrong side of Captain Ellery and he failed you on a question for which there was no answer. Captain Harding didn't want the others to see you would only be a few minutes in the seamanship room.'

I was now a *Master Mariner*.

My brother James had now completed his 12 months at Captain Brown's cadet course, and had taken the examination. Captain Brown called me into his office and showed me the exam papers – they were completely blank. James had not even tried to do any of the problems.

'I am afraid you have wasted your money on your brother Mr Donald, he will never do any good. But,' he added, 'he did well in the oral and practical seamanship tests.'

'That,' I told him, 'was all I wanted to know.' The main thing was he had the inclination and makings of a seaman. 'I will get him taken on as an apprentice in the firm I am in, Watts Watts of London.'

I wrote to them and the reply was favourable, subject to the usual medical tests and school reports. I laid down the law and told him if he wanted to succeed he would have to get stuck into his navigation and other work otherwise serving four years' apprenticeship would be a waste of time. I took him down the Broomielaw one afternoon and fitted him out. The cost was only one tenth of what had been spent on me when I joined the Anchor Line.

Chapter 14

Return to the Chertsey

and adventures in Russia

*I*t had always been my intention to get into one of the firms trading on regular routes when I passed for master, so I wrote, among others, to the New Zealand Shipping Company. I received a reply, then a telegram, calling me for an interview. I should have taken all my gear with me, but went with only pyjamas and shaving kit. I was passed and told to proceed directly to their ship sailing that evening from Southampton.

'I don't have my gear with me,' I told them, 'can I go back for it?'

'No, I am sorry, the ship will be sailing in a few hours, your name will be placed on the waiting list.' So that was that.

As I had time to kill, I decided to take a look at Watts Watts offices. The entrance door was wide open so I went inside. The silence was intense. I had turned to walk out again when I heard a chair creaking. Moved by a desire to speak to someone, now I was there, I looked into the room. A large man was sitting at a desk.

'Good afternoon,' he said, 'can I help you?'

'I should like to speak to the marine superintendent,' I replied.

'What is your name?'

'William Donald, I have been serving as second mate in this company and have just passed for master.

'Why haven't you notified us, you should have written. Captain Cox isn't here at the moment, I am Captain Musson, acting assistant. The *Chertsey*,' he said looking in a ledger, 'you have been in her before, she is at present under repair on the Tyne. You are now due for a first mate's birth, but there isn't one available at the moment so you will have to re-join as second mate, but do not, under any circumstances, leave that ship. I will send you a telegram when to join.' We shook hands and I walked out. So I had lost a fourth mate's position, with little hope of immediate advancement, in the New Zealand Shipping Company and found myself still a second mate, but with prospects of promotion. I got a shock though – the second mate's wages were now down to £12 per month from the £16 I received on the *Chatham*. I returned home that night.

The ship was laid in the usual repair berth and looked a shabby, forlorn object. Captain Mitchell and Mr Jackson had been sacked for hitting the bottle too hard, they were well on the way when I left in 1920. The new master was a Captain Randall, and the mate Tom Walsh. I was surprised to see by the articles that Captain Randall was only 55, he looked 70. He was an alcoholic, and the worst case I ever encountered.

When the repairs were completed we were directed to Hartlepool to load and then to Searsport USA to discharge.

Loading in Hartlepool didn't take long. The situation on board was much the same as it had been on the *Carston*. Captain Randall was no navigator and unless specifically asked he never came on to the bridge or into the chartroom. He was not interested in where the ship was or when she would arrive. Mr Walsh, even though he had passed for master, had spent four years sailing up and down the east coast but never, except in fog, out of sight of land, so he was not skilled in deep sea navigation. As mate, he took no sights but did learn in time to take and work out star positions morning and evening. The third mate had to be trained in practical navigation as it was his first time on the bridge.

When we left Hartlepool I asked Captain Randall which way he wished to go, north or south.

'What do you mean?' he said.

'Well,' I replied, 'it's a clean coast all the way up to the Pentland Firth, once through it's open sea and you can make a great circle track across. Going south you will have all the banks and shoals down the east coast and then the Channel traffic as well. As far as distance is concerned there is nothing much in it.' I did manage to get him into the chartroom and show him what I meant.

'We will go north,' he said.

'Shall I put her on course now sir?'

'No, head 25 miles off the coast then put her on course.'

'If we go out that far we will get mixed up with the fishing fleets.'

'Keep away from the land Mr Donald, always keep away from the land.' In the name of God, I thought, what have I met now. When Mr Walsh came up for his watch I told him what had happened.

'He's been too long in sailing ships and thinks he will get caught on a lee shore. Anyway he's drunk and has been since he came on board, but if he runs out of liquor he will go off his nut.'

We made a good run across and it was a relief to be in a ship that could move, even though she was only a heap of scrap. We settled into a routine and Captain

Randall never appeared during the passage. According to the steward he spent most of his time in his bunk ill, but there was always a bottle in the bunk with him.

While we were in Searsport the captain asked me into the saloon one morning and handed me a letter he had received from Watts. 'Write out a reply to this letter,' he said.

'That sir, is not part of a second mate's work and I have no idea what you want to say.'

'The second mate,' he said, ' is the captain's secretary; anyway you will have to learn to do this. Your letter does not go off the ship, I will type one out from it.' A while later he was out on deck talking to the mate, when I heard the clicking of a typewriter. In the saloon sat the steward typing out a copy of the letter I had written. Some ship I thought when the second mate answers the letters and the steward types them out. I found I also had to make up the sailing sheet, which was a return of cash drawn and issued with a complete report of cargo loaded or discharged and all other relevant data. What, I wondered, did Captain Randall do for himself? As I found out in due course, nothing at all. If ever a man held a job by false pretences he did, paid for doing nothing, only for being there.

Heading for Glasgow on our return trip I had a feeling of impending catastrophe.

'We will make up the account of wages this evening ready for the pay off tomorrow,' said the captain. I had kept the cashbook and knew that it was in order but when he handed me the wages book, it was completely blank. I can still remember the details of that night. Mr Walsh, myself, the third mate, wireless operator and steward were all round the table with the captain. It was around three in the morning when we finished, and by then the steward had carried the captain to his bunk. That night taught me a great many things. The pay off the following afternoon went off quietly enough; Captain Randall was, for once, sober and managed to sign the discharge books quite legibly.

After what had happened the only way to keep the ship's accounts under control was for me to take over and deal with all money matters myself. One day, when he happened to be sober enough, I put the matter to him and he agreed, so I took possession of the account of wages book, the stock of sailing sheets, cash book, insurance books and some of the portage account sheets. He agreed he would draw the money I asked for and give me a note of the amount he actually drew, with a copy of his receipt. The money was locked in his safe and the key hidden in a place he couldn't find. All this, coupled with having to go ashore on arrival and departure with Captain Randall, gave me a complete knowledge of master's business which few men had the opportunity to acquire before attaining command. It never occurred to me that the London office would get to know what went on, but they did, as I found out when I was eventually given command of the ship. It may seem a strange situation for a second mate but it was the only way with a confirmed alcoholic like Captain Randall. He was now drinking two bottles a day and spent most of his time in his bunk. He was not in a fit state to be in command of a ship, or to be in a ship at all. Mr Walsh, the first mate, should have called the superintendent's attention to the state he was in.

Early in August 1924 we eventually persuaded him to see a doctor in Port Said. He advised immediate removal to hospital, but Captain Randall refused. The doctor prescribed some medicine but told Mr Walsh he was in a very serious condition. The day after we left Port Said Mr Walsh came to me in a panic.

'For God's sake Bill come and have a look at this.' I went with him to the captain's bathroom. He pointed to the lavatory pan and whispered 'In heaven's name what's that?' It was guts, there was no mistake about that. I went in to see him and he was quite calm. There was nothing we could do for him.

It was only then that Mr Walsh sent a cable to London telling them Captain Randall was dangerously ill and would be landed in Malta. When we arrived he was taken straight to hospital and died the next day.

A cable was received from London stating Mr Walsh was to take over as master, with Mr Donald as first mate. That was how I obtained my promotion. I went ashore to the shipping office with the new Captain Walsh. This was a change of masters and I had to be promoted to first mate on the articles. We left Malta that afternoon.

I moved into the mate's room on the other side of the deck and Mr Walsh occupied the master's room. During the passage to Ipswich I collected the account of wages book, cash and tobacco books, sailing sheets, crew lists, voyage account and discharge books, then carried the lot to Captain Walsh.

'The mate of a ship has his hands full running the ship and has no time for keeping crew's accounts,' I told him. 'Anyway that's what you told me when you were mate.'

We were paid off on 5th September 1924. I remained by her until the cargo was out and repairs well in hand then went home for a week's leave.

Things were still the same, only James was away. Jenny was still in the Labour Exchange in charge of the women's department and was still going round with her boyfriend Jack Morrison. My other brother Alex was now out of his apprenticeship with Coats the yarn people, and waiting to be appointed as a salesman somewhere in South America.

Our next voyage turned out to be the longest yet. We headed south from the River Plate, through the Magellan Strait and up the east coast of South America. From there we passed through the Panama Canal and made for Norfolk, Virginia and across the Atlantic to the Mediterranean and Alexandria before going on to Russia.

I had never been to Russia, nor had anyone else on board, with the exception of the chief engineer, Mr Jacques, but in the next few years we were to get to know it well. We passed Cape Helles and entered the Dardenelles, and next morning we anchored in Constantinople* for clearance and permission to proceed through the Bosphorus. We had heard all kinds of stories about the Bolsheviks and we were all was a bit uneasy about what would happen when we got to Poti (on the eastern side of the Black Sea). When we arrived we were the only ship there and, except for the sounds connected with berthing, there was utter stillness. This was surprising as the other side of the narrow harbour was part of the town; there were people walking about but no traffic of any kind.

After we had made fast, the Control Commission came on board. The party consisted of about 20 people, including one woman. Only one of them spoke any English. We were all mustered on deck and checked off against the crew list and discharge books. Then each person had to make a list of *all* their effects, including books, magazines, toilet requisites and any money. When this was done the searchers checked every item, and the whole ship was searched inside and out. All books, magazines and newspapers, indeed all printed matter owned by the crew, had to be brought along to the saloon, put in bundles and sealed in a bonded store. Then we were issued with a pass to be shown to the gangway guard when going ashore or coming back on board. It all took a very long time.

I had everything ready to start loading the following morning. At 8 a.m. a crowd of men, mostly with long-handled ore shovels, came marching down the quay and went into a building – the workers' rest rooms I learnt later. Then they came out and sat in a circle singing but no one came on board. The next day the same thing happened, no one seemed to be in charge of them. I had had enough of this nonsense. I could see they were all experienced men who had probably been loading ore ships all their lives, so all I had to do was find out who worked on the ship and who filled the ore tubs on the quay. Going through a pantomime of driving a winch brought out the winch drivers, and by similar means we identified those who tipped the ore buckets and the hatch men. They were quite pleased to have someone to take charge and tell them what to do. Inside half an hour the loading was in full swing. All I had to do was blow my whistle at exactly 8 a.m. each day to start them off.

The reason why there were no requests for cash from the crew was the Lenin Club. The day after our arrival an individual, who could speak English, came on board distributing pamphlets. It was communist propaganda and everyone was invited to the Lenin Club. The bait was free beer and the tap was turned off at 9 p.m. when they were treated to a lecture on the benefits of communism. Of course the free beer drew in everyone with the exception of the mates, engineers and steward. It was not politic to sit drinking with the men under your command. The first night they all got caught and had to sit the lecture out. Then they got wise and were out of the club each night before nine when the beer was turned off.

Behind the ore heaps was some waste ground and in the evenings our apprentices, and some of the crew, amused themselves by kicking our football around. They

---

* now Istanbul

108

were watched intently by a crowd of Russian boys aged from about 12 to 16. Our lads could not speak Russian, nor they English, but they picked up most of the football jargon from listening, and the rules of the game by watching. One evening I saw a very good match between teams comprising half our boys and half Russian boys. They were very enthusiastic about the game but they did not have a football, nor could they obtain one. The Russian boys formed themselves into teams and, while we were there, we let them play with our ball. Just before we were due to leave a deputation arrived and through an interpreter they asked if we would we play them for the football. It was agreed and although they played well our team won, not surprisingly. However, after the game we presented them with the ball. As Captain Walsh said, we could always get another. Whether any of this contributed to the rise of football in Russia I don't know, but those boys certainly were keen.

Another port we visited frequently was Novorossiysk, which lies at the head of a narrow bay on the eastern coast of the Black Sea. It was a very busy port and, in normal times, handled most of the grain from the eastern regions. The Black Sea grain trade was a flourishing business and a large percentage of the British tramp tonnage was engaged in it. Quite a number of firms, whose entire fleets were in the trade, went out of business when the outbreak of war closed the Dardenelles. By 1925 the Soviets had entered into the grain trade again and they had plenty to sell. Our company rushed to buy second hand ships to capitalise upon the re-opening of this trade. It was said that from 1925 to 1928 we had 25 ships on charter to the Soviets alone, most of these trading with the Black Sea ports.

On one occasion we arrived in Novorossiysk at the latter end of January. It wasn't too cold in Constantinople but when we emerged into the Black Sea it was like entering an icehouse. The kind of still weather common in that sea in winter is a slight wind, clear sky and freezing cold. In the Black Sea when the winds were southerly one could go around without an overcoat. When they were northerly it was necessary to wear all that one possessed. A north-westerly meant remaining indoors, as to go outside was to risk freezing to death. Shortly after we arrived the snow clouds began forming over the top of the high tableland on the eastern side. An easterly blizzard blowing along the steppes to the north-east drove the snow before it like sweeping a floor, and Novorossiysk, being north of the Caucasus, had no shelter from it. The appearance of this snow, looking like a dense bank of cloud from below, heralded the advance of a blizzard. The temperature was so low that the snow was frozen hard, and the force of the wind was such that, when the snow reached the edge, it descended into the valley as invisible particles of ice. This condition usually lasted about three days and during that time no work was done by anyone. Looking out, not a soul could be seen anywhere.

It was my first experience of this kind of weather. I don't know what the temperature was as the mercury had gone down into the bulb of the thermometer. The fresh-water tanks were frozen solid and I had to take the manhole door off so that the water could be chipped out with a boat axe, and the lavatories could only be cleared with boiling water from the galley. By the time food reached the saloon it was frozen and had to be warmed up again in front of the saloon fire.

It was impossible to remain outside for more than a few minutes and no loading took place during this time. I sat in my room one night with three paraffin lamps and the steam radiator under the doorstep on full. As the door faced the wind the ice particles were blown through the bottom of the door on to the wooden cover over the radiator and built up in a heap on top of it. That's how cold it was. I had on three of everything, plus my overcoat, a woollen cap and fur lined gloves and was so cold I could hardly move. To open the door, step out and inhale was like having knives thrust into the lungs. I did that once but never again. The bad weather lasted three days, then the wind turned southerly and it actually began to rain. Within a few hours all traces of snow and ice had vanished. The warmer conditions lasted long enough for us to complete loading for home.

The ship was overdue for survey so, on our return in March 1926, we went up to the Tyne. One afternoon Mr Lang, the superintendent, arrived to go over the survey repair lists and made, what seemed to me, a very odd remark. Referring to something he said 'next voyage your mate can attend to that himself.'

'As I expect I will still be the mate here, I will get it attended to.'

'No,' he said, you are taking over as master of this ship.' He didn't say any more. Three weeks later I went home for some well-earned leave.

When I had last left home the family was still in Woodview Terrace; now they were in Gardenside. This was a large house, far too big for the two of them. It appeared mother had insisted a bedroom had to be kept for each of us in case we were all home together.

'How much,' I asked father, 'is this place costing?'

'More than I can afford, but mother insists.'

I arrived back on board on 2nd May. Everyone had assembled and a Captain Stoker-Johnson had arrived to take over the ship. The miners' strike had been dragging on and now there was talk of a national strike in support. Just after dinner a telephone call came to Readheads, the repair yard, from the London office. ALL PERSONNEL ON CHERTSEY TO RETURN HOME EXCEPT CHIEF ENGINEER AND THIRD MATE. AWAIT FURTHER INSTRUCTIONS. This was when I made a costly mistake. I decided to go home the following morning, all the others left that afternoon. It just didn't occur to me that the general strike would include bus and train services. When I reached the station next day a notice was pinned up saying 'Service suspended till further notice'. There was not a bus or taxi to be found, so I walked the 12 miles to Gateshead on the south side of the river. I arrived at Newcastle station to find the place crowded with people, but not a train to be seen. It was now early evening and I had had nothing to eat since the previous night. I managed to get a room in a hotel and had a meal at last.

On the third day I saw a notice saying that a train taking milk and newspapers would leave for Carlisle and passage could be obtained for anyone willing to help. I seized the opportunity and offered my services whereupon I was allotted the job of assistant guard. My job was to sort out bundles of newspapers and parcels for each station and drop them onto the platforms. We didn't drop or pick up passengers. In all I spent four days in Carlisle and father had to wire me money to keep me going. When I eventually arrived home I spent a further two weeks doing nothing.

I returned to the ship on 24th May and we sailed for Rotterdam. While there I had occasion to refer something to Captain Stoker-Johnson for his decision.

'Don't bother to refer anything to me about the running of the ship, just carry on in your own way. This is actually your ship, I am only here for the voyage.' So there it was again – *my* ship. We had two quick trips to Baltimore, then Alexandria and back up to the Black Sea and Novorossiysk for wheat.

Proceeding homeward up the English Channel Captain Stoker-Johnson came into my room.

'I hold your future in my hands, young man,' he said. He handed me a radiogram. CONSIDERING MR DONALD FOR COMMAND. IF YOU RECOMMEND PUT HIM ASHORE AT GRAVESEND TO PROCEED TO THIS OFFICE FOR INTERVIEW. WATTS.

'What shall I reply?' he asked.

'That sir is up to you.'

'I have already sent an answer, I will land you at Gravesend. They must be in a hurry if they can't wait for the ship to dock.'

When I arrived at the office it was still closed, so I had to wait around till 9 a.m. I made myself known and asked for Captain Cox, the marine superintendent, but he had not yet arrived. Time passed slowly. I was bored stiff and very hungry and at 1 p.m. I was told to have lunch. I asked what was happening about the ship.

'She has docked at Ranks Mill in the Victoria Dock. She struck the corner of the lock and dented some plates, Mr Lang is down there now.'

It must have been around three when Captain Cox beckoned me into an office. At the end of the room sat a very old man. So this, I thought, is the famous Stanley H. Burgess, the managing director of Watts Watts.

'Young man,' he said, 'do you consider you are capable of commanding one of my ships?'

'Certainly sir,' I replied.

'Confident, eh. Do you know anything about captain's business?'

'Yes sir.'

'Ah, you were second mate with the late Captain Randall, so no doubt you do.' He continued, 'A master of one of my ships is in sole charge and takes his orders only from this office, and is answerable to me alone. I do not wish to know anything

111

about crew troubles and other happenings, that is what you are there for, only get in touch with this office when you are unable to cope by yourself. I don't care what trouble you get into, what I will watch is how you get yourself, and your ship, out of it. Your commencing pay will be £32 10s per month. If you are a clever man you could double it. I don't mind whose pockets you put your hand into as long as you keep it out of mine.' He gave a ghost of a smile. 'That will be all.'

The following morning a gentleman came on board looking for me.

'I am from the office, they are all asking where you are. You had better come at once. You have to get your name on the register and attend to other things.'

'There is no one here but me,' I replied.

'That can't be helped, we have to open articles this afternoon and sign on a crew.' I got hold of the senior apprentice and gave him instructions.

'Can you tell me,' I asked, 'as no one else has bothered to, am I now a master and, if so, of what ship?'

'You were made master at your interview. You should have had the *Fulham* but now you keep this ship.'

When the three mates walked into the shipping office I got a surprise. The mate and second mate were considerably older than me. Mr Lake, the mate was in his 40s and the second obviously in his 50s, and I was the master aged 29! When I returned to the ship I went along to see Mr Jacques, the chief engineer.

'As you know by now Mr Jacques I have been given command of this ship. I have had to put up with your unreasonable animosity over the last two years but I do not bear any malice. I do not drink, run after women or make money out of people – all things you have seized on to get a hold over some of the masters that have been in this ship. I am not a person to be intimidated. It will be in the best interests of the ship, and ourselves, if we work together and not against each other, are you agreeable?' I held out my hand and he got up and shook it.

'I will assist you all I can,' he said.

That first passage as master, to Baltimore, was the toughest and longest I ever made across the North Atlantic. We left Rotterdam on 16th November and arrived in Baltimore 28 days later. There was one gale after another, first from one direction and then another. We were not the only ballast ship making the crossing and we had made a good passage compared to some.

We then returned to the Russian Black Sea trade and I was initiated into its financial aspects. As there were no foreign shipping agents in the Russian ports the masters of the ships had to attend to everything themselves, and pay all the disbursements. They were unable to contact their owners so everything had to be settled before a ship was allowed to leave. The battles had to be won or lost by the masters themselves – nothing could be left to be settled by arbitration later. I had

Captain Donald, on his first command.

already received a lot of information from other masters so I knew more or less what to expect.

Back in Novorossiysk the Russian winter was in full swing. Now that I had to go ashore to attend to ship's business I needed something warmer to wear in this kind of weather, so I decided to obtain a fur hat, similar to those the Russians wore in winter. I was informed that I would first have to obtain a permit from the Cheka (police), so I went round to their headquarters to acquire one. Then it had to be decided whether I was to be classed as a manual worker, white collar worker, or an official. Finally I was graded as an executive official and given a permit to purchase a fur hat as worn in that grade. I chose one made of leather and seal fur which cost 20 roubles, which worked out at about £2 4s. I then had to go back to the shop to complete the purchase, and to the Cheka again with the receipt. By this time I was on first name terms with the hat and cap department of the Torgsin store and the officials at the Cheka headquarters. All this fuss was because, under the regulations, anything bought by a foreigner had to be for personal use and not for sale outside Russia. It was the most useful purchase I ever made, for even in the coldest weather it kept me warm and comfortable.

As time passed, restrictions on foreigners were gradually relaxed and, as long as you had your pass, you could go more or less anywhere you wished, not that in Novorossiysk there was anywhere worth visiting. But you were always under surveillance. I found that out when I noticed one particular man hanging around the pier when I went ashore, and he seemed to be everywhere I went. I mentioned this to one of the captains who had been to Russia many times.

'That man,' he said, 'is your shadow. All he does is note where you go and what you do when ashore. Nod to him, or wish him good morning, and he will disappear, and you will find another in his place. You must not show that you suspect you are being watched.'

The masters of ships in port congregated at the offices of the Inflot, which was the agency department of the shipping control. They had offices in a large building on the waterfront. Inside was just a long space filled with desks and tables – everyone could see and hear what went on; the captains and a motley crowd of Russians, wearing sheepskin coats, knee high leather boots and fur hats, all smoked Russian tobacco, and the smell in that airless place was dreadful. No matter how warm it got no one took off hat or coat, it simply was not done. When I first went in I felt sick but gradually got used to it. Coming out afterwards into the cold clean air was a shock to the system. There appeared to be no toilet arrangements at all but somewhere outside the building would be a structure resembling a wooden sentry box. It was for one person only and was completely open to the weather. Inside was a wooden bar for a seat, and the structure was placed over a pit in the ground. It was not necessary to look for it – the smell was ample guidance as to its location.

Occasionally I had a meal ashore. Through the ship chandler some of us were introduced to an eating place – one could not call it a cafe – with bare wooden tables and benches. All that could be obtained was bortsch, their national dish. What it consisted of could not be ascertained, but the taste was wonderful. We got a large bowl of that, with a lump of black bread, without butter or salt, and Russian tea in a tall glass, with sugar and a slice of lemon. By the time the bowl was empty, and the bread eaten, one was so full it was only with great effort that movement was possible.

By the time we were loaded and ready to go we discovered the ship had frozen to the pier. We got the mooring ropes in and started the engines. I put them SLOW AHEAD, but the ship did not move; HALF SPEED, no movement. I rang FULL SPEED, then FULL ASTERN for a minute or so, then FULL SPEED AHEAD again. Suddenly we felt a wrench and away she went.

Our cargo this time was 5400 tons of oil cake and grain for four ports in Denmark. I found out when we reached Copenhagen that the discharge was going to be a very leisurely business as no night or weekend work was done. Weighing machines were set up at each hatch and everything carefully weighed out in small lots and sold to farmers at the ship's rail. From Copenhagen we sailed to Nykøbing on the island of Falster, Åbenrå in Jutland and finally Kolding. Everything took so long I would not have been surprised to find another master waiting to take over. It might have been considered that I hadn't been able to look after the ship efficiently. However the letters I received on our subsequent arrival on the Tyne contained only instructions for the forthcoming voyage.

I was pleased to see Mr Bryson, the second mate, leave at this point, because everyone addressed him as captain and it was getting too much of a strain. People were surprised to find that the younger man was actually the captain. The only time I could attain any dignity was when the third mate was around, at least I looked older than he did.

Our orders were to deliver coal to Ancona in Italy and then to proceed to the Black Sea. We arrived in Sulina on the west coast late one night. This ship had not been to the Danube before and now I was introduced to what I had only heard about, Romanian bribery and corruption. A crowd of officials poured on board dressed in fabulous uniforms. There was nothing for most of them to do; they were after tins of cigarettes and must have pocketed them by the thousand. I protested to the agents, but was told if I continued they would find a way to delay the ship.

As this ship had not been up the Danube before she had to be measured for the Danube Commission dues, but we finally got away around noon and headed for Braila. To avoid the many bends in the river a canal had been cut through for some distance. The canal was very narrow but there was plenty of room in the river when we reached it. The current was strong and it was slow work pushing up. From Sulina the distance to Braila was 105 miles, but the bends and twists of the river made it much more.

The procedure was the same as at Sulina – Danube loading was an expensive business. Customs and immigration, police, agents, captain of the port and searchers all had to be dealt with. A tin of 50 cigarettes had to be placed alongside each one of them. When they absentmindedly put the tin in their pocket another one had to take its place. This dragged on all morning.

We laid for some time in Braila where there were also a number of Greek ships. I began to go ashore with their captains and, as a result, gained a great deal of knowledge of the Black Sea grain trade as practised in Romanian and Bulgarian ports.

One captain advised me. 'If you have to tear your signature off a bill of lading, or an account, do not throw the scrap of paper away. Eat it, then no one can get hold of it.'

'Why,' I asked, 'should it be necessary to tear your signature off anything.'

'Figures can be altered after you have signed. So that is the time to tear your signature off and eat it. Protesting will be no use.' Interesting places these Danube ports. With a full cargo of yellow maize we were again bound for Danish ports before returning home.

On arrival there were crew changes. Mr Jacques, the chief engineer, left for a long leave, and Mr Charles Walker arrived as first mate. We had known each other since we were boys and our families had holidayed together.

'As long as we are on the ship, Charlie,' I told him, 'you are Mr Walker, the mate, and I am the master. Ashore together is a different matter.'

'Of course,' he said, 'that is the way it has to be.'

We loaded coals for Alexandria then proceeded to the Black Sea as usual, it was becoming a routine voyage. There was no indication that this would be the longest, and also the last voyage the *Chertsey* would make for Watts Watts.

In Alexandria with us was the *Beckenham* commanded by Captain J.C. Hill. It was his boast that no man ever made two voyages with him; if they survived the first one they were lucky. I could see he had a great sense of humour, and I had a feeling we would get on together. The way to deal with him was not to take him too seriously. He gave me several pieces of advice, which I always remembered. 'Never be subservient to the owners, speak your mind and give them the impression you don't care whether they keep you in command or not. In that case they will not let you go. They will keep you on till they finally convince you they are the boss. If they succeed in doing this they will sack you, if not, you will remain master. It is a question of psychology.'

Another piece of advice was on the subject of voyage accounts. 'Make up the account to the nearest penny and draw your money. It is advisable to keep in hand a little of theirs, then they will inform you at once that you owe them money, and how much, so you can get a settlement. If they have some of yours they will not bother to settle, sometimes for years.' There must have been something in what he said as I remained master with them until I retired, 34 years later.

There was still a lot of ice in the Sea of Azov and an icebreaker and two pilots were waiting to take us up to Mariupol. It was a bright, clear, sunny day but intensely cold. We had to keep close behind the icebreaker, but in following him through a narrow lane in the ice we got stuck on a floe. He went round and round us pushing and shoving but we were stuck in the middle of it. Finally as a last resource he backed down ahead of us and put a towing wire on board. This was taken round the bitts each side and round the windlass. When he took the weight and went full speed I thought the forecastle deck was going to lift off, but it held. He dragged us off that floe by main force; I could hear the screeching and whistling as she went through the ice. We couldn't help with the engines as the propeller was jammed solid in the ice. Once we were clear the icebreaker took in his towline and we resumed our way, with many stoppages, until he broke his way through.

We loaded salt for the Far East and embarked on the long voyage to Vladivostock via Perim* and Singapore. There was an immediate outcry from the sailors who had hoped that they were going home, but they had signed articles for three years and there was nothing they could do, short of deserting.

---

* Perim – a rocky island which commands the entrance to the Red Sea. It is now known as Bab-el-Mandeb.

Approaching Vladivostock we ran into loose ice and the weather was as cold as it had been in the Azov. There seemed to be a different atmosphere here to that I had been used to in the Russian Black Sea ports – there didn't seem to be any restrictions. Money could be drawn and there were plenty of shops, cinemas and cafes to spend it in. The police were no more evident than in any normal town, no passes were issued and there were no guards on the gangway. We were there about a month because the Russians just took the salt out as they required it. In addition, the *Beckenham*, our sister ship, was unloaded first as she was first to dock.

When we finished discharging I was directed to Saigon to load rice for Cuba, then via the Tsauganu Straits, thence to Vancover Island and the Panama Canal. This surprised me as the usual route from Saigon to the West Indies was via the Cape. As it was now a summer passage across to the Juan-de-Fuca Straits it would be fine weather all the way. I intended to make the great circle tract, just south of the Aleutian Islands, to take advantage of the Kuro-Siwa current which flowed across to the North American coast. In Japan, I had taken more than sufficient coal for the passage with a good reserve. While there I had received a typhoon warning for the west side of Japan. As we were right on its track, and unable to deviate, all we could do was try to keep ahead of it until it petered out. It was then that the chief engineer came along to see me.

'Do you know the coal consumption has been 27 tons per day?' he asked.

'You're joking, we are only doing the usual eight and a half knots.'

'The coal we got on the previous occasion was good, this time knowing we would not be back they have filled us up with rubbish.' We found, by trial and error, that on 14 tons she would still do seven knots and that was the consumption all the way across the north Pacific. We also discovered that we had been considerably short weighted when in Havana.

We had heard reports of a violent hurricane which had curved off towards Florida where it caused utter devastation. On the way to Montreal with a cargo of sugar we passed Miami and I kept close inshore to look at the hurricane damage. It was awe-inspiring. Some of the skyscrapers were now only a mass of twisted girders, and the wreckage of wooden and brick houses had not been cleared up. There was an air of desolation everywhere.

I was now going into a part of the world I had never visited before. I had experienced winter weather in the USA, the Black Sea and the Baltic, but the night we took the river pilot at Father Point, in the Gulf of St. Lawrence, seemed to me the coldest I had ever known. It was only the latter end of October but the cold was intense. Montreal was full of ships loading grain, but by 12th November we were loaded and on our way. We had a fine passage across, but as I remarked to the chief engineer, 'one good stiff gale would finish this ship.'

'Yes,' he said, 'and if the propeller commenced racing heavily the engines would collapse.'

From Montreal we headed east. On the morning we arrived in Gibraltar to load coal, a Lloyd's surveyor came on board. He showed me a cable from Watts: DETAIN AND SURVEY CHERTSEY ON ARRIVAL. COMPLAINT UNSEAWORTHINESS FROM CREW.

'What goes on?' I asked Mr Walker.

'The crew think the ship is out for a three year voyage and hope she will be held up here so they will get paid off and sent home. I have the ringleader washing down the fore topmast to keep him out of the way.'

'Why didn't you tell me before?'

'I only got to know yesterday,' he said.

'As far as I can ascertain,' said the surveyor, 'there is nothing wrong with the ship. She has made the Atlantic passage without trouble. I will make out a certificate for three months.' In view of this I thought it advisable that the owners should know exactly what condition the ship was in, and enclosed a list. On it I put everything I knew about the ship's condition including the fact that she had cracked right across between the after end of the engine-room and No.3 hatch coaming. That was what I meant when I said she would not withstand a stiff gale. I was told, when I visited the London office, that my list had prompted them to put the ship up for sale.

We made our usual trip to the Black Sea and then headed for Denmark, topping up bunkers in Dartmouth, Devon. Leaving there the temperature went down and down. As we went toward the Skaw the ice floes were getting more numerous, then it was a case of pushing through them. From the Skaw to the Kattegat it was a slow business. The ice was in solid sheets and it was a case of putting her nose into a crack and pushing until it was wide enough to get through. We spent days doing this. It was now February and we had only managed to reach within a few miles of the entrance to Odense Fjord before we came to a standstill. I radioed London, UNABLE TO REACH ODENSE FJORD ICE IMPASSABLE AM PROCEEDING SOUND TO AWAIT ORDERS. I sent a similar one to our agents in Copenhagen, but received no reply from either. The charter party gave the option, 'if unable to enter port of discharge owing to ice conditions vessel can proceed to nearest ice-free port within 100 miles and there discharge'. Copenhagen was not ice-free but it could be entered. I managed to get into the Sound and anchored.

Then began the nightmare. Every few hours dense masses of ice would come down from the Baltic and up one side or the other of the Sound. We were pushed along by the ice and dragged anchor. We upped anchor and looked for a clear space, then anchored again and this continued for two days and nights with the ice getting denser until finally remaining at anchor in the Sound became impossible. To my requests for instructions I received no answer. In the end I informed the agents in Copenhagen that I would put the vessel into Helsingborg on the Swedish side as a port of refuge. That brought a response. The orders came, PROCEED COPENHAGEN.

Within half a mile of the breakwater (mole) the pilot came out in a tug. There were no berths available so we were pushed up to the Langalina Mole. The sky was cloudless and the temperature, until two days before leaving, was 8°F. The Baltic had frozen over and the whole area, from the Skaw down, was dotted with ships stuck fast in the ice. We had sustained plenty of damage but, so far, only the forepeak showed any leakage.

In the mornings I would walk up to the agent's office for news and watch what was going on, which was plenty; the freeze-up had caused complete chaos. Then I went to a cafe for lunch. The port was absolutely full and this cafe was doing a roaring business. Each table was decorated with the flag of a different country and the one that bore the Union Jack was attended by a waiter who spoke English. I got into the habit of buying a Danish newspaper each morning to see the latest ice reports. I acquired a Danish-English dictionary and, had I persevered, I think I would have been able to read and speak Danish quite well. In all we were there nearly a month.

When we discharged the Odense and Kolding cargo the ship had risen enough for us to see what damage had been sustained. From the stem to the shoulder of the bows, on both sides, the portion of the frames and plating that had been compressed by the ice were pushed in about two feet just back of the stem, gradually tapering off to an inch or two by the fore end of No.1 hold. The leak in the forepeak was due to the plates being pushed in two feet. The rivets along the lap had sheared and a two-inch gap had appeared between the plate edges. However, until the ice in the forepeak melted nothing could be done.

It was now well into March and there was no sign of the ice breaking up. One day I heard that the Russians had agreed to lend their largest icebreaker, the *Yermak*, and she was on her way. She was to clear a channel from the breakwaters up to The Sound and the ships were to follow in her wake, one behind the other. We were at the tail end of the procession. The *Yermak* went through the ice like a knife through butter. If any ship got stuck the line halted while the *Yermak* went back and broke her free again. It was evening before we cleared harbour and almost daylight the next morning before we turned off for Aarhuis. I had been told the ice in the Kattegat was now loose enough for navigation by large vessels, and hoped it was true. There were indeed open passages between the floes and we got across without any more trouble. The anticyclone which had caused the freeze-up was moving away and the temperature rising.

The weather turned warm and wet just before we left Aarhuis, spring was now on the way. We arrived back on the Tyne looking like a shabby old wreck which, in truth, she was. I was not sure what view Watts would take of the ice damage incurred in Denmark, and sure enough a few days later I received a telegram. ARRANGE TO BE IN LONDON OFFICE TOMORROW MORNING. INTERVIEW WITH CHAIRMAN. I presented myself at the office and was greeted with pitying looks. Captain Musson warned me to be careful with young Mr Watts, who was now in charge, as he was not easy to deal with. I was taken into the same boardroom where Mr Burgess interviewed me. The only occupant, who looked very young, sat reading at the head of the long table.

'Captain Donald, sir,' said Captain Musson.

There was no reply from the figure at the table. Captain Musson shrugged his shoulders and went out leaving me standing. I found myself a chair and had just sat down when the figure at the table turned to face me and pointing at me said, 'I have sacked you.' The action was so funny that I couldn't help laughing. He stood up and I saw a young man about my own age.

'This is no laughing matter,' he shouted. I stood up.

'To me it is sir,' I said, 'as I intend to hand in my resignation.'

'You do, do you.'

'Yes sir, my father wants me to go into his business instead of continuing at sea.'

'So you think you can sack yourself, I will decide about that. I sent for you to find out how you came to incur such heavy ice damage.'

'Because the ship is so old and frail she could not stand up to ice navigation.'

'What do you mean by ice navigation?' he asked. I walked over to the table and, on a sheet of paper, gave him an explanation of the ice conditions in Denmark.

'As you must realise sir, as long as a ship can make her way through ice she must do so even at the expense of damage. The charter party only allows deviation if a ship is unable to enter a port, but she must first arrive off the port. To do that in Denmark meant ice damage.' With pencils and matchsticks I illustrated to him how an icebreaker worked a convoy through heavy ice. He rang the bell and Captain Musson appeared.

'Bring me a list of the ships; I am going to give Donald another ship.' He came back with the list and I could see he was highly amused. Mr Watts went down the list but I had objections to each one of them.

'So you are not satisfied with any of my ships.'

I want six months leave, I have only had a few days at home since 1922.

'All right,' he said, 'you can have six months.' We shook hands and I left with Captain Musson.

'Am I fired?'

'No,' he replied, 'you were never fired, he was trying to see what reaction he could get out of you. Now I am going to tell you what you are going to do. Go home for a month's leave, then you can take the *Medmenham* when her repairs are finished.'

I had heard a lot about this ship and none of it good; there were problems with her stability.

'Why that ship?' I asked.

'Because no one else will have her and your performance in the *Chertsey* indicates you are the right man for the job.' Now I knew I was settled in as one of the firm's masters. The salary, plus what came in from various sources, was considerably more than I could earn by taking over my father's business, and it would be foolish to throw away 17 years training and experience at sea.

I explained this to father and he saw my point though he was disappointed. I told him it was time he packed it in, he was now 67 and it showed. He told me quite a lot of people owed him money and repeated requests for settlement had, so far, had no effect. He gave me the particulars and I began writing to them. To my surprise they began to settle up. When I left home to join the *Medmenham* I could not know that I was never to see the house in Gardenside again, and it would be another couple of years before I saw my parents in a place a long way from Uddingston.

Chapter 15

A bone of contention

*W*hen I took over the *Medmenham* I asked the retiring master about the ship. 'What,' I said, 'is supposed to be wrong with this ship? I know she is 25 years old but so is most of the fleet.'

'She is,' he told me, 'a comfortable ship with a good speed of nine and a half knots but she has one fatal fault, she will not remain upright, even in ballast. The list she takes on frightens everyone. She was built during the period when a long, thin, deep-legged ship was fashionable, the theory being that such a hull would give more speed with lower coal consumption. The long bridge deck is the trouble. When you put cargo in there, it is the same as putting it on deck.'

When we moved out of dry dock she took a list with only the double bottom tanks in. We were bound for Leningrad to load a cargo of dry bones, consigned to the Texas Chemical Company, to be discharged in Houston, Texas. It was summertime and a quiet fine weather run up to Kronstadt at the head of the Gulf of Finland; from there a canal runs up to a dock in Leningrad.

The bones arrived in small open mule carts. The mule was unharnessed and the back end of the cart lifted out. The cart was then slung over the hatch and upended letting the contents cascade down into the hold. Quite often nothing would drop out, the bones having become interlocked, in which case the cart would have to be lowered on to the hatch and the bones pulled out piecemeal. The cows' skulls were the problem. For some reason the horns were still attached, and they could cause a jam. There was no smell but legions of flies kept buzzing around the holds and the carts waiting on the canal bank.

It was my first time in Leningrad. I went into town only once and had a look at the Nevisky Prospect, said to be the broadest street in the world, and the Imperial Winter Palace. The passage to Norfolk, Virginia, was north through the Pentland Firth and we had fine weather all the way.

From Galveston on the coast of Texas, a canal runs 48 miles inland to Houston.

S.S.Medmenham

The discharging berth we were allotted was in the canal, which had been widened to form the port. The water was a dull brownish green colour and stank of oil. The stevedoring company, which discharged the cargo, had taken the ship on a lump sum basis, and later the manager told me they had lost a considerable amount of money on the deal.

They began by using grabs. The grab was dropped with its jaws wide open but, when coming together they would jam on a skull which prevented them closing fully, then when the grab was lifted, the smaller bones fell out. When after a couple of days nothing much had been achieved the stevedore was becoming alarmed. He came to me.

'How, for God's sake did the Russians get this mess into the ship?' I explained to him how it was done. 'You mean I have to put men down below to fill tubs? That will certainly cost money.'

'You could use rope cargo nets for the skulls and larger bones,' I said. 'Get the large ones out first, then the small ones will then fall to the bottom and can be lifted in tubs using the ship's winches and derricks.' He realised it would be the only way.

'There's going to be plenty of trouble getting men to go down there. I would not like to say when you will be finished.'

Some of the ship's crew, as a joke I suppose, gave out a story that the bones were those of Russian aristocrats executed by the Soviets after the Revolution. Newspaper reporters got hold of it and they headed for the ship to get stories from the crew. The local papers were full of the story. Before the stevedores were satisfied that only animal bones were on board, and old ones at that, they suspended all discharge until samples were taken away to be examined. They did indeed prove to be old animal bones in dry condition. Work was resumed, but then a human skull was found, followed by several more. A government inspector was then stationed on the wharf to examine the slings as they came out of the ship to make sure no more human bones were discovered. All the human skulls had to be collected and properly buried. At last the bones, skulls and all were discharged and we were ordered to Tampa, on the west coast of Florida to load phosphates for Helsingborg and Malmö in Sweden, bunkers to be taken at Norfolk, Virginia.

One morning, several days out from Norfolk, Virginia, the radio operator handed me a radiogram from Watts. REGRET TO INFORM YOU FATHER SERIOUSLY ILL. HAVE ADVANCED YOUR MOTHER MONEY AGAINST YOUR ACCOUNT. PLEASE CONFIRM. I didn't know what illness father had gone down with but mother asking Watts for money I could understand. I heard later he had suffered a stroke. He went to bed one night in his usual good health but the following morning he could neither move nor speak. In time he recovered the use of his hands and legs but could not write, and spoke only with difficulty.

Ever since I started earning money I had left the major part of it to my father; he gave my mother an allowance for her personal use, and banked the remainder. We had a joint account to enable father to draw and send me money if necessary. He had his own private account and paid all the bills and housekeeping. The bank manager refused to advance anything to my mother so she asked Watts Watts if they could advance her cash against my account, which they did.

Some time later, in Alexandria, we had trouble with a deck cargo of bones. I went to have a look at them and found they were in rotten bags, stank to high heaven and were alive with maggots. Something had to be done so I instructed Mr Richards, the mate, to put up fencing forward and aft to contain the bones. I took care to be out of the way when it was being erected. Boards were lashed to the rails and bulwark stanchions, with other boards lashed crossways to them. As the bags of bones were very light the fencing, by itself, would be sufficient to contain them. The stink was horrendous. The apprentices and catering staff, living in the poop, had to shut forward doors and ports to keep out the smell.

I can still remember those bones; someone said they were from camels. They were not old and dry but fresh ones with flesh still attached, that was what made them stink and provided food for the legions of maggots which infested them. The bags were so full of holes that the maggots came out and began working themselves along the deck. This had to be stopped somehow as they would be in the after bridge accommodation in no time. A barrier of planks, twelve inches high, was laid across the deck – we discovered a maggot could not leap higher than that! Then the planks were thickly coated with heavy Vaseline, from the engine-room that acted as a flypaper and prevented them getting over. For some reason the maggots did not attempt to jump backwards so that no precautions had to be taken to keep them away from the poop accommodation. To lessen the stench the bosun tried hosing down the bones one day and as soon as the water touched them the maggots came jumping out of the bags into the air as if they had gone crazy.

We went into the South West India Dock in London and then the fun began. The stevedores complained of the stink and said the maggots were getting up their trouser legs, sleeves and down their necks. After some delay the discharge was resumed. The men now had lashings round their cuffs, trouser bottoms and collars to keep the maggots out. I believe the promise of extra money was the inducement that brought them back. The Public Heath Department got to hear about the situation and men from the insect infestation section came down to collect specimens for examination. When all the bags were off the ship they sprayed the decks and wharf with insect killer, then swept up all the bodies and burnt them. Later Watts stated that none of their ships would be allowed to carry Egyptian bones on deck again.

Some months later, while in Cardiff, I was told my mother was on the telephone and wished to speak to me. I naturally assumed she was speaking from Uddingston.

'I want you to come down here and look at a house.'

A house; where are you speaking from?' I asked.

'Torquay, in South Devon.'

'What are you doing down there?'

'Looking for a house,' she said, 'The doctor says father has to get into a warmer climate.'

'I will see what I can arrange and will call you back.' I wrote down the telephone number. That was the first time I had ever heard of Torquay. It was now Friday and there was little happening as the Christmas holidays were approaching. I rang the office, was granted a weekend leave and left for Torquay that afternoon.

My mother met me at the station and took me to the hotel where she was staying. Someone had given her a list of places and Torquay was one of them. The next morning I was taken to see the semi-detached bungalow on St. Marychurch Road. It was not fully built, but far enough advanced to enable me to see what it would be like. The price was £1250 which I considered rather steep, but I could see mother had set her heart on the house, so I agreed. Next we visited the solicitors to arrange a deposit and mortgage. I put £700 into the house and a mortgage was arranged for the balance. I also arranged for the house to be in her name in case it had to be sold when I was not on hand. This proved to be a very unwise thing to do as I found out years later. There was nothing further to be done so we returned to Cardiff that afternoon and as she wanted to have a look at the ship I put her into a hotel until she left for home.

My father had not much money left. He was always an easy touch and misplaced trust in people, a trait he had not passed on to me. He had lent money to quite a number of people and, now they knew he could not write or speak properly due to the stroke, they sat tight and said nothing. The money was never repaid.

Some time later, during a visit to Plymouth, I managed to get home to Torquay for a short visit. My brother James was at home sick, and my sister's boy Stanley was there too. Jenny had managed to foist him on to the old people when they moved down there. I had received many letters from Jenny during the year, her shop was not paying and she was in debt to moneylenders. She asked if I could advance her sufficient to pay off her debts. In all I had advanced her over £1000 and never saw a penny back.

My brother James, after recovering from a badly gashed arm, had gone back to sea as second mate in the *Denham*. While on this ship a cargo of sulphur in one of the holds caught fire. He went down with a hose to put the fire out, got caught by the fumes, and had to be hauled out. The violent coughing caused by the fumes damaged his right lung and he contracted tuberculosis. He did not recover and was sent home. Fortunately, my mother was in good health. She had already quarrelled with the neighbours on either side and was now at war with those across the road, so she had regained her usual form.

The *Medmenham* was laid up for a long time in the River Fal and finally towed to the Clyde and scrapped. During her career she had scared the life out of everyone who sailed in her, but the ship herself never came to any harm. My two years in her had made me an expert on trim and stability. I had to be, just to remain alive.

Chapter 16

S.S.Finchley

I intended to give myself a holiday as I hadn't had a proper one since I had been at sea. I calculated I should have around £1000 which I could afford to spend. This was why I had not accepted the offer to stand-by in the River Fal on laid up pay. After I had settled down and made up the last voyage account I went down to the bank to have a look at my account. I received a shock when I discovered there was only about £400 remaining. On enquiring what had happened to the other £600 I came up against a wall of silence, but in course of time I managed to piece events together. Father had very little money in the bank. He had, it seemed, been persuaded to buy mining shares which turned out to be worthless. His uncle, John Copland, had fleeced him in the first place but that did not appear to have taught him anything. So my money, being in an account to which he had access, had been used to pay all the expenses of the removal to Torquay, and that was what they had been living on since. All he had now was his army pension plus their combined old age pensions, but that was not enough to keep them. Now I had my father and mother to support, as well as James and Jenny's son Stanley. James had no money and could not help. The first thing to be done was to have young Stanley sent back to his parents. Clearly the intention was to get him off their hands and put the expense and trouble of raising him on to me, through the old people.

Now my brother Alex arrived home. This was the first time I had met him since he went abroad. He had come, or been sent, home for treatment. While in Cuba he had owned a horse. One wet night his horse had stepped into a hole and thrown him against a tree and he was not found until the next morning. Several ribs were fractured, but the serious damage was his right hipbone which had been fractured in several places. He developed pleurisy and his lungs were affected, so he was advised to return home where he could be treated properly. He didn't pay mother anything towards his keep; he said he had very little left after paying for doctors and hospitals. Some years later I found out his firm, J. & P. Coats, had paid all his expenses. My long time dream of owning a cabin cruiser would now be out of the question.

My mother, true to form, had got to know her neighbours. Across the road a large house, called *Leaholme*, was run as a boarding house by a Mrs Heap, whose husband was an invalid. My mother was invited there to a garden party one afternoon and, as a result, she invited Mrs Heap over one evening. She came and brought with her one of her daughters. This was my first meeting with the girl who would become my wife. Her name was May. She was a widow and had been married only a couple of years when her husband died. She had a lovely voice and had been trained as a singer at the Manchester College of Music. Before her marriage she did a lot of concerts and broadcasting when the Plymouth station was operating, but now she was home again and working as a manageress in a steam laundry. When I told my mother that May and I had become engaged there was a fearful scene – she thought I would never marry – but things quietened down when James became ill. When I called the doctor I learned James had pneumonia. He did not improve and the infection spread. Just 14 days from the time I sent him to bed he died; he was just 25. The shock of James's death caused father to have another stroke so now he had to be nursed as well. As that took up most of mother's time I had to do the housework.

May and I had intended to get married before I went away again and the date had been set for 2nd February 1932. I was to command one of the vessels on the Dominion Coal Trade commencing in April. Being so soon after James's death it was decided we would be married in the Registry Office in Newton Abbot. My brother Alex had returned in January so he acted as my best man. He had been appointed to the agency in Durban, South Africa, but was not required to go out there for some time.

We stayed a few days in London on our honeymoon and spent the remainder of the fortnight with May's sister in Cricklewood. During that time we visited all the sights and I enjoyed every minute.

The day before we were due to go home I decided to call at the office to see which ship I would be taking over. May was convinced that if I did they would catch me for some job in the meantime. I didn't think so as everything seemed to be laid up. I left May in a Lyons teashop and went to the office. Captain Anderson was surprised to see me.

'What brought you up here?' he enquired. I told him I had just got married and was on my honeymoon.

'Good God,' he exclaimed, 'I thought you were a confirmed bachelor.'

'You left me too long at home. I just called in to see which ship I have been appointed to.'

'You are to take the *Finchley*, now laid up in the Tyne, but I will not require you until the beginning of April. Ah, Torquay isn't far from Truro. We are bringing the *Datchet* out to load in Barry Dock. Tomorrow when you go back you could carry on to Truro and take her to Barry.'

I told May what had happened.

'It will only be for a few days and you can come through to Barry.'

When we finally went home May settled in with my parents at *Glenkindie*. Wives could travel on board during the summer months and so it was arranged that she would come out to Montreal at the end of May. She came up to South Shields with me. The ship was laying at Readheads wharf waiting her turn to dry dock. After coaling we would go to Narvik, in northern Norway, to load iron ore for Sydney Cape Breton, Nova Scotia, then after discharge run between Sydney and Montreal. I took a dislike to the ship as soon as I set eyes on her, she was filthy and ugly. A more depressing looking vessel would be hard to find.

The two mates had been with her some time, Mr Garlick, the first and Mr Foster the second, so had the chief engineer, Mr Renshaw. Mrs Garlick was very pleasant and friendly but I didn't like Mrs Renshaw at all. She and May were polite to each other but never friends.

We had fine weather on the run up to Narvik and arrived there to find everything was under several feet of snow and deadly cold. There was no ice in the fiord, as part of the Gulf Stream runs along the Norwegian coast and keeps the sea warmer than the land. The ore we loaded was magnetic and some of the pieces weighed several tons. Every time one of these landed in the hold the ship shook like a leaf. We made the passage across to Cape Race between the Faroes and Iceland. The iron ore was indeed magnetic and the compasses went haywire. I had to use anything that was soft iron to act as magnets. Marline spikes and pieces of soft iron were tacked to the deck all round the standard compass to try and reduce the deviation to controllable limits. As we went down to the south-west, under ordinary conditions, the deviation of the compass should have returned to normal, but now the ship's magnetic condition was affected by the iron ore. For several trips I had to ease down off Red Island, in the St. Lawrence River, and adjust compasses. This was necessary until the ore magnetism gradually worked out of the ship.

We arrived off the entrance to Sydney Cape Breton harbour one dull, gloomy morning. There was plenty of sheet ice floating around but nothing to impede a ship. The land around the harbour is mostly flat and now, all covered in snow, it was a depressing sight.

If I remember rightly there were, in that season, 22 ships on the coal run. In a full season this vessel, according to her logbooks, made 20 round trips, the last one up to Montreal making 21 cargoes. With this ship the run up to Father Point, entrance to the St. Lawrence River, took on average two days and six hours. From there to Quebec was about 22 hours depending upon the tide. Quebec to Montreal required 18 hours which gave a total of four days. Discharge usually occupied two days, and then there was the three-day passage back to Sydney. This went on, trip after trip. Ships on the coal trade were away nine months each year and sometimes voyaged to South America and back to the trade, without returning to the UK. In all, they could be away for almost two years.

S.S.Finchley

The masters had recently been granted permission to be accompanied by their wives, subject to certain conditions. The wives were not allowed to cross the Atlantic with the ship so they had to make other arrangements. Masters had to sign a declaration agreeing that the owners were not responsible, in case of any accidents involving wives, and not liable for compensation. A victualling charge of 3s 6d per day had to be credited to the owners. In view of this, it had been arranged that May would come over during June and stay till the end of September. I was not keen on her coming over at all that season, as it was my first, and I wanted time to settle down and find out what the conditions would be like, but she insisted. My real reason was because she was carrying our first child, and I considered it too risky climbing around a ship in that condition. Her contention was, if she did not come over this year, she would not get another chance after the baby arrived. As that was true enough I had to agree and advised her to make application to the Canadian Pacific Steamship Company, and it was arranged she would take passage on the *Empress of Australia.*

The Mission in Sydney Cape Breton had a large hall suitable for concerts, dances and occasional cinema shows. It had become the social centre where locals and ship people met and May made a lot of friends. I think she was the only captain's wife on the run that season and, being young, was a novelty to them. During the time we were out there Sydney was a round of parties and house visiting. In Montreal a Mrs Jacobs took charge of her and the only time I had her to myself was on the passage between ports.

May on board the S.S.Finchley.

Captain Pendred of the *Watford* had formed a band and they considered they were pretty good. While both ships were in Sydney he somehow managed to persuade the Sydney Broadcasting station to allow his band on the air. Having heard May sing at the Mission they refused to go on air unless she went along too. She agreed and rehearsals went on all weekend. I was allowed to sit at the back of the studio and watch. It was May who carried the whole show along with her singing. Congratulations poured in and the newspaper comment was mostly about her. She was offered a singing programme of her own from the station but, as the ship's times in Sydney were uncertain, she had to refuse.

The ship had been on the trade some years but we didn't have a football team and we were not a member of the league. By chance, May had been goalkeeper in a girls football team at school, so she was easily persuaded to help found the *Finchley Football Club*. Everyone in the ship found they were members, whether they wanted to be or not, and had to pay a subscription. The wireless operator was elected manager, May became chairman, and a committee was voted in comprising members from each department. The money raised went to buy shirts, shorts and socks, also a ball for practice. A team was formed. The second mate, wireless operator, third and fourth engineers and one of the cabin boys had all played for their schools. Oddly enough two of the firemen joined, both large men, and as full backs formed an impregnable defence line. The remainder were made up from the sailors and apprentices. The colours chosen were green and white vertical striped jerseys with

The S.S. Finchley football team.

white shorts and socks. We were accepted into both the Montreal and Sydney leagues. As far as I recall the *Finchley Football Club* didn't make a name for itself that season. I was not allowed to do anything but had to pay the subscriptions for May and myself as she insisted in attending every match, so I had to go along too.

Toward the end of August we were to take the winter supply of coal and stores to Belle Island in Conception Bay, Newfoundland. It was a small island with high cliffs all round. The loading berth on the eastern side of the island was a narrow wharf clinging to the bottom of the cliff. The main occupation on the island was fishing. The large cod were out in the bay but along the narrow jetty the smaller codling were plentiful. May and I spent every day fishing from the jetty. The local fishermen lent her a large lobster pot and some of the lobsters we caught were very large, one in particular was huge. A photograph of it shows one claw covering the whole of a dinner plate! The fishermen said that to attain that size it must have been a hundred years old.

Before the end of the season we returned with a cargo of ore for Rotterdam. Unfortunately there were no sailings to the UK from St. John, Newfoundland, at that time. It would have been necessary for May to stay in St. John until she could get a ship to Halifax, then on to Montreal and a passage home. So she had to make the passage to Rotterdam in the ship. It was no use writing to Watts for permission – we would be in Rotterdam before a letter arrived in the UK, so I decided to say nothing and explain if I was asked. The matter was never mentioned. In the rough weather from Rotterdam to the River Fal, May had jumped out of bed to rescue a tray of sandwiches and a heavy roll of the ship threw her against the side of the cabin, but she never mentioned it.

We went to lay up in the River Fal. I heard later that there were more ships on the trade that season than were necessary. The demand for coal had fallen off so much that it was cheaper to lay the *Finchley* up and pay the hire to the end of the season, than to keep her running. So ended my first season on the St. Lawrence Coal Trade.

We arrived home in the middle of September; the baby was due in November. Father had recovered from his second stroke but was now unable to walk and his hands were not much use, so he required constant care. Midst all this, mother had acquired a lodger. I didn't like the idea and asked her to dispense with him. She would not, saying the house was hers and she could do as she liked; in fact it was my money that had bought the house but that did not seem to count for much.

One day May had gone into the back garden to put out some washing and slipped on the steps. I was not told of this either but three weeks later labour pains started and she was rushed into the nursing home. Unfortunately we lost the child and it was several weeks before May was able to come home. Whether the falls contributed in any way to this loss is hard to say.

By the end of the year we had reached the point where we were thinking of a house of our own. The presence of two strong-minded women in the same house simply would not work. At the back of our house lay the Cedar Court estate, where 26 semi-detached houses were being built. One Sunday afternoon we went to have a look at what was going on, and particularly at the house we could see from our garden. We took an immediate liking to the property and, even though it was Sunday, decided to have a word with Jack Lloyd the builder.

'What price are you asking?'

'Eleven fifty freehold, including road charges.'

'What discount will you allow me for spot cash?'

'If you could pay cash on the nail you can have it for nine fifty,' he replied.

'I will give you my cheque tomorrow,' I said.

The house was named *Chertsey* after the ship where the cash was earned for its purchase. Mother was horrified when I told her what we had done. She probably thought it was a waste of money when we could continue to live at *Glenkindie*, but we wanted a home of our own. When I left to rejoin the *Finchley* we had furnished one room downstairs, the front bedroom and the kitchen.

May didn't come over to Canada the next season. She was not well enough and had the house to put in order. In any case there simply was not enough money.

Towards the end of March 1933 I went down to the Fal to take the *Finchley* up to the Tyne for survey and May came with me. We steamed out of Falmouth Roads into dense fog which dogged us all the way to the Tyne. Fortunately we had from a mile to two miles visibility through the Dover Straits but apart from that it was only half a mile. Up the east coast I simply steered from lightship to lightship and then from fog signal to fog signal. From leaving Falmouth to arriving in the Tyne I never left the bridge. That was the worst coastal fog I ever encountered.

The survey did not take long. Mr Davies was the superintendent in charge.

'Make a note of how many plates are dented on each side,' he said.

'I don't need to make a note,' I told him, 'every plate is dented from stem to stern, both sides.' Nothing was done. 'How about new winches?' Nothing doing. 'If you will not do anything else will you put an extension piece on the rudder, it's too narrow for the size of ship and makes her nearly unmanageable in the St. Lawrence River.'

'She seems to have managed all right for 10 years in that river,' he said. I gave up.

I had been through the Pentland Firth on many occasions and had no fear of it, but I hadn't been through in ballast. I had intended, if the weather was at all doubtful, to go up and make the Fair Isle passage between the Orkneys and Shetlands, but the chief engineer changed my mind.

'Are you going through?'

'If I were sure,' I replied, 'that this ship could hold 10 knots for about three hours I would try it.'

'There's no sea and very little wind,' he said. 'With the ship in ballast we could hold 10 knots easily.' I should have realised that the tide, running with the wind, had ironed the sea out flat. Unfortunately I believed what he said, so in we went. We managed to struggle past Stroma Island but she was not doing 10 knots. It took a long time but she was making headway. Suddenly she fell off with the wind and sea on the port side. We were now heading for the cliffs on the west side of Hoy and she would not come up to the wind and sea again. I summoned the chief engineer. 'Why has the speed been cut down?' I demanded.

'The third engineer shut her in to ease the racing.'

'Go down and open out again or we will be into the cliffs.' I had no wish to add to the number of wrecks on that coast.

I still couldn't get her round. Emergency measures were called for. I realised that when the engines were astern it only needed a push on the bows to get her head round to the east. A staysail was hastily constructed out of a tarpaulin, folded cornerwise with a rope runner on each corner and hoisted on the starboard side, forward of No. 1 hatch. When the sail was up I went astern again and round she came. We managed to get under the lee of Hoy and I had decided to try again to make westing when the chief engineer appeared on the bridge. His face was not white, it was green.

'We will have to stop,' he gasped. Just then there was a thump down below and the engines went dead.

'What's happened?' I asked him.

'LP bottom end has spewed out, the engines are useless.' He ran off the bridge. It was now nearly 4 p.m. The west running stream was now nearly run out. We came round beam on to the wind and sea again and hung there for some time. The silence was eerie. Then as the tide turned we started to drift back through the Firth.

'Mr Garlick,' I said, 'the sailing directions say that a vessel left free to drift will never go ashore in the Pentland Firth; we are about to find out if that is true.' As far as the *Finchley* was concerned it was. We drifted beam on to the wind and tide past the north side of Stroma Island. After some hesitation she went past the north side of the Pentland Skerries which were just a few hundred feet away from the stern. She drifted back through the Firth faster than she had steamed through earlier in the day. I went down to the engine room. The four engineers were sitting in a row on the bench in silence, just staring at the engines.

'Well gentlemen, we will not go ashore, we are now clear of the Firth and out in the North Sea. Can you make a repair?' I asked the chief.

'Yes,' he said, 'we have a spare LP bottom. It should be ready in three or four hours.' When we got under way again I hauled up for the Fair Isle channel. I would not attempt the Pentland Firth again with this ship in ballast trim.

Approaching the Newfoundland banks we ran into the usual fog. I was on the bridge when, in the third mate's watch, I began to hear a tinkling and crumping sound alongside which changed to a sound of breaking glass. I looked over the side; it was ice, and gradually getting heavier. I hauled down to the south and was some 70 miles south of Cape Race before I got round the ice field.

This was the only full season I had on this trade. It was just up and down, up and down, every trip the same.

Three ships were moored together at the buoys in the centre of the Tyne Basin, the *Twickenham*, the *Finchley* and the *Blackheath*. Only one officer and one engineer would be required, I could if I wished take the standby. The conditions were half pay and 3s 6d per day victualling allowance. I hadn't sufficient money to remain at home so we decided to manage. No rates were payable on an unoccupied house and we had no other immediate expenses. The apprentices would be kept on. On 30th January I received a telegram from mother to say father was seriously ill again. As I could not leave the ship I asked my sister to go down. He died on 12th February, aged 72.

On 5th March we were ordered down to Readheads for dry-docking and repairs, we were going back into commission. We had been laid up for two months and five days. We would go out in ballast to Takoradi, a West African port, to load ore for the USA. Mr Grist came as mate and Jimmy Travis as second. Fine weather greeted our departure on 17th March and remained so all the way. Takoradi was not a natural harbour, just breakwaters enclosing an area of water, where the swell rolled in and caused vessels alongside the quays to roll and surge up and down continuously.

135

The ore was very heavy so all the weight was low down. She started to roll as soon as we got under way and never ceased till we arrived in the USA. When we came beam on to the north-east trades the rolling was such that it was difficult to remain in bed, and sleep was impossible. I tried lying on a mattress cross ways in my entrance lobby but simply slid up and down with each roll. In the end I fixed a plank down the middle of the bed and jammed myself in, then I managed to get some sleep.

It seemed that during the time we were in the USA and Canada anyone that had anything to do with this ship ran into trouble. I have no doubt that the discharge of the *Finchley's* cargo of ore was long remembered in Newport News*. Originally we were to proceed to Norfolk, Virginia, but the authorities in Newport had protested about Norfolk getting all the ships, and they were backed by the Chesapeake and Ohio Railway who demanded their share. The reason they were not getting any ships, they were told, was they had no facilities for discharging ore cargoes, something they vehemently denied.

During the war a wooden pier with a gantry had been built to ship war supplies to Europe. This was fixed and could not move along the pier. On this gantry was a travelling grab worked by an electric motor. This, said the port authorities, could discharge ore faster than Norfolk. Because this grab could only go up and down and in and out, the ship's winches had to be used to trim the ore to the centre of each hold. The whole structure had not been used since the end of the war, 16 years previously.

This was not my first visit to Newport News and I had got to know the place well. Before we completed discharge here I got to know the place very well indeed. Trouble was not long coming; already the grab had broken down several times and this was only the first day, and so it went on. When the grab was working our winches were under repair and vice versa. Instead of discharging in two days it was now a question of being able to discharge at all. Then the last of the spare motors burned out leaving the grab suspended in the cross bunker hatchway. It was eventually got out and we were moved to Pier No.2. I didn't think this pier would stand the weight of wagons loaded with ore, but time would tell.

The local newspaper was giving lurid descriptions of what was happening in the battle to unload the *Finchley's* cargo of ore. Every day a large photograph appeared on the front page together with a progress report. The reporters enjoyed themselves as this was showing up the neglected state of the cargo piers and targetted the Chesapeake & Ohio Railway who owned them. The pier winches hadn't been used for a long time and were giving as much trouble as ours. The breakdown of the electric grab and the condition of the piers and their winches were getting so much publicity that the chairman of the railway company made an inspection. He arrived on the scene just as the pier began to give way under the weight of a locomotive pulling a string of wagons. This incident caused the suspension of all discharge.

* a city and port in southeast Virginia.

I was now a well-known figure in Newport News. People pointed me out to visitors. 'That's the skipper of the *Finchley*, she's the ship that made the C. & O. Railway plan to spend a million dollars building new piers.' Suffice to say we did eventually finish the discharge. On our last day I received a cable from Watts to proceed to Sydney Cape Breton – a time charter for Dominion Coal. I was shocked, I had hoped we were finished with that trade.

On the second day out from Newport the ship developed a juddering sound – it felt as if the vessel was shivering. The chief suggested we should stop and have a look. We did, and discovered we had lost part of a propeller blade. We resumed the passage. Difficulties arose over the propeller and eventually in Montreal a Lloyd's surveyor was called in.

'I am not,' said the surveyor, 'concerned with what speed your propeller can drive. As long as it can produce enough speed to control the vessel, and keep it out of danger, I am satisfied. A propeller is not part of a ship.'

'What is it then?' I asked.

'It is something you can change if you wish, therefore it is not part of the hull or machinery.' We were, in his opinion, seaworthy and were issued with the relevant certificate.

Later when the chief engineer and I arrived back at the ship we found loading had ceased as the ship had a heavy list to starboard. I was told the second mate had pumped out half the ballast tank when the pump broke down. All the coal being loaded was now running down to the low side and he had to stop the loading. For an hour the chief did everything he could think of but the pump wouldn't work.

'Have you actually tried it?' I suggested.

'The third said it wouldn't work.'

'Well you have done everything but start it, try that.' He turned the steam on and away it went pumping normally.' He stared at it, shrugged his shoulders and went to have a word with the third. Arriving back in Sydney Cape Breton we dropped the port anchor, and dropped was the right word. As the anchor went down I heard a roar of cable running, which should not have happened as we were in shallow water. Then the mate shouted 'Anchor gone sir, cable parted at the 15 fathom shackle.' Anchor bearings were taken and for two or three trips, each time we were there, we kept on dragging but had no success.

We were on the trade for three months, and it was to be three years before I saw Sydney Cape Breton and Montreal again.

After a trip to Alexandria the ship was laid up again, and Mr Grist, the mate took the first month's standby. When I returned with May I found Mr Grist had left for a berth in another company so I had to remain. But this was not the case, as the ship was put up for sale and I was sent to take out the *Maidenhead*. When we left in the launch I never even looked back, I was never so pleased to leave a ship as I was that one.

I had heard about the *Maidenhead* many times but had not seen her until now. The *Chertsey* had been a wreck, but her equipment and gear had been kept in good order. The *Maidenhead* was also a wreck but her equipment had not been kept in order. I asked if any repairs were being done.

'No,' said Mr Davies, the superintendent, 'bottom scrubbed and painted, forecastles distempered out, that's all. You are only going to run with coal to Alexandria and back with grain or iron ore, so you will not need your gear. I made three voyages in her after which she was sold. A couple of days after Christmas I handed her over to the new Greek owners. That was the last old ship I commanded, from then on most of my ships were new or only a few years old.

Chapter 17

War for a second time

*W*hen I left the *Maidenhead* Captain Musson did not hold out hope of employment in the near future; times were still bad and the fleet was being steadily sold or scrapped. May was now carrying our child which would be due towards the end of September. We just lived quietly and did not spend any more than was necessary. Late in February I had a letter inquiring if I would be prepared to take command of the *Star of Cairo*. I wrote in reply that I was not prepared to serve under a foreign flag and, if there was nothing else, I would have to try and obtain employment elsewhere. This resulted, a few days later in a telephone call from Captain Musson. He was giving me command of the *Dartford* when she arrived back in the UK. I was to remain on that ship for four years and three days, the happiest years of my life. Everyone in that ship seemed to stay for a long time. The Maltese firemen had been several voyages and so had some of the sailors. The people who did not stay were the masters, but I was to break this record and was promoted out of her to the large ships, but I did wonder what fate had instore for me.

The first voyage was a routine one to the River Plate and back, then we went to the Black Sea again. When we arrived off Mariupol I was amazed. The last time I had been there in 1930 there were only a few buildings and we had to go five miles to Mariupol town to do business. Now in 1936 there was a fairly large town, public buildings, shops, factories and a railway station. The harbour had been completed, a grain silo built and the transporter system brought up to date.

The money situation had changed and now, instead of drawing roubles for crew advances, we were given Torgsin stamps. These could only be tendered in the Torgsin stores for buying goods, but they would also accept foreign currency. One afternoon I was in the large Torgsin store and noticed a display of beautiful fur coats. One in particular fascinated me – a squirrel coat, an exquisite creation – and I asked the price. It was 600 roubles, around £70. I didn't have that amount and could not tender a cheque so I had to pass that up. Then I saw a sealskin coat, which had not been priced. They wouldn't take Torgsin stamps, as this coat was for export, but I could have it for £7 cash. Noticing one of the sales girls was about the same size as my wife I asked her if she would try it on; it was a perfect fit. I was now the owner of a sealskin coat. The bill of sale had a broad green stripe running diagonally across which allowed me to take the coat out of the country. For myself I bought, very cheaply, a fleece-lined leather overcoat, partly with cash and stamps. When we arrived back home the sealskin coat gave the customs a problem they could not solve. They did not know what duty was chargeable. The following morning the customs officer came back with two large books under his arm. Sealskin was not listed. I would either have to take it out of the country again or call it something else. So the manifest was altered to read one fur article and the duty was 30*s*.

It must have taken a fortnight at least to load the anthracite for Boston, but at last we were ready to leave. We had fine weather for the passage across the Mediterranean, but half way across the Atlantic we began to receive reports from US weather stations about the progress of the season's first hurricane. It seemed to have struck Cuba and was heading for the Mexican Gulf, but then changed its mind, hit Florida and then swung out again and followed the coast. The last weather report stated it would pass over Boston the following morning. Working out its speed and ours I reckoned we would both arrive at the same time. I was not going to be caught inshore in that kind of weather. The wind would start as a south-westerly, then swing round through south-east and east till the centre passed making a lee shore.

Forty miles from Boston we reached a position that I considered would give me shelter from the worst of the sea where we would be in shallow water. I stopped the ship and lay to. Everything had been lashed down and lifelines stretched fore and aft. The barometer had been going down rapidly and was now below 29 inches. We heard a low roaring sound which gradually grew louder, then we saw a white line along the horizon advancing rapidly. I got the ship under way and headed round to bring this advancing white line ahead. This spread until it covered the sea and a huge swell, topped with white scud, bore down on us. Then came the wind. Getting over that swell was like a horse taking a high fence, the ship practically stood on end. By 9 a.m. the hurricane was at its height. Every time the gusts eased off for a minute or two the sea rose up almost vertically. When that happened the speed had to be eased down and the seas kept just off the bows; my hand was never off the handle of the engine-room telegraph. I had to give helm orders by hand as it was impossible, with the screaming of the wind, for the helmsman to hear anything. After four and a half hours the wind suddenly dropped away and the sky cleared to a cloudless blue, this was the centre passing over. In less than an hour the scream of the wind began again, now from the westward, then gradually it eased down. By noon the wind was moderate and by 1 p.m. the weather was quiet and we were making for Boston at full speed. We boarded the pilot around 6 p.m. The harbour was a sight, covered with the wreckage of boats, yachts, club pavilions, houses and all kinds of other debris.

'Well,' said the pilot, 'that twister sure dusted Boston off. The city should be clean as a new pin now.'

About a week out from Boston I received a radio message from my mother-in-law. HER LADYSHIP HAS ARRIVED. BOTH DOING WELL. I had been getting worried as I knew the time was near but had heard nothing. So I had a daughter. When I arrived in the River Plate I found she had been born on 2nd October.

We were somewhere between Recife and the Leeward Islands when one of the firemen came to me complaining of a swelling in his stomach. He was a tall thin man and the swelling in his middle made him look like a snake which has swallowed an apple. He had no temperature and his pulse was normal, he complained only of constipation. He had eaten scarcely anything for days but he was swelling up gradually. It was not just his stomach, it was all round. When I poked him with my finger it was hard and made no impression, but when he moved I thought I detected a gurgling sound. It was a puzzle. I tried giving him laxatives but that had no effect. I told him to eat his food dry and take as little liquid as possible. The strange thing was, even in this tropical weather, he did not sweat, his skin was as dry as paper. The nearest I could get to his symptoms in the *Shipmasters' Medical Guide* was dropsy but according to the book dropsy started round the ankles and worked up; he was swelling round the middle. He got larger and larger and the skin round his middle was tight as a barrel. I got in touch by radio with the doctor of an American passenger ship and he advised siphoning off the fluid, but I had neither the knowledge nor instruments for that kind of surgery. The man was unable to work and only got round with difficulty. He was now like a barrel with arms and legs sticking out. I then contacted a doctor on one of the mail ships who confirmed what the other doctor had said. I was to give him hot salt water baths every few hours to make him sweat and land him as soon as possible. He now had to be wedged in the bunk otherwise he just rolled round and round. He was so heavy and unwieldy that only Mr Stevenson, the mate, could lift him in and out of the bunk. The patient did not lose weight but Mr Stevenson claimed he lost two stone.

We were now coming up to the Leeward Islands so I decided to put into Barbados, if he was still alive. I wirelessed the owners and also the Barbados Port Authorities, advising the latter that I was coming in to land a sick man, non-infectious. Their port doctor boarded at daylight and was amazed at the condition of the man, he had never heard of a case like it. It proved quite a battle to get the patient off the ship and into the launch. When the doctor in charge of the hospital saw him he was delighted, it was a unique case he said. Then he telephoned every doctor on the island to come and have a look at what he had got.

'What chance has he of surviving doctor?' I asked.

'He will be alright now we have him here, we will drain him out shortly.' Luckily I had kept a complete record in the official log for every day since the man reported sick, and also made a few copies just in case. I gave one to the doctor who said it would be invaluable in treating the patient. The man recovered although the cause

S.S.Dartford

of the condition was never discovered; I met him in the Cardiff shipping office a year or two later and he was fine.

When we arrived back in Cardiff I met May at the station. She was carrying an elongated bundle, well wrapped up. Out of the top stared two small blue eyes.

'Your daughter,' she said as she handed me the bundle. She had been given the names Mary Jeanette and was now three months old.

The next few years were very happy ones. I had home leaves and May and Mary came over to Antwerp and all the home ports.

In July 1939, shortly before the outbreak of the Second World War we were heading from Rotterdam to Cardiff. A French tanker, loaded with benzene, as I afterwards heard, discharged his pilot off the Hook of Holland at the same time as we did. He was also bound down the Channel and kept station about a mile away on our starboard beam all the way down. About 6 a.m. dense fog shut in. I was on the bridge and rang HALF SPEED then SLOW when we were abeam of the Eddystone lighthouse. The French tanker's whistle still sounded on our starboard beam, he must have reduced speed at the same time. About an hour later we heard the whistle blasts of an approaching vessel. From the direction of the sound he was on our starboard bow and so would pass clear, albeit close. His whistle sounded louder and louder. Then there sounded three short blasts from the tanker followed by one short blast, then three blasts from the approaching ship followed by a sickening crash, the hiss of steam, an explosion and the sound of fire.

'My God,' said Mr Travis, the mate, 'they've collided.'

I stopped the engines, got all hands out and the lifeboats ready for lowering. I edged as near the sound of burning as I could. The fog was so dense nothing could be seen. I sent out a message, ALL SHIPS. A COLLISION HAS OCCURRED IN MY VICINITY. and gave the position. DENSE FOG. ALL SHIPS KEEP CLEAR OF THIS POSITION. I AM STANDING BY.

As the sun gained strength it dried up the fog and we could see a dense mass of smoke, then the bows of a ship, the tanker, projecting vertically out of the water, but upside down. An area of burning oil was spread all round. I edged in until we were on the fringe of the burning oil but could not see anyone or boats in the water. Now the fog cleared to about two miles visibility and we saw a ballast ship, stopped, with her bows stove in and her bridge vanished. Alongside her was a lifeboat full of people. At the same time they saw us and the boat pulled away and rowed over to our ship. They were the survivors of the *Sunik*, 24 of them with the mate in charge. Ten had gone down with the ship including the captain and the chief engineer. They were in a bad way, some naked, most with only trousers on, just as they had come out of their bunks, and all covered with oil. None that I can recall had been burned, the fire had not spread to the sea until after they got the boat away. Mr Heavers, the steward, got to work giving them coffee and food and getting them cleaned up. He, along with my wife, organised a collection of spare clothes for them.

While all this was happening a boat from the Swedish ship *Grangesborg* came alongside with her mate asking if we could render assistance. Before they were able to get clear of the tanker, the bridge caught fire and was gutted. The mate and helmsman had jumped off the back of the bridge but the captain couldn't be found. They now had no compasses or navigation instruments, everything in the chartroom had been destroyed. His collision bulkhead had gone but, being in ballast, he was still buoyant. I instructed him to put his hand steering on the poop into gear – he could then steer as close to me as possible. This was necessary as I had to blow fog signals for us both. He was now 'in tow' – this was known as invisible towage – and had to depend on me as he had no compasses. I adjusted my speed to his and headed for Falmouth.

So we got underway. I radioed Watts that I was making for Falmouth to land survivors, gave our time of arrival and asked for tugs to stand by. Then I notified the French Consul to say I had survivors from the French tanker *Sunik* onboard. As the *Grangesborg* could not do so I radioed his owners and the Swedish Consul. During that short passage the fog sometimes closed in to a mile but when we neared Falmouth it cleared again.

They were all waiting for us: pilot boat, tugs, the French Consul in a launch and boats full of newspaper reporters. We put the *Sunik's* lifeboat into the water and the survivors into the consul's launch. The tugs took charge of the *Sunik*. Then we resumed our passage to Cardiff.

I pieced together what had happened from the accounts of the mates of the *Sunik* and the *Grangesborg*. The *Sunik* was at slow speed, as we were. The *Grangesborg* was at full speed until they heard the whistle of the tanker. At first they assumed there was only one ship ahead as our whistle and that of the tanker followed each other. Thinking that the ship, i.e. us, was on his port bow and going clear, he was still at half speed when the tanker loomed ahead. The tanker captain, knowing he had no room to swing over on my side, had gone hard to starboard and full astern when he sighted the other ship. This put him across the Swede's bows. The Swede struck him on the port side in the way of the cofferdam between the after tank and stokehold. The cofferdam bulkheads were crushed and the benzene poured into the stokehold. That was the explosion, then the fire swept over the tanker and the *Grangesborg* before he went astern clear of the tanker. Everyone in the tanker's stokehold and engine-room died. She listed over to port and they were only able to get one of the bridge deck lifeboats away. The captain refused to get into the boat until he was certain everyone was off the ship, but the ship suddenly turned over and the captain was not seen again. I heard later he had been awarded a posthumous Legion of Honour.

While we were in Cardiff Watts put in a claim for salvage, quoting invisible towage. The claim was granted and the award was £1000, of which I received £75. The wireless officer had put in the busiest morning of his life. In addition to the messages I sent he was inundated with calls from other ships offering help. The

S.S.Dartford leaving Barry Roads, South Wales.

admiral in charge of Devonport demanded a full report and the big daily newspapers asked me to reserve them rights to the story. I did not reply to any of them.

At the beginning of August 1939 we loaded for the Argentine. I was now carrying a sealed envelope in the safe only to be opened if a certain signal was received from the Admiralty. The passage was uneventful. We were lying at anchor waiting for a berth when, on 2nd September, I heard over my radio the announcement that Great Britain was now at war with Germany. This was the second time in my life. Having served through the First World War I could not share the enthusiasm displayed by the younger members of the crew on receipt of the news, I knew what was coming. The news of the sinking of the *Athenia*, with heavy loss of life, which came through later confirmed my foreboding – it was to be sinking without warning.

After discharge we were ordered to proceed to San Lorenzo and San Martin to load a part cargo. These two small ports were about three miles apart and were merely jetties jutting out from the bank. I also received a telephone call from Mr Middleton, our agent, to come down to Rosario as the British Consul wished to see me. San Lorenzo was not far from Rosario so I could get there by bus. The consul informed me that I must insist, before signing bills of lading, that the final destination of the cargo be put in writing. It was part of the blockade regulations resulting from the state of war.

Buenos Aires was full of ships, rumours and wild stories. The British Consulate was now the pivot around which we all revolved. From the Admiralty came the order for ships to be painted grey all over, as in the last war. We finished loading a cargo of bagged grain but the final destination on the bills of lading caused trouble. At first the consignees refused to name the cargo destination stating it was no business of mine. The port of discharge was to be Antwerp. I refused to sign. Finally Lausanne in Switzerland was put in as the final destination.

'You have a very interesting cargo captain,' the consul remarked, 'somehow I doubt it will ever see Lausanne.' I had my doubts as well, it had to be something out of the ordinary if I was involved in it.

We were now to call at Montevideo for orders as a naval control station had been established there. I had to proceed to Sierra Leone and keep off the usual route as a German raider was in the South Atlantic, and I was given a code book which I had to destroy if captured by the raider.

We arrived at Sierra Leone one afternoon. A boom had been laid across from the mud banks fronting the town over to the main shore line and behind this was assembled the largest concourse of ships I had yet seen in one place. After a while a launch came out flying a pilot flag. A young RNR lieutenant clambered on board and came up on the bridge.

'I have been put on this job captain, but have no experience in handling ships, I was only a junior officer in the Royal Navy. I can show you where you have to anchor but you will have to handle the ship yourself.'

'I can manage that,' I told him. 'I was stationed here in a fleet collier during the First World War and so know something about this place.' That was an unwise statement to make as I found out later. The anchorage and town did not appear to have changed since 1918. The only difference was the anchorage was now full of merchant ships not naval ones.

The naval control headquarters had been established in an old Union Castle liner, the *Edinburgh Castle,* and I had to report there for orders. A naval captain was in charge.

'I understand, captain,' he said, 'you were stationed here in a fleet collier in the last war.' Instinct warned me to be careful.

'I was only the second mate, sir.'

'Maybe, but you would get to know the harbour; colliers were always on the move, and since then you have had years of experience in handling ships. As you probably know there was no pilotage for this anchorage in peace time, the masters on the West African trade took their ships in and out themselves.'

'I know that, sir.'

'We have no experienced masters to serve as pilots, only young RNR officers from the mail boats. When a convoy leaves, the masters take the ships out themselves. It is bringing them in and putting them in berth where we need experienced men. Also to put ships alongside the colliers and bring them away again.'

'When I was on this station, sir, the whole crew went down with malaria. We lost seven dead out of a crew of 34. I had six bouts of it, was classed unfit for further service and discharged on medical grounds and advised to stay away from West Africa. I do not intend to get malaria again.' I didn't mention that the incident had actually occurred in Lagos.

We were there a long time waiting for escorts and colliers. Things had not been properly organised as yet. The ships homeward bound from the Argentine and round the Cape usually fuelled or coaled at St. Vincent, in the Cape Verde Islands, Dakar or Las Palmas. Now as all ships were ordered here the question of fuelling and coaling became acute and we had to wait our turn.

The day came when we were ordered to attend a convoy conference and bring our wireless officers with us; it was going to be a very large convoy. The naval captain led off by giving a lecture on ship handling and station keeping in convoy. This was interrupted by an elderly master from one of the Blue Star passenger ships.

'Sir,' he said, 'we have not come for a lesson on ship handling, we are all experienced seamen and of an average age to have served in the last war as ships' officers so we have experience in convoy work. All we want to know is our stations and instructions as to what to do in case of enemy attack.' He sat down.

'Thank you captain, for reminding me. I am not yet used to dealing with merchant ship convoy routine.'

We were to leave the next morning. We were anchored the furthest in and would have the longest way to go so we were to get underway first, at sunrise. We would lead the inner ships out and those nearest the boom would be the last to move. I knew what would happen. It was well after noon before we got sorted out into our stations. Many of the slower River Plate ships never got into station at all as the commodore, as usual in the fastest ship, went up to nine knots before they had a chance to catch up. By sunset about a third of the convoy had dropped out of sight astern. Many more were just, like us, hanging on by our teeth. I spent all that day and night teaching my three mates the art of station keeping. At daylight the signal to commence zigzag was hoisted. There were no collisions but near misses a plenty. The next day we were in the north-east trades and by late afternoon we were on our own proceeding as per instructions in 'envelope C'. We had a quiet passage to the Channel and never sighted another ship, and late one afternoon arrived in Weymouth Bay. The examination steamer came alongside.

The boarding officer examined my papers.

'Ah yes, you are the ship we have orders to detain, you have contraband cargo. The pilot will board and put you into Portland Harbour.' We lay there eight days and May came through for a long weekend. German planes were over at night dropping mines, and a trawler was kept busy sweeping the bay and harbour. Quite a number must have been swept up and also sunk by rifle fire, judging by the amount of shooting that went on.

The cargo was eventually allowed to be discharged in Antwerp, with a proviso that it was not to leave Belgium. We left Portland early one morning with an armed trawler for escort. By the time we reached the Dover Straits a south-westerly gale with driving rain reduced the visibility to only a mile or two. Where our escort got to and what became of him after dark we didn't know, nor was he in sight at daylight. The Downs* was packed full of ships and the only anchorage I could find was in the small bay in the south-west part of the Goodwin Sands. After we anchored the examination steamer came alongside and checked our papers.

'You are the contraband ship, awaiting orders.'

Apparently we were becoming a headache to the contraband control. The weather was unsettled, one gale after another. One morning an envelope was tossed on board saying I was to leave for Antwerp by the route given, from the North Goodwin Lightship to Flushing. Just when it was coming in dark we picked up the Fairway Buoy for the channel into Flushing. An apprentice on the starboard side of the bridge reported a buoy or something close alongside. I had a look, it was a large mine painted yellow, about 15 feet away from the ship's side. It had probably been

---

* a convoy assembly area inside the Goodwin Sands, off the east coast of Kent

thrown off by the bow wave. Had it been moored, it would have swung back in again. That gave me a nasty shock. It was quite dark when I eased down off Flushing and the pilot scrambled aboard.

'Full speed, captain, full speed, we must get into the river as fast as we can. Floating mines have broken adrift from the minefields in the gales and are coming in on the tide.'

There was a feeling everywhere that people were just waiting for something to happen. German planes were flying low overhead and the Belgians appeared unable to do anything about it. The day before we left I couldn't find a taxi to take me to the British Consul. I telephoned the agency and the clerk came down in the agency car.

'Is anything happening?' I asked him, 'there are no taxis anywhere.'

'The Belgian Army has been mobilised and all the young men on the office staff have been called up; they are now on the frontier somewhere. If things continue like this the office will have to close down.'

The pilot office told us that the pilot boat was off station, owing to floating mines and we would have to take the ship out ourselves. We were told not to leave before daylight as we would be unable to see the mines at night.

'How about mines in the anchorage?' I asked.

'You have your choice,' was the reply. It was just over 60 miles to the Downs. If we left now we would be arriving there at night and with everything blacked out we were quite likely to end up on the Goodwin Sands. We said we would leave at daybreak.

As soon as we berthed in Cardiff I received a letter which stated AS YOU ARE NOW ONE OF OUR SENIOR MASTERS WE REQUIRE YOU TO TAKE COMMAND OF THE BEACONSFIELD WHEN SHE ARRIVES IN HULL. THIS IS AN ORDER NOT A REQUEST.

I never saw the *Dartford* again. I heard sometime later that she had been torpedoed and sunk in the North Atlantic. That was a little ship of happy memories. From now on I was to be on big ships and long voyages.

Chapter 18

Nothing but trouble

*W*hen I arrived home after leaving the *Dartford* I went down with a dose of influenza. I had been home three weeks, and still had not got over it when the call to Hull arrived so May came along with me. It was a very severe winter, snow and ice everywhere. We stayed the night at the Station Hotel before going on board. I don't remember much of what went on during that stay in Hull as I was still recovering from the after effects of 'flu.

We went down river to anchor off Spurn Point to await the coastal convoy. The pilot cheerfully announced that a couple of ships had been mined leaving the anchorage a day or two earlier. We were to wait for the convoy and fit in where we could. That was a nightmare passage. We speeded up and eased down, twisted and turned avoiding suspected mined areas, and the German planes were over at night dropping mines along the route. I didn't hear of any ships in this convoy being damaged but some ghastly sights were to be seen as we went along.

We arrived in the Downs to await the London ships. The convoy was in complete confusion as usual. When off the Scillies, the commodore gave the convoy speed – nine knots. They gradually drew away from us and faded over the horizon. It was then I discovered the *Beaconsfield* could manage only eight and a half knots. She had a clean bottom, she had been dry docked and she had a full head of steam, but could manage nothing more.

The passage down to the River Plate was uneventful, one could almost forget there was a war on. One afternoon, when we were south of the equator, we had target practice. Mr Martin, the mate, would not go anywhere near the gun and stayed on the bridge, his ears plugged with cotton wool. The firing was carried out just before sunset and, when it became dark, I made a large alteration of course which I held for several hours, just in case any of the lurking raiders might have heard the gunfire. We discharged in Buenos Aires and loaded cargo for London. We had to call at Montevideo for coal and route instructions. Lying in the shallows to the west of the entrance channel we could see the wreck of the *Graf Spee*.

When I reported to the Naval Control on arrival at Sierre Leone and filled in the usual particulars including speed, I put down "only able to do eight and a half knots". The naval captain became annoyed.

'I do not like this kind of joke, kindly put down your correct speed on the form.'

'That is my correct speed, sir.'

'Lieutenant,' he called to one of the officers, 'take a launch and examine that vessel and her log books.' The lieutenant came back.

'The captain is quite right sir, that is her speed. She is only 17 months old. I was amazed when I looked down into the engine-room. Her engines must have been made for a tugboat. She burns less than 20 tons for a 9000 dead-weight, an economy job all right.'

'I will put you in the seven knot convoy,' said the captain. We managed to stay with it to the Channel.

As we were London bound we were ordered into Portland harbour to be degaussed. This was a protection against the magnetic mines used by the Germans. Some of these mines had been washed ashore and their magnetic nature discovered. The magnetic field created by the steel hull of a vessel was sufficient to activate any mine over which it passed. It was easy, knowing the polarity of the mine, to reverse the ship's magnetic field by passing current through electric cables, which were laid and made fast around the edge of the upper deck. When the current was switched on, the polarity was reversed.

Then we went out into Weymouth Bay for trials. What happened was not, I believe, on the agenda. Suddenly there was a tremendous underwater explosion close to the ship. Although loaded, she seemed to be lifted up in the water. In the wheelhouse were the naval officer in charge of the degaussing, the pilot, compass adjuster, helmsman and myself, with the watch officer on the wing of the bridge. The shock lifted us off our feet and my head hit the wheelhouse deckhead. The steering compass bowl jumped out of the gimbals, then fell back into the binnacle. A trawler engaged in sinking mines was firing at one near us and instead of piercing the buoyancy chamber had, by chance, hit one of the horns and exploded the mine. Everyone one cleared off as fast as they could get the tug alongside.

I had already received the route orders but the convoy had not arrived.

'Get the hell out of here,' advised the naval officer, 'and pick up the convoy on the way. The trawler will pilot you through the minefield, it is too dangerous to wait around here.' Somewhere between the Downs and Margate we passed the half submerged hull of a ship with the degaussing coils round her.

'The coils didn't protect her,' I remarked.

'The coils are all right,' replied the pilot, 'the human element lost that ship. She is a tramp with the usual single dynamo. Coming in during daylight the second engineer, as usual, shut the dynamo off. Having no protection she struck a mine and that was that.'

S.S.Beaconsfield

We went up to the Tyne for survey and May and I went to stay in Glasgow with my mother who had returned to Scotland after father died. Back in South Shields a Marlin machine gun had been mounted in each bridge wing – our air defence!

The passage to the River Plate and across to Sierre Leone was uneventful but trouble struck to the west of Ireland. Our route was round the north of Ireland and it was getting near time for meeting the destroyer escort. At 6a.m. one morning I was called to the bridge. A Morse signal had peen passed down from the commodore that a severe south-westerly gale was imminent and all ships were to take precautions. We were in for the worst thrashing I have ever received in the North Atlantic. It was the first time I had been in a gale in convoy. I was wondering if I should have the boats swung in, but then, if we were torpedoed in heavy seas we would never get them out again, so I decided to leave them where they were. Before long a tremendous sea was running and the after deck was continually swept by heavy seas, and the crew accommodation was flooded when the weather decks were smashed in. By evening the seas were sweeping over the ship, ladders and hand rails were torn away and the saloon alleyway doors smashed in. The second engineer couldn't be relieved and he reported water in the stokehold and difficulty in keeping steam owing to the violent rolling. There was nothing for it, we had to heave to. By midnight the wind was in the north-west and blowing a full hurricane, and I could no longer keep control of the ship through lack of steam. The only thing to do was bring the wind and sea astern and run towards the Irish coast. She laid in the trough with the seas pouring over her, I thought she would never come round, but she did degree by degree until the seas were astern. Now she was under control but both lifeboats had vanished and, as seen in daylight, everything else that could move. By daylight, with a rising barometer, the wind and sea had begun to ease a little but there was still a huge swell running. There was no sign of the convoy. The sky was now clear and Mr Martin obtained a star sight. We couldn't hold this course for long as we would reach the west coast of Ireland before sunset. We could now see what condition the vessel was in. The lifeboats had gone and the davits were bent and twisted. Everything moveable had been stripped off. The hatches had held, if they had gone it would have been the end of us. The degaussing wire had been torn adrift and hung in bights over the side, so we had no protection against mines, and could not attempt to reach Liverpool as that area was thick with them. I decided to make for the Clyde for boats and DG repairs.

It was now November and darkness came early. We came up to the boom from the Cumbraes to Bute after sunset. I had no mind to cruise out in the Firth all night, a sitting target for any submarine, as we had no boats or DG protection. I called up the boom defence vessel and informed him of our condition and that he must let us through. He kept the gate open and, as no pilot was available, I had to anchor in Rothesay Bay for the night. I had been on my feet since the gale commenced and was so tired I was unable to get down the bridge ladder. The steward, Percy Heavers, carried me to my room and gave me a large tot of hot rum. I didn't wake up until the pilot boarded next morning.

We anchored off Greenock and found most of our convoy there and what a sight they were, not a boat to be seem amongst them. We lay at the Tail of the Bank* for 10 days while our DG coils were reset, but that was all. Then I was ordered to proceed to my destination.

'How about boats and rafts?' I asked.

'We have none to give you.'

'What are we supposed to do if we get mined or torpedoed?'

'Swim around and if you are not picked up you will just have to drown, you are not the only ship in that condition.'

When the ship had discharged in Manchester I handed over command to Mr Martin, then went home on leave until I took over the *Teddington*, the third of the new ships being built in Dundee.

---

* the convoy anchorage point just off Greenock which was also used in emigrations during the 19th century.

Chapter 19

S.S.Teddington –

an ill-fated ship

My instruction for Dundee did not arrive until the middle of February 1941, so I had two months at home. During this time the German bombers were busy night after night destroying Plymouth. We could see from our upstairs windows the glow from the fires and the flashes of the exploding bombs. We heard the drone of the bombers as they passed over Torquay, but we had not been raided. Everything was dreary and dismal and food was short.

May stayed at home while I was in Dundee as expenses only allowed for me to live in lodgings or hotels until the ship was ready. I went up to London by the night train travelling on a first class voucher from the London office. I had applied for a sleeper and got one. When I boarded the train the attendant informed me I had outranked a colonel! Shipmasters at that time appeared to be more important than army officers.

I arrived in the early morning – a raw cold day with a biting east wind. There was only Mr Wardman the chief engineer, who I had not met before, standing by. He was lodging in a house not far from the yard and had booked me in there. For the first three or four weeks there was nothing much to do, then the ship was moved down to the quay at the Caledon Yard to complete fitting out. We completed the sea trials but over the measured mile the average speed did not even come up to 10 knots. However, she steered and handled well.

We were ready to go and had hauled over to the wharf at North Shields to take on bunker coal. It was a bright moonlit night. Most of the crew were ashore and May and I were the only ones on board in that part of the ship. About 9 p.m. the sirens went, then searchlights and gunfire – it was a full scale raid. Two of the gunners asked if they should man the machine guns on top of the bridge wing houses, but I told them the planes were far out of our reach and firing would only serve to draw attention to ourselves. A new cruiser, the *Manchester, w*as lying moored at the buoys on the opposite side of the river just abreast of us. When the bombs started falling around South Shields the cruiser got into the act blazing away with

S.S. Teddington in the North Atlantic

her anti-aircraft armament. May was sitting in the smoke-room and I had gone outside on deck to watch. Then a bomb landed in the water between the cruiser and ourselves. It must have been a large one as when it hit the bottom it went off. It acted like a depth charge, the ship appeared to lift out of the water, then drop back again. I was standing on the deck outside when the shock hit the ship and fell flat on my back. May was lifted off the settee and thrown across the table, but was not hurt. I got up and went inside to see if she was all right.

'Where have you been?' she asked.

'When the ship jumped I fell flat on the deck. I have come to see if you are all right.'

'That was 10 minutes ago,' she said. So I must have been knocked clean out when I fell on the deck but fortunately did not feel pain anywhere.

We joined a coastal convoy to Methil in the Firth of Forth and from there were instructed to proceed to Halifax, Nova Scotia, for orders. Ships bound across the Atlantic would join a convoy being made up in Loch Ewe on the east coast of Scotland.

We were approaching the Pentland Firth when we heard a plane and saw it skim over the water, barely high enough to clear the ship. It was obvious we were going to be hit, but when our gunner opened fire the pilot must have realised he had lost the element of surprise. He banked away and dropped his bomb on the after deck of the ship astern of us. The vessel dropped out of line and the convoy continued on its way. I could only hope that he managed to reach Wick, which was just a few miles distant.

Nothing seemed to go right in this ship. We had had a minor collision in Loch Ewe and then engine trouble. Now while loading ore No.2 hold feeder collapsed, causing further delay.

'This ship is fey,' said the second engineer. That word in Scots dialect means *marked out for death*. As it turned out he was right.

We returned to Halifax and left in the largest convoy I ever joined. Not all the vessels were out of Halifax, some came from the St. Lawrence, Sydney Cape Breton and other US ports. In the middle of the convoy was stationed the battleship H.M.S. *Ramillies*. Several days out, in a dense fog, the battleship disappeared. How he found his way out of that mass of ships I don't know but it must have been superb seamanship. Shortly after his departure we were again in fog which lasted for 24 hours. During that time we had 16 large alterations of course at full speed. The column leaders blew their numbers when they put their helms over. The next astern, when they came up to the point where the leaders had turned, indicated by their wake, blew theirs and so on. It was frightening work, a delay of seconds in altering could bring your next abeam alongside you, or seconds too soon and you were alongside your beam ship on the other side. What the reason for all this was no one knew at the time. I found out later, when we arrived in the Clyde, that the German ship *Bismarck* had been in action with the *Hood* and the *Prince of Wales*. *Ramillies* had been called out to join in the hunt. The alterations had been to try and keep the convoy away from the area where the *Bismarck* was assumed to be. In fact we were turning circles and marking time.

In Glasgow I handed over the ship to Captain De Courcy and went to stay with my mother until I had made up the voyage account, then I went home.

I heard the story of the *Teddington's* demise some time later. She had been proceeding up the east coast in convoy and, during an E-boat[*] attack at the notorious Sheringham Buoy, a favourite spot for the E-boats, she was torpedoed. She didn't sink. In No. 2 hold there was a quantity of carbide and when the torpedo struck this caught fire. The ship was abandoned and eventually drifted on to Cromer Sands, where she settled in the quicksands. I subsequently heard that she re-appears for a short time every few years, then sinks again. Her career had only lasted a few months during which time she loaded and delivered just two cargoes – a most unfortunate vessel.

[*] a German motor torpedo boat

Chapter 20

S.S.Blackheath

the ship that always came home

*T*here was a legend in the Britain Steamship Company that only company-built ships carried the names *Blackheath* and *Twickenham*. Further, they never lost a ship of that name, they were either sold or scrapped. When I arrived in London as relieving master for a couple of weeks I was to spend the longest period in the *Blackheath* of any one ship during the Second World War.

The *Blackheath* was laid in the Surrey commercial dock where she had been discharging, and the following afternoon moved into the South West India dock to commence loading. This vessel was now attached to the 8th Army Maintenance and the cargo to be loaded was for that purpose. She was five years old and had never undergone her first survey and, since being taken over by the Sea Transport Department (Army division) at the outbreak of war, no maintenance had been carried out. She was dirty and shabby with rust everywhere. No work had been possible on the engines and boilers as she had been under notice for steam since she had been taken up by the Sea Transport, and everything down below was now in a bad state, especially the boilers. It was a case of 'why waste time chipping and painting when the bloody thing could be sunk any time'. That had become the attitude among all ships' crews – officers and engineers as well.

I was lucky to have officers I knew well. Mr Fletcher was mate and had been second mate in the *Beaconsfield*, and Mr Jarvis was second mate. He had been apprentice and third mate with me. The chief engineer was Mr Leybourne who had been second engineer in the *Medmenham*.

The cargo to be loaded was too varied to be described but all was necessary to the conduct of war. In Glasgow a tank landing craft had to be loaded on deck in four parts, one part alone was said to weigh 120 tons.

The magazines under the saloon house were being reserved for special cargo. The port side magazine was stowed with cases of coins. These stood on lorries on the dockside with no one in charge for a night and part of a day. I was told by the

S.S.Blackheath

agents for the Sea Transport that they were filled with bullion valued at five million pounds. The Sea Transport staff in London and in Port Said never knew, nor did Watts Watts.

We went down river to Greenhythe and moored alongside an explosives store hulk in the river. All fires had to be put out and no smoking was allowed. The No.2 after magazines were filled with small strong wooden cases with **TNT HANDLE WITH CARE** stencilled on them. The men who handled them wore canvas shoes and gloves. From the invoice we had 200 tons, a nice little oddment. If we got hit not an atom of ship or crew would be left. I could visualise a queue of crew members reporting sick when we arrived in Glasgow, and I was right.

I had to join the northbound coastal convoy for passage to Glasgow, and it so happened that I was the leading ship for the inside, or port column. At 11 p.m. we were rounding the notorious Sheringham Buoy when our beam ship, the leader of the starboard column, opened fire with his bridge machine guns firing at low altitude. The moon came out just then and we caught sight of a large plane, not much above masthead height, flying parallel to the line of ships. The alarm was sounded and all hands went to stations; it could be the first of an air attack covering an E-boat raid. As he went down the line each ship in turn opened fire, and from far down the column we heard a heavy explosion but could not see any flash. Perhaps he had dropped his bomb or torpedo without scoring a hit. Our motor launches were racing round like terriers, convinced an E-boat raid was developing, but nothing happened. The plane, I assumed, was just on a scouting patrol. The next scare came the following night when we nearly ran into a half sunken wreck which suddenly loomed up right ahead of us. As usual with the coastal convoy, ships dropped off as we passed the various ports and a few deep sea ships joined on. I had to break off at Loch Ewe and as commodore take five ships for the Clyde.

After the tank landing craft came on board in Glasgow her crew arrived, 13 in all, including the captain.

'Where is our accommodation?' they demanded.

I got hold of the Sea Transport officer. 'I have only,' I informed him, 'one two-bunked room, which is supposed to be the ship's hospital.'

'But the crew must go with their craft, they have to be there when it is put together.'

'Well that,' I said, 'is your problem.'

In the end they were sent to another ship but the chief engineer had to go with the craft. He agreed to my suggestion that he lived in his own quarters on the TLC and had his meals in the saloon with us. As if that was not enough on deck, four planes were lashed down, two either side of No.1 hatch. We were an object of curiosity to the other ships around us. Telescopes and binoculars were focused on us trying to find out what we had on deck. Then we were taken down river to the Tail of the Bank to await convoy. There I had a compass adjuster off to see what could be done with the standard and steering compasses. The forward part of the TLC was only a few feet away and all the metal was playing havoc with the compasses. Watching them on the way down the river I could see we were going to have a nightmare time with the deviations when we were on our own. Round and round we went all afternoon.

'It's hopeless captain,' the adjuster said, 'every time I put her round I get a different set of deviations. Even if they are high they should remain constant as long as the course is not altered.'

'What if we have to zigzag?'

'God help you.'

After we passed the latitude of Sierra Leone the convoy dispersed and we were on our own. I had no option, with the condition of my compasses, but to make one course down to Table Bay; to try anything else would have been chaos. We arrived early one morning, the Bay was empty. We were taken in and berthed immediately and coaling commenced. No one, not even myself, was allowed ashore and I noticed a motor launch which seemed to have nothing better to do than idle up and down close alongside the ship.

In Durban, no vessels were taken in or out over the Bar at night, and I was working into an anchorage when out came the pilot boat and two tugs, and in we went and berthed at the coal quay on the Bluff.

'How come,' I asked the pilot. 'it is against harbour regulations for vessels to enter or leave after dark, or so the Admiralty sailing directions say.'

'This ship seems to be a special case, you are to commence coaling at once.' We did. As at Cape Town, no shore leave was allowed. There were police on the gangway and quay, and a launch patrolling off side. I began to wonder if the Sea Transport people out here knew what was on board. As I found out later they could not have known, it was something else that was causing all this commotion.

We had a quiet uneventful passage up to Aden, with only one incident. One evening about 8.30 p.m. the third mate and I were standing in the starboard wing of the bridge when a loud voice came out of the darkness, 'What ship is that?' I got a shock. There could be no enemy vessel in that area. Before we could answer the voice came again.

'HM vessel speaking, identify yourself.'

'British cargo vessel *Blackheath*, bound Aden.'

'Thank you,' came out of the darkness. I came to the conclusion we had been challenged by a submarine.

We coaled at Aden and when we got into the Red Sea we were warned that nothing white or light coloured must be shown on deck at night and no white cap covers were to be worn. The German long-range planes were raiding down as far as Jebel Tier. We arrived in Suez Bay during the afternoon and next morning, at daybreak, we got underway and entered the Canal. We had a plane flying low ahead with a huge ring hung underneath. That, said the pilot, was to detonate any magnetic mines, the Germans frequently mined the Canal at night. There were no other ships, just ourselves.

'Full speed,' said the pilot when we entered the Canal, 'and the best you can do. We have to go full steam all the way to get into Port Said and berthed before dark.'

We arrived late in the afternoon and before we had time to moor up a small lighter came alongside and a number of army units climbed on board and tore off the hatche covers. The officer in charge requested me to deliver Case No. so-and-so, the one which had come on board in Glasgow. I heard later, true or not, that a consignment of tanks had been put on a convoy for the Middle East. The tanks were complete except for one vital cog-wheel which had not arrived by the time the convoy sailed. The tanks could not move without it, and this was what all the fuss was about.

Nothing happened for several days then along came the 150-ton floating crane. This took off the bow part of the TLC and placed it on a barge. I went on to the bridge to watch what the compasses would do when this mass of metal was lifted off. They spun round like tops. The square section on No.3 hatch was lowered into the water and left to float. It appeared to me to have only a few inches of freeboard and I pointed this out to the Sea Transport officer.

'It will be alright,' he said, 'we will tow it to the fitting-out berth later, it should come to no harm.' The after section was placed on the deck of the floating crane and the part on No.5 hatch was put into the water and towed away. No one bothered about the other section left floating around. Next a lighter came alongside and, under the supervision of the Royal Engineers, to whom the explosives were consigned, the TNT was discharged. I was glad to see that go. Nothing happened for several days then someone came on board to enquire how many parts of the TLC had we discharged.

'All four of them,' I informed him.

'We have only had three sections delivered to us.'

'That,' I said, 'must have been the one I saw floating away on its own very low in the water. The Sea Transport officer said it would be towed away later.' They never did find it. The swell from passing craft must have lapped into it until its buoyancy was lost and it sank, but no one knew where. Divers were sent down but nothing was found. Then the lighter returned with the TNT with instructions to put the stuff back on board as the harbour authorities would not allow it in the harbour. I refused and the Sea Transport upheld my refusal. Finally it was put in the furthest part of the lagoon where it could blow up, if so minded, without damaging the town or harbour.

One day what looked like an armoured truck arrived on the quay. It was full of soldiers, led by a captain no less, who came on board with fixed bayonets. I was ordered to discharge into the captain's care the cases of coins taken on board in London. They were checked and found to be correct then loaded on to the truck.

'You are taking a lot of trouble with these cases, one would think they were filled with gold,' I remarked to the captain.

'I have no idea what is in them, my instructions are to take them to Jerusalem and deliver them. We are to be locked into the truck and not allowed out till we get there. Provisions and water have been put in for the journey.'

Discharged at last I was to make my own way to Alexandria, but I would be given an escort. As we cleared the channel a small craft, about the size of a herring drifter, pulled up alongside.

'Who are you,' I asked, 'and what do you want?

'I am your escort to Alexandria.' He had, as far as I could see, a tiny gun, possibly a two-pounder, and a couple of machine guns.

'Have you any depth charges?'

'Yes sir,' he said, 'two.'

'You couldn't fight a submarine on the surface with your armament, could you?' I said trying not to smile.

'I could try,' he replied bravely.

Finally when the time came to leave Alexandria I went to the naval control for route instructions. The lieutenant in charge was very depressed.

'Submarines are swarming around here just now and a ship has been sunk. There's no official route to follow, just skirt round the sand banks and keep zigzagging.' There was no escort. We went through the Canal to Aden to coal and then to Cape Town and Sierra Leone for convoy back to the UK. There were no incidents and on the way through the North Channel, the Clyde and Belfast ships left us. Off the Isle of Man we were dispersed with the signal from the commodore BEHAVE LIKE GENTLEMAN WHEN MAKING UP FOR THE PILOT.' Next day we docked in Liverpool. The ship that always came home had done so again.

I would have liked some leave, as I hadn't been home since the previous July, but was told to remain in the ship. The Sea Transport would not release me as they had found out I had been in the Fleet Auxiliaries in the last war. The Navy never lets go no matter how old you are.

This turned out to be one of those voyages one would rather forget. I did manage some leave, about six days, but then had to return. May returned with me as now I would have to remain with the ship.

The ammunition and bombs had to be loaded first, and as soon as the crew saw these coming on board they took fright. There was a constant flow to my door with crew members armed with doctors' certificates stating they were unfit to make the voyage. Replacements from the pool were signed on and then, after a day on board, became ill and had to be paid off.

Shortly after we started loading, three men dressed in civilian suits, but quite obviously police detectives, came on board one evening. Their documents identified them as officers of the security department. They asked to have the third wireless officer brought in. I sent for him and the security men took him over to the corner table. May and I were making up a crew list at my desk so all we heard was a murmur of voices. Then one of the men, who appeared to be in charge, came over to me.

'We are taking Mr _____ away with us, he will not be making the voyage in this ship.'

'What's it all about?' I asked.

'He is someone we want. We have been tracking him for some time, examining innumerable ships' articles, comparing signatures and finally found what we wanted in the signature of your third wireless officer.' I never heard any more about that strange affair.

The ammunition and bombs were in the bottoms of the lower holds, with the lorries and cars on top, one layer on top of another, each vehicle fully loaded. They were assembled on the open ground at the back of the sheds. My wife was convinced they could not be got into the ship, but they were, some 600 of all sorts and sizes. Then there was another consignment of those cursed NAAFI stores, which always got pilfered, in No.2 port magazine. A layer of detonators and cases of hand grenades were placed on top to try and ward off pilferage. The other magazines had small arms ammunition.

We were now loaded and ready to go – when we could get a complete crew together. The pool officers said the only thing to do was to get the ship out to an anchor with what we had and to send them a list of replacements, which they would send out in a tug. I could sign them on on board –and that is what was done.

The convoy conference was held in the Royal Liver Building and we were told to join up with the Clyde ships, then with the east coast ships. By 4 p.m. we were on our way back to our ships. A sea was running and it was a dangerous job getting on board up a rope ladder. This was not a promising start to the voyage. When I had time to take stock of what I had for a crew I was by no means reassured. There will be plenty of trouble with this crowd I thought; I had never had a tougher looking, or more useless, collection of men.

Four days out from Sierra Leone we were dispersed and on our own to Cape Town, a small convoy of six ships with a corvette in charge. Before dispersing the captain of the corvette informed us we were the worst convoy he had ever seen. Station keeping had been non-existent, the convoy speed was not maintained and signalling had been dilatory. He was thankful to be rid of us.

One evening, I was on the bridge with Mr Davies the mate. We had another Mr Davies, the chief engineer and they became known as Davies the Deck and Davies the Engines.

Just after sunset as it was growing dark Mr Davies said, 'I think I hear something banging about in No. 2 forward end.' We both listened and there it was, each time the bows went down after a pitch. It sounded like a door banging, but the magazine doors were bolted and padlocked when they were filled up. Mr Davies went along to listen. He was away for some time.

'It was the door of the port magazine. The padlock has been forced and the cases of detonators and grenades have been thrown aside and some of the NAAFI stores have gone. The fools could have blown up the ship.'

That night thinking the affair over I remembered that the magazines had been filled first before loading in the holds commenced. With the crew changes that took place there could not be anybody aboard, except the second and third mates and the engineers, who were in the ship then. But there were the four with the London discharges who had joined when we first signed on. I got their discharge books and examined them. This began to get interesting. The four of them had served together in the same ships, ships that carried army and navy stores. The next morning when everyone was out on deck we searched the crew quarters but nothing was found. Then, as far as possible, I made certain there was no means, except by opening the hatch, of getting into that shelter deck. The only thing to do now was wait for the inevitable informer and, when least expected, make a spot check search of crew quarters. In Durban we decided to make the check. We found nothing until we came to the carpenter's room. The steel wardrobe was packed from top to bottom with cartons of cigarettes and under the bunk was a case of whisky. I fully expected

The ship that always came home.

these four to desert in Durban and was very surprised when they didn't. I suppose a clean discharge book was of more value than a fine or a month's imprisonment. I was unable to get the Sea Transport to take any action.

'If you have a crew that enables you to leave, let matters rest until a later time,' was all they said.

Two nights out, on our way to Bombay, I woke about 3 a.m. with the feeling we were running into danger. I dressed and went up on to the bridge. A radio message had just come in saying one of the Anchor Line Bombay ships had been sunk by a raider and gave the position. I laid it off – it was right on our course. Whether the raider was there by chance, or had knowledge of our route, it was safest to take avoiding action. I altered course to close the land around Cape Corrientes, about two miles off. The downward traffic I knew was routed close to the land but I had to take the chance. I considered a raider was more likely to go for the northbound traffic which would be carrying munitions and military stores, rather than the southbound which could be in ballast or commercial cargo. We closed the land about 2 p.m. in the afternoon and then kept in close as a line of reefs ran up the coast as far as Mozambique. Nothing was seen that night nor the next day, but that night the moon had not long risen when we heard faintly, but distinctly, gunfire away to the east. It only lasted a few minutes. It was about where we should have been on the route we had been given.

The next night gunfire was again heard out to the east, but louder this time. The next evening I was on the bridge with Mr Davies when we sighted two vessels coming towards us, close together. Well, this was the southbound route so that was not unusual, but why were they so close together? The sun had just set when the outside ship commenced firing at the inner one. At the distance they were apart he could not miss. The gun flashes reflected on our bridge.

'We will be destroyed, we will be destroyed,' cried Mr Davies, 'we can't get away with our speed. If we see him, he sees us and will come after us when he finishes with that ship.' I had a look at the chart. We were passing a small island situated inside the line of reefs. In line with its northern end was a clear opening through the reef, not wide, but wide enough. The channel, between the island and the mainland, was half a mile and the depth given there was four fathoms and we were not drawing more than 20 feet aft. All this took only a minute.

'Get forward Mr Davies and prepare to anchor, I am going behind that island.' The apprentice on bridge lookout was ordered, 'STAND BY THE ECHO SOUNDER and when it shows four fathoms let me know.' I put the helm hard over to port and rang STAND BY on the engines. If the chart was not reliable, or if I miscalculated the distance, I could take the bottom out of her, but that was better than gunfire which would set off the ammunition in the holds and blow the ship apart, and us with it.

We were two miles off the reef, three and a half in all to reach behind the island. The light was fading fast but it was just sufficient to get there if I held full speed. The ship had been blacked out as usual at sunset so the raider would be unaware of what I was doing. We made it and anchored, the stern lifting in the swell as it rolled in to the beach. From the time the gunfire commenced the radio was blaring out RRR (the raider warning signal) and giving name and position, he was Greek. The raider must have missed the wireless cabin and the operator was a brave man. By the time we anchored all had gone quiet again.

'He must have finished off that ship by now,' I told Mr Davies. 'he will not try to come in here but might wait for us to come out at daylight, but I don't think so. Now he has been reported and his position given he will get out of this area as fast as he can.' I called all hands on deck and when they were assembled I gave them the choice of going on to the beach in case anything happened.

'Are you going to stay on board sir?' someone asked.

'Of course,' I replied.

'Then we will all stay, is everyone agreed?' They all agreed.

'I have a rough fix on our position and find we are within the port limits of a place called Parapato,' said Mr Davies. 'It's a small Portuguese port and the mouth of the river is just opposite the opening in the reef we came through, that was the way in.'

'You would come up with something like that,' I told him. 'In any case we will be out of here come daylight.' I suppose I must have fallen asleep on the chartroom settee as I remember nothing until Mr Davies called me at sunrise.

Next day we resumed our passage. I half expected to see the Greek ship's lifeboats but they were not to be seen anywhere. We assumed they had made for the small port during the night. I hoped they survived.

There was nothing in sight all day and by sunset we were off Mozambique. When it was fully dark I altered course at right angles to the eastward and held on that till daylight next morning, then made a course to pass south of the Comorin Islands. From there I made my own course to Bombay. The incident proved that my theory of keeping close in to land was a sound one. I considered the raider would know our secret routes so the thing was to do the unexpected. As Captain Hunter of the *Gryfevale* used to say, 'Do everything wrong, that is the safest way'. When I reported to the naval control in Bombay I handed them a report on what had happened. This was returned to me with the remark 'we are not interested it's not our area.'

I also visited the Sea Transport to enquire when we would berth. 'Do you know Captain, there are over 200 ships here in Bombay, when you will berth we simply do not know.'

'In that case I will require fresh water.'

'Yes, you and 150 others, we only have one water boat.'

In these circumstances I had to put the crew on water rations. I also decided to adopt an old practice of mine – visit the Sea Transport office so often that they would get sick of the sight of me and be driven to do something, anything, to get rid of me. We had no water sail in this ship but we could improvise. It began to rain, continued for 48 hours and then eased off. Fresh water was no longer a problem.

In due course I was sent for by the Sea Transport, I was not the only one putting on pressure. The battalion whose transport I had on board were screaming for it. There was no hope of getting alongside here but Madras was empty and the ship could discharge there if I agreed. I could not be ordered to as the Bay of Bengal was an unsafe area with no sea or air cover. The battalion said they were willing to send a company to Madras to take possession of the vehicles, so it was up to me. Would I volunteer? I would and I did.

'What,' I asked, 'is causing the congestion?'

'An army contract with the Indian State Railways. They carry all vehicles across India,' said an officer, 'but they don't have the rolling stock to cope with this lot.'

'All my vehicles have wheels, they could go by themselves.' The officer merely shrugged.

We arrived off Colombo just after sunset one evening. There was too much risk in going close up as a Japanese submarine would very likely lie in wait and, if the searchlights picked us up, we could be fired on. I kept about 10 miles off and moved round slowly in large circles to baffle any lurking submarine. The searchlights were continually quartering the sky over Colombo which gave the impression that an air raid was expected. We were there two days. My further instructions were to keep close to land round the Ceylon coast then, at my own discretion, to Madras. This we did and when across the entrance to the Palk Strait we hugged the Indian coast in depths which allowed only a few feet of water under the bottom. I had two reasons for doing this. First, to be in water so shallow that a submarine would have to come within torpedo range on the surface, in which case it would be who hit who first. I could take more punishment than a submarine. Secondly, if torpedoed or holed by shellfire the ship could only sink a few feet, which would give the crew a chance to get away and the cargo could be salvaged. Also a ship close in under the land could not easily be picked up by a vessel any distance out to seaward.

Arriving off Madras we located the swept channel and went up to the breakwater. The pilot who came out was drunk and I refused to let him handle the ship. He merely pointed out our berth and I did the rest. A number of soldiers were waiting on the quayside and as soon as we moored up the major in command came aboard.

'I am pleased to see you in berth at last and able to deliver our vehicles, we have been waiting long enough. Now we will be vehicle borne troops instead of muscle borne.'

'Have you brought enough men to drive them away, we have about 600 of all sizes.'

'I have a full company and a copy of the invoices and know how many vehicles you have.' They could not have been stationed too far away as 200 men proved sufficient to take away 600 vehicles, so they must have delivered and returned several times.

I had been wondering what we would be given to do when this cargo was out. Empty tonnage was scarce on this side of India so I was not surprised when Sea Transport told me I had been handed over to the Ministry of Transport, who in turn had chartered me to Andrew Weir & Co., to load in Calcutta and Colombo a general cargo for Durban.

At sea, in wartime, I always kept the third mate's watch with him. Somewhere off Coconada about 9.30 p.m we saw a light some distance away, and seemingly near the surface of the water. It called up with a series of dots, the peacetime merchant ship call sign. Then it spelled out slowly 'what ship.' We both read it. If this was a British or Allied vessel the coded challenge should have been given. I did not like the look of this at all. The weather at the time was broken cloud with glimpses of a half moon, southerly wind and rising sea. At this time we were steering a straight course so I put the helm hard a starboard to bring the position of the light astern, then called the engine-room for all the speed they could give and alerted the gun deck. As I steadied up, from astern came a gun flash and a shell whistled well past us. The moon was then hidden by cloud. I instructed the leading seaman not to fire back as whoever it was had lost us in the darkness. Now that we were

166

stern on I was not going to give my position away by a gun flash. Another shell went wide. I commenced zigzagging. By now all hands were standing by and the machine guns were manned. The next flash and shell came from wide on the port quarter and the last from astern. Four shots in all. Nothing more happened. The wireless officer came up to the bridge and handed me a signal – RRR (raider), the name of the ship and gave a position. I asked Mr Davies to give me our position as I was going to put out an SSS submarine alarm. To my astonishment the position was the same as the one on the RRR signal. After an hour I resumed course and normal speed and ordered the crew to 'stand down.' Had the ship who sent the raider message fired the shots under the impression we were a raider? But that did not explain the call up and signal by lamp. I was convinced the call up came from a submarine. The Naval Control officer in Vizagaptam wanted to know what had happened. The ship that had sent out the RRR signal was, he said, an American ship bound south from Calcutta. We must have passed while I was being fired at, but I was still puzzled. A report from the leading gunner as to the calibre of shells fired at us could confirm they came from a submarine. The American had a 4-inch gun but, like me, he didn't open fire. The mystery remained.

In Calcutta I received a request to attend at the Naval Control and bring my leading seaman gunner with me. When I arrived I was informed the admiral wished to see me. I had been expecting something like this and had made out a report.

'Are you sure, captain, it was a submarine that fired at you?'

'No sir, I do not know what it was as we only saw the light that signalled and afterward the gun flashes. If it had been a raider we would have been able to locate him when the moon came out. There was only one gun firing and by the sound of the shells I judged it to be a 12-pounder.' The leading seaman gunner had been through the hoop as well, but stuck to his belief that it was a submarine. So that was that. The other ship's version would not be known till she arrived in port.

Our next cargo was mixed but very valuable. So much so that Andrew Weir had detectives working in the holds as cargo wallahs. It came to light later the gang were also watching where various things were stowed and started pilfering again. Andrew Weir informed me cargo was being broached and missing but nothing was being taken ashore. Now I knew the crew were at it again. I realised by this time Mr Davies was not greatly concerned whether cargo was pilfered or not. Who could I trust in this ship? The engineers could be ruled out, also the wireless officers. Mr Newton, the second, I could trust but who else. All the sailors and firemen lived in the poop so everyone aft was in the swim, and the apprentices and catering staff could be as well. Where was the stuff being hidden? I would sit studying the ship's plan but could not see any place that had not already been examined. But I did not know then about the wooden flooring in the DEMS* quarters. When that accommodation was fitted up the bare steel deck had been covered with a wooden

* DEMS – Defensively Equipped Merchant Ships. Ratigs were supplied to man the guns.

floor. This, I got to hear long afterwards, had been raised. The original four-inch beams had been raised on blocks by another 12 inches, thus giving considerable stowage. I heard about this we were on our way to the USA. When I went to look, the blocks had been taken out and it was just the normal height.

When we were ready to leave there were no firemen, donkeymen or sailors on board. I contacted the police and asked them to round up my crew as the ship was about to leave. Nothing happened until 6 p.m. I was sitting in my room writing when a lieutenant of the military police came in. He looked exhausted.

'I have your crew in a troop carrier on the quay, they refuse to come on board and want to resume fighting my men.'

'How,' I asked, did the military police come to be mixed up in this affair?'

'The civil police could not handle that crowd, they were in a brothel and refused to come out, so the police asked us to take over. Your men had drunk just enough to make them fighting mad. It took 18 of my men to hold them down. I am afraid you will need a doctor.' I informed them if they were not on board in five minutes I would ask the lieutenant to order his men to knock them all out and carry them on board. That quietened things down. They were all battered about and hardly recognisable. I signed a receipt for them.

The river pilot came on board about 8 p.m. and we went out against the last of the flood. Even with the full ebb behind her we were only making eight knots, so we had to anchor in the river for the night, and the pilot set up his bed in the dayroom. The fan was full on and, as I passed round the camp bed to reach my bedroom, I caught the full blast. When I reached the bedroom I was shivering with cold. I remember dropping on to the bed just as I was. When I woke it seemed about sunset and I could feel the ship lifting and rolling. I got up feeling as light as a feather and saw we were at sea. I went up on to the bridge and had to climb the ladder on hands and knees. When I got there Mr Davies was looking like a walking corpse.

'Just as well you have come up,' he said, 'I can't last out much longer.'

'What has happened and why was I not called when we left the anchorage?'

'That was yesterday morning. No one could wake you. I have been on the bridge since four this morning.'

'Where are the second and third mates?'

'Both unconscious. Everyone is sick and I don't know what has happened. There are no watches on deck or below, the men are just coming out when they are able. The ship is barely crawling along at three or four knots.' We managed to get the third mate up on to the bridge.

My left arm felt heavy and I was not able to lift it. We had all had inoculations in Calcutta and the area on my upper arm had swollen up like a boil and burst, so the vaccine must have been at fault. The bursting of the boil must have let the poison out and that was when I came to.

The next morning Mr Davies and I ran a first aid post cleaning up and dressing the arms of all the crew. No one was capable of any sustained work for several days, only watchkeeping. As well as the faulty vaccine we now had a rash of ringworm. This was confined to the junior mates, engineers and apprentices, and was considered to have been connected with the open air swimming pool at the Merchant Navy Club.

The night before we arrived in Colombo we passed a tanker bound on the opposite course. A couple of hours later the wireless room intercepted a radio message that a Dutch tanker had beaten off an attack by a raider, and miraculously had received no damage; it must have been the one we passed. 'The *Blackheath's* luck still holds,' I remarked to Mr Davies.

My cousin Alex Stewart had been on the staff of *The Times* of Ceylon for a number of years and was now the editor and practically the owner of the newspaper. Having a day or two in hand I decided to go and see him. I rang the office and asked if a Mr Stewart was still there. A voice answered. 'Hullo Willy, I was expecting a call from you, come right over.' It was then about4 p.m.. When I arrived I was shown into the editor's office.

'How,' I asked, 'did you know I was here?'

'An editor of a daily paper knows everything that goes on, that's his job, he also knows everybody. The harbour office gave me the name of the ship and told me a Captain Donald was in command.'

'You are not supposed to get that kind of information in wartime.'

'We don't print that kind of information. When I looked up in Lloyd's register and found she was owned by Watts Watts of London, I knew it was you.'

I stayed the week-end with the Stewarts and spent most of my evenings there while we were in Colombo. On my next visit to Colombo, some six years later, Alex had retired and gone back home to Scotland.

We were ready to leave, if the crew could be found. By the following morning they had all returned with the exception of four firemen. These I learned were in jail on manslaughter charges. They had beaten up a rickshaw coolie and he had died from his injuries.

'I cannot go to sea four firemen short,' I told the Naval Control, 'What can you do?' The naval officer had a conference with the magistrate and the trial was suspended indefinitely. In times of war the death of a coolie was of no importance where the sailing of a ship was concerned.

While we were in Durban the notion that the ship was to proceed back to the UK in ballast got around. This suited me as now I had no difficulty in getting good replacements for the men who had deserted. With the cargo finally out we were to leave for Trinidad to join a convoy for the USA.

For some time I had been pestering the Sea Transport to allow us time for boiler repairs, but they refused.

'It was quite possible,' I said, 'that the boilers will give out when we get to sea.'

To that they replied, 'if that happens the ship could drift down with the Agulhas current to Cape Town.' Since Calcutta, the buck was being passed from port to port and no one was going to be responsible for delaying the ship.

The following morning our two cooks were missing with all their gear. It was too late to do anything about it, we had to go. How were we going to manage now? The steward knew nothing about cooking, but as always when a crisis blows up, someone emerges. The second steward offered to take over. He had once been a galley boy and assistant cook before changing over to stewarding. I had no choice. All I can say is we did manage to eat the food that was served up.

I made another attempt to get boiler repairs done in Cape Town. I even asked the Ministry for permission to call in a Lloyd's surveyor, but it was useless. Now, to add to everything else, we were having condenser trouble. As nothing would be done I insisted on filling both peaks and a ballast tank with fresh water. I informed the Ministry that we had so many leaks in the boiler tubes that the condenser could not cope with the heavy loss of water in the boilers and, as no repairs were allowed, we must have the water. We were independently routed to Trinidad where we would pick up the convoy. It was a long way to go and, at the speed we were reduced to, it would be a long passage. The speed was now down to eight knots as the chief dared not carry a full head of steam owing to the condition of the boilers. Nine days out of Cape Town we had to shut down the boilers.

'What is the matter now, chief?'

'Come down into the stokehold and see.' Water was pouring out of the three furnaces of the starboard boiler.

'I have been warning of this for months,' said the chief. 'I have filled the auxiliary boiler and am setting the fires away.' By the time 100 pounds of steam showed on the gauge, seven tubes had gone, so that boiler had to be shut down. That left only the port boiler, and the tubes in that were not good either.

Vessels were being sunk all round us. I plotted the positions on the chart as they came in and wondered when our turn would come. Now I didn't turn in at night as I was convinced we could not get away with it, crawling along at five knots we were a sitting target. I dozed in my armchair in the sitting room with my life-waistcoat on complete with light, flask in pocket and watertight bag with my personal papers strapped to my forearm, and the ship's papers in a bag by my side. I was now sick to death of this ship and the struggle to keep her going.

Then the dynamo packed up. Since arriving in the tropics it had been run continuously to keep the temperature down in the domestic refrigerated spaces, which were situated on the weather deck, but it was just too much. The temperature on deck was now in the upper 80s. In a day or two the chief managed to get it going, after a fashion. But in the meantime, as we had over 2000 pounds weight of fresh meat, something had to be done. Awnings were rigged over the area and the deck hose was kept continually spraying. Despite everything we did the temperature in the meat room could not be brought down below 45°Fahrenheit.

I had a conference with the chief and suggested we put into Pernambuco (Recife) for boiler and dynamo repairs. It was a port of distress and should be able to handle all we require. We managed to contact the signal station and informed them we had only one functioning boiler and were unable to proceed until repairs had been effected. After we had moored, Watts' agent in this port, who was also Lloyd's agent, came on board with an engineer from the repair ship attached to the coaling plant. The result of the inspection showed we were fortunate to get here, we could not have gone much further.

Inevitably, all the meat had gone bad and none could be obtained here, the US navy had commandeered the lot. I made application to them for some but they would not part with any. As a result, my main occupation every morning was going round all the shops I could find buying tins of meat to make up for what we had lost. Other stores were running out and could not be obtained in any quantity here. Always the same story, the US Navy had taken everything. I eventually received some food but only enough to last until we reached New York.

When the starboard boiler tubes were tightened up and stood the test, the port boiler had to be done, and the auxiliary. By the time they were tested the starboard boiler went wrong again and so it went on. The surveyor said the boilers would have to be retubed before long. However, the dynamo came back rebuilt.

The next morning we left in a convoy of around 30 ships, across the Caribbean and up to the American Naval Base at Guantanamo, where more ships joined, together with escorts for the USA.

The *Blackheath* was doing very well and had gradually been promoted to the position of column leader, but I had forgotten the rule of *three of a kind*. The boilers had shut down, the dynamo had broken down – that was two – there had to be a third. Sure enough, just north of the latitude of the Bahamas the fan engine failed, the eccentric strap had broken. As this ship depended on forced draught to maintain a full head of steam this meant speed would drop until the fan engine was running again. I passed a shaded lamp signal to my next abeam for the commodore, eased out between the columns and let the convoy move ahead. I now had to open my envelope marked C, that contained route instructions for vessels that dropped out of convoy. We now had to zigzag all the way. This meant our 10 days of stores were inadequate, but as I had cautioned the steward to keep the crew on the Board of Trade allowance I did not worry. Our luck held and we came to an anchor in Staten Island Roads on Christmas Eve 1942.

It was then that the steward informed me there was no food left; the men had kicked up such a fuss he had given them the usual quantities. Tomorrow was Christmas Day. All we had left were lifeboat stores, tinned milk, meat and biscuits. By the time we cleared immigration and received pratique (our health certificate) it was too late to get in touch with the shipchandler. The customs officer lent me $20 which he said should be enough for the crew to get a meal at a drugstore. That was one of the kindest things I have ever seen done, he was a true Samaritan. I had a few dollars of my own and was able to issue everyone with $1.50, officers and crew alike. We, the chief and I, were invited home by the customs officer and gladly accepted. It was one of the most enjoyable evenings I have ever spent.

We had arrived in New York on 24th December, but it was to be the middle of February before we left with a general cargo bound for Cardif. The passage of the convoy down the harbour and out to the Ambrose Lightvessel was orderly enough, but slow, and by the time it was formed up it was dark.

'I don't like the look of the weather Mr Davies, it's too quiet for February. We are going to have plenty of fog.' Then the wind died away and in came the fog that lasted for days. To cut down noise, only column leaders were to blow the column number and, when altering course, only the turning blasts were to be given by each ship. When the fog eventually cleared, our column was intact but no other ships were in sight. Then a corvette appeared escorting several ships and the convoy appeared some miles to the north of us and we formed up again. It was now March 1943; we had left Liverpool in April 1942. In response to my letter asking for leave, London informed me that I was to be put on as relieving master and my first job was to stand by this ship, then I would be able to have a month's leave. As May had come to see me, bringing Mary with her, I didn't mind.

Chapter 21

Time on my hands

*I*n May the previous year, 1942, May, Mary and my mother-in-law had spent a holiday on a Dartmoor farm two miles from Postbridge. Now May had arranged to spend three weeks up there, and this time I was to go. We went by train from Newton Abbot to Moretonhampstead and then by taxi to the farm.

The farm comprised about 90 acres, half planted to crops and the rest grazing. In addition to the usual farm animals, they also boarded horses and Mary learned to ride during her two visits. The farm house was a modern building, but the farm buildings were very old, as was the original farmhouse. Mr Hooper said the farm buildings dated from the 12 th century and he showed me a parchment that described the place as a fortified manor house. It was quiet and peaceful which was what I needed – nothing to think about and long walks over the moor. One day May and I walked to Widecombe and back, the longest walk I have ever made. But all good things come to an end and when the three weeks were up we arrived home to find a letter on the hall floor. Fortunately it had only come the day before. It contained instructions for me to go to Sunderland, via London, to take delivery of the *Chiswick* from the builders, Messrs Pickersgill & Sons. It was the end of June and I would go up there alone. When things were sorted out I would send for May and Mary.

While in London Mr Watts stressed the fact that the *Chiswick* was a standard model and he had had to take her as she was, he couldn't alter anything. 'She is not,' he repeated, 'a ship of my design so don't send in any complaints to this office.' When I took her over I found the accommodation was very good. One afternoon we had a front seat view of the launching of another Watts ship the *Greenwich*. She was in the berth opposite us. Princess Mary, the Princess Royal, performed the naming ceremony. As it turned out I was to be nearly four years in command of that vessel.

For some reason, mishaps always happened to ships I was on when going into the dock at Sunderland. Damage in the *Maidenhead*, sinking of a tug in the *Dartford*, so I wondered what would happen this time. I soon found out. The tugs let the stern drop in at too great an angle when the engines were going ahead. As the stern overhung the quay, one of the propeller blades came into contact with the quay wall and the upper part of the blade snapped off.

We went out for trials, and got out of the dock without further mishap. We were run over the measured mile but that could not give a true indication of speed with a damaged propeller. The compasses had to be adjusted and then we proceeded on our course to West Hartlepool. Then the armament testing started. We were at breakfast while this was going on. The guns fired a couple of rounds and the machine guns rattled, then suddenly there came a tremendous jar, the whole ship shook like a leaf. Mr James, the mate, dashed out to find what had happened. There had been a misunderstanding about testing the rocket launching stands. When we left the dock the stands had been loaded with a full complement of six rockets each. Instead of one from each stand, as was intended, they had fired the lot. Besides losing 12 live rockets the force of the blast nearly tore the stands off the deck. The propeller, the rocket stands, what on earth was going to happen next?

I received orders for New York and learned we were under the Ministry of Transport now. We joined the coastal convoy for the run up to Methil and I was asked the usual question. 'What accommodation do you have suitable for a commodore?' I replied that the master's sea room on the bridge was available, but had no accommodation for staff. The commodore for Loch Ewe chose the *Chiswick* as his ship and was very satisfied with the sea room as it allowed him to be available at once. We were just passing the Pentland Skerries in the approaches to the Pentland Firth when a violent thunderstorm broke, followed by torrential rain. The ships were flying their balloons at the time. Usually the balloon wire was attached to the main mast, but in this ship it was attached to the top of a derrick post amidships. That was the cause of the trouble. A violent flash of lightning struck and burnt out our balloon, and then came down the wire. Immediately there was a shout from the helmsman.

'Compass spinning round sir.' I sent the second mate to look at the standard compass – that was the same. Both the commodore and I assumed the compasses would gradually settle down again, and they did, but not on the previous heading. Now we didn't know what had happened to the deviations. The commodore signalled one of the armed trawlers escorting us to take station ahead and steer the convoy course. Three other ships had the same trouble. I realised later that the ship had not shed her induced magnetism after building, nor had she acquired her permanent magnetism. The other ships settled down again, but the *Chiswick* never did, and compasses became a permanent headache. That was the third accident. My second new ship and now this.

The stay in Loch Ewe was only a few days then we set off on the Atlantic crossing. That passage was a nightmare, as fog engulfed us for almost the whole journey. We were the third ship in one of the inside columns and because of our compass condition had to hang on to our next ahead's fog buoy by day and night. Chasing a fog buoy towed by the ship ahead, which was subject to the erratic steering of our next ahead's helmsman, and our own, was enough to drive anyone round the bend, especially when making course alterations.

Then we had another problem. The soundings in the forward holds began to show water in the bilges. The rain, it appeared, was coming through some of the deck rivets and plate edges in the shelter decks. I reported to the Ministry of Transport that we would require rivets and plate edges caulked before loading. The surveyor who came onboard was the same one who put the *Blackheath* through survey.

'So you have a new ship now and are still in trouble,' was his greeting.

'Trouble,' I replied, 'is my middle name.'

'Wartime workmanship,' was his only comment.

We laid at anchor for several days with repair gangs on board before the Lloyd's surveyor was satisfied and gave me a certificate.

The loading was fast; wheat and flour in the lower holds, vehicles in the shelter decks, and our port of discharge was to be Alexandria. The only problem was that the wheat was not consigned to anyone and this caused problems.

On our way into the harbour in Alexandria we passed the surrendered Italian battleships anchored at Mex just outside the harbour. There were many naval craft including the battleship *Howe*. The question now was what to do with the wheat and flour. It seemed the bagged cargo had just been put in to fill up the ship. Then one day I was called in to a convoy conference at Ras-El-Tin. The convoy was going to Bari on the east coast of Italy, and it had been decided to feed the starving Italians with the wheat and flour. So off we went but some days later I received a signal from the commodore requesting us to detach and head for Malta. We were one of a number of ships anchored there.

Our discharge was fast as the Maltese were in desperate need of food. The harbour was full of wrecks of all kinds. Not far from us was a sunken floating dock and just inside the breakwater the American tanker *Ohio* was lying with decks awash. We went outside to anchor and await the convoy from Alexandria. Passing Europa Point we received a signal to detach from the convoy and anchor in Gibraltar Bay. We were now bound for Sierra Leone, then Lagos and Port Harcourt.

The heat in Port Harcourt was sickening. I started issuing malaria tablets as soon as we left Sierra Leone and were fortunate to have no cases while we were on the coast. We loaded palm kernels and ground nuts topped up with bags of cocoa beans on the return to Lagos.

For the convoy back to Sierre Leone I was requested to take over as commodore, but had to refuse as the compasses were not reliable. When I came to heave up, the ship was lying with her stern to the boom entrance. This would have been a simple manoeuvre with any ordinary ship, but not with the *Chiswick*. I thought I would never get her round, but eventually did. She was what seamen call a hard mouthed bitch.

It was January and the worst passage home I made during the war, decks awash most of the time. The nights were the worst, pitch black with only the wake of the next ahead showing faintly as her stern rose on the cresting seas. How the ships kept station was a mystery, I suppose now we were all getting expert at the game. I was sick, tired and fed up, there seemed no end to this war, and it was now over four years since it had started.

When we docked in Liverpool I was told to go on leave, but call in at the London office first.

'We are bringing you ashore,' I was told, 'to stand by to bring back a Liberty type ship from the USA, one has been allocated to us for management. You are the best man for the job. You will have to remain ashore till the end of April before the ship will be ready and a passage arranged.'

'Will the pool allow me to remain ashore that long?'

'Get a sickness certificate.'

'But I'm not sick sir.'

'Then see a nerve specialist and arrange a certificate somehow.' I contacted our doctor who arranged an appointment.

'I want,' I said, 'a certificate to stay ashore for three months as my firm requires me to go to the USA to take delivery of an American ship. I am only allowed one day's leave for every week of my last voyage and, if not re-employed by then, I would be taken into the shipping pool and sent away on any ship available. As I am medically fit the only thing I could do was try to obtain one from you.'

'Well,' he said, 'you sound all right to me but I will put you through the routine.' He tested my reflexes and called in his partner to check as well. He then went behind my back and let off something which made a loud bang.

'There is nothing wrong with your nerves,' he said, 'I doubt if you have any at all. The war has had no effect on you, nor will have. You have a bovine constitution and the gift of not being able to think about a thing long enough to worry about it, in other words you do not have a worrying nature.' I think he had me taped alright. 'I will give you a certificate saying that, owing to strain and exhaustion, you require three months complete rest, that should do it. I will forward the certificate to your doctor.' We shook hands and that was that.

Torquay is not a deep water harbour, only suitable for yachts. The inner basin dries out completely and the outer has only a few feet of water at low tide. Only very small vessels could lay on the inner side of the outer breakwater, and even they were on the bottom at low water. During this period small steamers were coming into the harbour during the day to load, as part of the D-Day build up. In a small harbour like Torquay the customs officer also had to act as the shipping master when necessary. The customs officer, at that time, was a friend of mine and had no experience in shipping office work. With these small ships wanting to sign men on

176

S.S. Chiswick waiting for high water at Lagos Bar.

and off, and with overtime arguments, he was unable to cope. One day he rang me up and asked if I would come down and help him out. As I had nothing else to do I agreed and for several weeks became the unofficial and unpaid shipping master at Torquay. All the customs officer had to do was sign his name.

Chapter 22

Mediterranean miscellany

I went up to London by the night train. In the office I was told I was now in the hands of the Ministry of Transport and all they knew was that I would leave from the Clyde. They understood I had to take possession of the ship and bring her back to the UK, it should only take a few weeks. I was to contact their agents in Glasgow for further instructions. In Glasgow I found I had three days to wait around so I went out to my mother's place in Burnside and stayed there over the weekend.

Before going down to Greenock I was introduced to Mr Brown, the chief engineer, who was going with me. We were part of a group of 12, six masters and six chief engineers, who were going to take over Liberty ships. We had been told we were in the first class category, and couldn't believe it when we discovered that all 12 of us had to share one room! Eventually we reached what would have been a stateroom when the vessel was originally fitted out. By now, of course, we realised we were on the *Queen Elizabeth*. The room was just four bare walls with a wooden floor. There were four rows of three bunks, upper, middle and lower, each with a straw mattress and two straw filled pillows. On the inboard side were wash-hand basins and toilets. There were showers but no baths. Alas, no water could be had from the taps and the toilets would not flush. The lounge was empty and what would be the main dining room was now filled with trestle tables and benches. The canteen was closed. The ship was dead. There must have been a maintenance staff on board but we saw no one. We could see now we were not going to get anything to eat, and a more lonely, hungry, miserable crowd of men it would be hard to find anywhere. A printed notice tacked up on a bulkhead in the room proclaimed:

Fresh water will be turned on between 7a.m. and 8 a.m. each morning and for one hour in the evening.

Two meals per day, breakfast and dinner.

Breakfast 8 a.m. to 9 a.m.

Dinner 5 p.m. to 6 p.m. in two sittings.

No coffee or afternoon tea.

No smoking allowed below decks.

I heard later that the *Queen Elizabeth* was known to service people as Uflag L.23, and that was an accurate description – it was like a prison camp. The room was chilly and the two thin blankets did not give much warmth.

We must have slipped away sometime during the night as when we woke up we were at sea. I didn't get much sleep. The air conditioning blower on the bulkhead only gave out cold air and, as it swept from side to side, the cold blast passed over my face. Finally, by keeping the blanket over my head, I managed to get to sleep. For a very large vessel with mighty engine power and four propellers, there was very little vibration, even over 30 knots.

Our day commenced with the order to rise and dress blaring through the loudspeakers. The water was on but there were only two basins. Six to a basin in one hour meant each man had ten minutes to wash and shave. Then a steward came in and gave us each a small card, to be shown at the dining room door. Blaring through the loudspeakers came *This is the first call, take your places in line and proceed to the mess hall.* I got the first sitting and Mr Brown got the second. There were two courses, porridge or cereal, then kippers or powdered scrambled eggs on toast. Sometimes it was hash or fish, then tea or coffee, both weak, and not much of anything. I never left that saloon feeling really satisfied. At 8.30 the loudspeakers told us to leave the mess hall. Dinner was much the same, vegetable soup followed by meat or fish and a milk pudding of some kind. Coming to the table not having eaten for eight and a half hours and then not having sufficient, was not enough to satisfy one who had to wait another 14 hours for the next meal. As one of the captains remarked, 'This ship has got the hardest case of Cardiff tramp licked on victualling.'

After breakfast there was nothing to do except walk up and down the promenade deck, and that was quite a distance. When you tired of one side you could cross over and walk on the other. There were no seats, all you could do was sit on your lifebelt. We could also walk right along to the after end and lean on the rail to watch the four wakes. As the ship was continually zigzagging it was interesting to watch. We were not allowed to go anywhere else on deck. Down below was a rabbit warren and I never returned to the berth by the same route twice.

The lounge was a very large place with small tables round the sides. If you were early enough a table and chairs could be occupied but if a chair became vacant someone else would get it and that was that. The lounge tables seated four and we formed a group, a Captain McPherson and his chief and myself and Mr Brown and except for meals we were always together. To keep a table and chairs we often played bridge from after boat drill until dinnertime.

The six masters were invited into the officers' smoke-room for morning coffee by the staff captain, but this was not a social visit. It was a rule, when groups of masters were carried, that each had to take over as captain of the day, and from the crews was selected bosun of the day. During this time the captain was responsible for the crews and, with his bosun had to inspect all crews' accommodation and settle all complaints and arguments – in fact, carry on as if the crews were his own. To distinguish him he was given a large round metal badge with 'Captain of the Day' printed round the edge. When my day came round I found the metal badge allowed me to go anywhere I wished. It was during this time I found the galley, a wonderful sight with rows of cooks standing over stoves and working tables. I also had a look at the hospital and the engine-room; I really enjoyed that day.

I believe several notable and famous persons were a among the passengers. One day, in the lounge, somebody said. 'Do you see that chap over there, that's James Cagney, the film actor.' I had thought the face was familiar. Another time a small slim blonde woman was pointed out.

'Do you know who that is?'

'No,' I said, 'I do not.'

'That is Unity Mitford.'

'Who's she?'

'She is said to have been a friend of Hitler before the war.' She kept herself apart with only an older woman companion. I never saw her smile.

We knew the passage was coming to an end when we were lined up and had to file past the sick bay for injections. I think we had two, or maybe three, and my arm was numb for a long time. The evening before arrival a concert was given by the captain, and it was held in the lounge. James Cagney acted as master of ceremonies and very good he was too. Next morning we berthed in New York.

The 12 of us were sorted out by one of the officials, put into taxis with our luggage, and taken to the Prince George Hotel. We didn't expect to be put into a hotel like this, it was the kind of place where film stars would stay. We were given $5 25c each for a week's tipping, it worked out at 75c per day. Any cash required for personal use would have to be drawn from our firms' agents. That evening we all had dinner in the dining room, the waiter was in full evening dress. When dinner was finished we had a conference as to how much we should give the waiter as a tip. As we only had 75c per day, it was decided to give him one dollar. I placed the dollar on the table for him as he was clearing away.

'What's this for?' he enquired.

'That's your tip,' I said.

He smiled and handed the dollar back to me. 'Buy something for the children,' he replied. I got annoyed.

'What,' I enquired, 'is the usual tip in this hotel?'

'For dinner a five spot, $5.' I picked up the note and put it in my pocket. We decided we would not have any more meals there. The lounge bar served snacks which were, in fact, full meals. As we had to fetch and serve them ourselves the business of tipping business was unnecessary.

The next morning I took Mr Brown downtown to the agents, Funch, Edye and Co. I was well known there and had no difficulty in drawing cash for the chief and myself. As the Ministry of Transport was in the same building I went to see them as well.

'Your ship,' I was told, 'is the *Samoland.*' This was the first time I had heard her name. She will be built in Brunswick, Georgia. As soon as accommodation can be arranged we will send you and your chief down there. A week later we heard that a start had been made in putting our ship together and accommodation had been obtained for us in Brunswick. Sleeping accommodation had been reserved on the afternoon train from Pennsylvania Station leaving at 3 p.m. We would have to change trains at Nahunta Junction.

Penn station was a very large place on two levels and we had some difficulty in finding our train, but eventually did so. The sleeping car had an aisle down the middle, I was on one side of the aisle and the chief on the other. The train slid away without noise or fuss and before we realised it we were on our way. We found the wash rooms and toilets and then the buffet car where there was a sign on the counter, mounted on a revolving base. On one side it said *'Dry State'* and on the other *'Wet State.'* If the sign was on Dry, all we could get was soft drinks, when it was turned to Wet we could get beer but no spirits. Prohibition was still in force.

The train was crowded. The sleeping car attendant asked if we wished dinner served in our berth as the dining car was full up. This was served on a drop table between the two seats. After dinner we returned to the buffet car while our bunks were made up. The attendant said we would stop at Nahunta Junction at 5 a.m., he would call us at 4 a.m. with coffee and toast.

At 5 a.m. the train just stopped. There was no platform, no buildings, nothing to indicate this was a station. It was full daylight and no one was around. We stepped down to the ground beside the tracks with our luggage round us and the train moved on. In the distance we could see what appeared to be a town of some sort. Some way toward the town was a drugstore and book stall, it was open and yesterday's newspaper could be obtained. It was now Sunday. We sat on a seat under a tree and waited. Sometime later a porter shuffled along. We learned that the Brunswick train would come along sometime. Sure enough, two hours later, along came a diesel train consisting of two carriages. We were the only passengers so we sat up front with the driver. When we arrived in Brunswick he got out of the carriage and disappeared, so we had to drag our luggage on to the platform. Once again there was nobody about, but then I heard a snore and discovered a porter fast asleep on a pile of crates. I woke him and ask how we were to get to the hotel. He pointed to a wooden gate in a fence at the back of the platform. 'There is the hotel garden.'

Reception was expecting us and we were shown to our room and, as in New

York, we had to share. It was a huge place with fans in the ceiling. There was a shower room and toilet. The luggage cupboard was a fair sized room itself. It was the most spacious accommodation I had ever seen.

On the ground floor a large hall extended from front to back with verandas covered with mosquito netting. The dining room was on one side, and opposite, the bar. When we went for breakfast the waiter pointed to a notice on the wall which said *the wearing of jackets in the dining room is not allowed.*

'No one,' said the waiter, 'wears a jacket in summer and anyone doing so would look out of place.'

Later I found the agent for the British Ministry of Transport waiting for us in the hall.

'The people here do not seem over friendly,' I remarked, 'it would appear we are not welcome.'

'They don't like to see foreigners taking away the ships they have built,' said the agent. 'Britishers have been too free with their opinions and criticism. These people here do not understand ships and shipping matters, they are trained to do only one job, it's like an assembly line. I will take you down to the yard tomorrow, but be careful, they are very touchy. Don't talk about your ship, she is only being lent to the Ministry, and don't ask questions.'

The yard was only a short distance from the hotel and at the gate we were checked by security guards. It was the most unusual shipyard I had ever seen. All the buildings were of wood and situated on platforms in a long row, and all of them were on wheels. We were introduced to the manager.

'So,' he said, 'you're for the lease lend ship. She has been launched and is at the completion wharf but you can't go on board until the ship's completed. Anyway she is the same as all the others. At present she is only a number, the name has not yet been hung, but it will be *Oland*, one of the river class of names. Don't ask me where the river is because I don't know or care, its just a name to me.'

'I was told her name would be *Samoland*.'

'The SAM stands for Standard American Marine. You are free to wander in the yard but don't ask questions.'

Just inside the entrance of the shipyard was a large hoarding with all the required information. Each trade had its own colour hat that was compulsory wear in the yard when working. A light green hat denoted an electrician, a black one a general labourer, red for an engineer and blue for a welder and so on. On the front of the hat was its owner's name.

The ships were in four sections. The stern section, complete with rudder and propeller, was landed on the ways and pushed down into place. The other three followed, then they were welded together. After launching the hull was moved to the outer end of the fitting out wharf to receive engines and boilers. Then followed the superstructure. Each deck of the midship house was lifted on board complete, even to the cabin furniture. Then she moved to the end of the wharf gathering en route the funnels, masts and derricks. She was then ready for trials after which she berthed on the other side of the dock for stores and furnishings. When that was completed she was ready to go and fuel and fresh water was taken aboard. I watched the forward section of a ship going along slung between two 150 ton cranes. The windlass was on and the anchors in the hawse pipes.

My crew arrived in the first week in June and the sea trials were to be held the next day, and would go on until late afternoon. I went to the yard manager and said I would like to go out on the run with my officers.

'Remember captain,' he said, 'until the ship is handed over she is not yours. You can go with your officers as one of the trippers, but it will cost you a dollar each, you go on board the same as everyone else.'

Everyone was onboard by 9.30 a.m. It was a very hot day and the ship was packed; everyone was in a holiday mood. The testing of the guns was the big attraction for the trippers. Everything went well, no failures of any kind. The next morning the handing over took place. Seated on one side of the table was the yard manager, the surveyor for the Standard American Marine, and the representative of the US Government. First the manager handed over the ship's documents to the surveyor who signed a receipt for them, also accepting the vessel on behalf of the SAM. He in turn passed the documents over to the US government representative, as they were the people dealing with the Ministry of Transport as representatives of the British Government. They in turn handed the ship over to me as the representative of the operating company. I was offered a cigar from a box on the table and we all shook hands.

The crew went on board during the afternoon. No one was very enthusiastic about the ship, I wasn't either. Nobody who had been standing by would give us any information, they just walked away without so much as wishing us 'Good Luck.' We left the next afternoon, 8th June, for New York, unescorted.

We were put into a berth in the Eyrie Basin in Brooklyn to load general cargo. When I reported to the Ministry of Transport they told me we were loading army stores for discharge in Algiers. I knew then that this was going to be an extended voyage. I was advised to take 12 months' stores as nothing much could be obtained in the Mediterranean. We also fuelled to capacity. When loading stores in Brunswick the mate had received the plans of the ship and all the other data, including a book called *Liberty Ship* which proved very useful. In due course we left in a large convoy composed mostly of Liberty ships like ourselves and US Navy escorts.

After discharging in Algiers, there appeared to be uncertainty about what was to be done with the ship so we anchored out in the Bay. I was now handed over to the Sea Transport and fitted out to carry 200 troops on a shuttle service, probably between Naples and Algiers. The steward had been worried about feeding them, but he need not have been; they brought their own stores, cooking stoves and cooks.

'I do not have lifeboat and raft capacity for all these extra people,' I informed the Sea Transport.

'Do not be difficult captain,' was all the answer I got.

Next day radio orders told us to hook on to the eastbound convoy as it went past. Because of Italian minefields the convoy route was along the African coast to Cape Bon, then past Malta, round the toe of Sicily, through the Messina Straits and then up to Naples Bay. A minefield stretched across the Bay of Naples leaving only a strip around the head of the Bay some two miles wide. The only way into the anchorage were narrow swept passages through the minefield, one each north and south. There we found a great fleet of ships and it was no easy job working through that mass in search of enough space to anchor. This was when I found a Liberty ship was a joy to handle, as long as she was moving she would steer and I now knew I could do anything I wanted with this ship.

Mr Brown, my chief engineer, left me here and went home on compassionate leave. His wife had been killed in an air raid and his daughter was missing, but later found to be staying with relatives. My new chief was Mr Cook, one of the oldest chiefs in the firm and only used to sailing in coal-burning ships.

'No one told me,' he complained, 'that this was a water-tube boiler oil-fired ship with quadruple expansion engines.' Thankfully the second engineer had the necessary experience, but I could foresee difficulties.

Meeting other masters of Liberty ships I found they had insisted on taking 1500 tons of sand ballast before loading. But they had come from ports where sand was available and it had not caused any delay. My case was different. I didn't know until I had been in the port some time that I was going to the beaches. My request for solid ballast was brushed aside.

Under the US Water Transport Department we loaded stores, ammunition and vehicles for the south of France. I also received an American artillery lieutenant as Berthing Officer Troops, BOT for short . The bottom of the lower holds were stowed with 1000-pound bombs. Then small arms ammunition, hand grenades and mortar shells. We also loaded cigarettes, chewing gum and Coca Cola, everything necessary to keep an American army going. No. 4 shelter deck was fitted out to take 200 troops, the others were stowed with the vehicles. When no more could be got in they were stacked on deck. When all the cargo and vehicles were on board, squads of US soldiers began to form up on the quay. I was standing at the rail with the BOT.

'How many,' I asked the officer in charge of troop embarkation, 'are we taking on board? We are only fitted out for 200 and there are more than that down there.'

'All these,' he said, 'about 600. They have all got their lifebelts and will sleep anywhere they can spread their rolls. Others will lean against something and doze. If you are worried about feeding they have cooks and gas stoves.'

I took the BOT aside and said, 'The lower holds are stowed with bombs, grenades and shells and other temperamental things. Please impress on those in charge not to fool around with gas stoves down below.'

Just as we were unmooring another party of troops came alongside.

'Who are they?' I asked.

'They are a company of Rangers and they have to return to the beaches,' was the answer.

I didn't like the feel of the ship when she started to move but all went well until we were on the northerly leg past Corsica. The weather could not be considered bad but the ship began to lurch over, not roll, every time a larger than usual sea came along, and she lurched over at a gradually increasing angle each time. I was considering slowing down and dropping astern to enable me to bring her up to the sea till the weather eased, when she took a larger than usual lurch and went right over to an angle of about 25°, and hung there. The sound of moving objects came from all over the ship. If the vehicles on deck hadn't been lashed those on the lee side would have gone overboard. There were shouts and yells from all over the ship. I put the helm hard over to give her a helm list, then eased back as she began to come up. We were not going to stand another one like that. Just then the signal light for a four point turn to port (windward) flashed from the commodore. Evidently his ship was suffering in much the same manner and they had all got a very nasty fright. That was the fastest turn I had ever seen. Every ship hauled round at once without waiting to follow the next ahead. Conditions were now more comfortable. The wind and sea died down at sunrise to a complete calm, and the convoy resumed its course again.

I never did know how many people were on the ship, officers of all ranks from colonels downwards seemed to appear from nowhere. I found a row of colonels on stretcher beds occupying the wheelhouse. Then a major or two, some captains and lieutenants. The captains got into the gyro room and the after rooms on the crew deck. The lieutenants, being young men, had made friends with the mates and engineers and were given their settees to sleep on. The settees in the mess halls were occupied presumably with NCOs. The rank and file occupied the No.4 shelter deck and the trucks. The galley was in use for all 24 hours and it was a wonder the galley fire unit held out. It had been ashore for repairs in New York, Algiers and Naples!

During the forenoon the commodore arranged the convoy into sections for the various beaches. We drew the Gulf of St. Tropez section and were moved to the port side of the column. We arrived just after midday and found the Gulf, which was only a medium sized inlet, packed with ships. A motor launch told us to follow him and he led us right to the top of the inlet before he gave the signal to anchor. Then a fleet of troop landing craft came to ferry the troops ashore. By sunset they were all off the ship including the BOT. The discharge continued day and night.

Tank landing craft ferried the vehicles ashore and the DUKs dealt with the stores and ammunition; in all we were there for five days. One evening a tank landing craft, came alongside with ramps raised and punched a hole in the starboard side of No. 2 lower hold. Fortunately the hole was above the water line. I reported the damage. The unconcerned reply stated 'If you are sinking haul out of the assault area.'

We had completed discharge of all but the 1000-pound bombs and these had to be taken to Port-de-Bouc 20 miles to the west of Marseilles. This little harbour consisted of a basin behind breakwaters and some distance behind there was a lake. The basin was connected to the lake by a canal three miles long. Along the westward side of the canal were the wharves for deep sea ships. Before they left, the Germans had blown up the transporter used for loading bauxite, effectively blocking the canal and preventing ships from reaching the wharves which lined the bank above the transporter. They had also mined the basin and blown out one of the spans of the railway bridge, but a pontoon bridge had been laid across, just below the bridge, to keep traffic moving. There was a large airfield not far away and this was where our bombs were consigned. Two berths were available below the transporter but due to the number the ships it was a slow process.

Another part of the trouble was transportation away from the wharves. The area along the side of the canal had been strewn with land mines through which a narrow lane had been cleared and marked with white lines on each side. This necessitated single line traffic for the army trucks taking away the cargo. To get the canal cleared a floating crane was sent up from Marseilles. Its arrival was watched with extreme interest. Motor launches towed the crane and a small red-funnelled tug took over to tow it up the canal. About half way across the basin the tug struck a mine and was blown to pieces, killing all eight crew. The turbulence from the exploding mine caused the floating crane to roll violently, so much so that we all expected it to turn over. The crane lost two men. It was now floating loose in the basin, but eventually the motor launches ventured in, got hold of the crane again, and towed it out. This incident caused a sensation as it had been assumed the basin had been cleared of mines. As the mine was of the old fashioned horned type D.G. was of no use as a protection. Everyone was now in a state of panic as it was thought the mine had broken away from the minefield outside and drifted into the harbour. If that was the case there could be others – no one felt safe. The American army engineers then moved in with mobile cranes and were not long in clearing the remains of the transporter out of the canal.

Finally our turn came to go inside and discharge. When the French pilot came on board he was shaking with fear. I asked him what he was so afraid of as he had taken ships in and out since the tug was sunk.

'Yes, captain, but this ship is full of big bombs, not so the other ships. If this ship strikes a mine everyone will go.' Strangely, this had not occurred to me. 'The cargomen will not like to work in this ship,' he added darkly. Now that he mentioned it I didn't like it either. The local French labour leaned on a fence watching the unloading. It was just as well they were not handling the bombs – that was dangerous work. The American labour company was experienced in that type of cargo.

We left Port-de-Bouc about 20th September. We were to proceed to Toulon for convoy back to Naples. By the time we had discharged the pilot it was well toward noon. We had to go at reduced speed through the minefields, the stick buoys were not easy to pick up until they were close, and we only had five hours of daylight left. As I had to find the passage through the minefield off Toulon I asked the engine-room to give her all they could for the last 50 miles. We must have done 12 knots and I found the fairway buoy while we still had daylight, but by the time we got through into the bay it was pitch dark. Creeping through the mass of blacked out shapes trying to judge when there was enough space to anchor was a nerve-wracking business.

Back in Naples I found we were once again answerable to Sea Transport. I decided now was the time to put in a request for 1500 tons of sand ballast, I didn't want a repeat of what had happened on the way to St. Tropez.

When the soldiers went ashore in St. Tropez they left behind them all their unconsumed rations. The steward was told he could have them. So they were collected and put in the storeroom and amounted to quite a quantity. What we seemed unable to obtain, because of the number of ships with similar demands, were fresh vegetables, fruit, fresh eggs and meat but there was little hope of anyone obtaining them. The Italians were short of food themselves. By now everyone was sick of tinned vegetables, dried egg powder and that most repulsive item of all, tinned potatoes.

In Alexandria I got a surprise, when I discovered that we were now on an UNRA charter to Greece.

'What,' I asked, 'does that imply?'

'The Germans are pulling out of Greece so we are sending up food supplies for the starving Greeks along with other things. You will have quite a number of people going along with you as well.'

'What part of Greece?'

'We don't know yet.'

We took on our sand ballast and loaded 4000 tons of foodstuffs. The greater part was bagged flour, but we had dried egg powder, milk powder, tins of bully beef and bags of beans as well as medical supplies. Then we moved up to Mex to take vehicles in the shelter decks, for delivering the food to the villages, two ration craft on deck with more trucks and a few cars.

The personnel were interesting. A guard company of 100 soldiers, 14 military police and 40 Palestinian labourers to discharge the ship as the Greeks would be too weak from starvation to do any work. Two majors and various other officers, a paymaster captain and a lieutenant in charge of the labourers also joined us. In addition to all this there were about half a dozen UNRA officials getting a passage up to Greece. The soldiers and labourers had their own food but the officers and other officials came into the big mess-hall for their meals which our cooks had to prepare.

We went back to Augusta, in Sicily, to await another convoy. I then found our destination was to be Kalamata, in the western Peloponnese. We went first to Taranto in Italy, where we were taken ashore for a conference. From what I heard it appeared to me that we were to take over Kalamata entirely and run the place. I had been under the impression we were just going to deliver a cargo of food for the people in that part of Greece. Now I could understand what the soldiers, military police and others were for – occupation.

It appeared that there were mines in the Gulf of Kalamata and we had to keep close to the land on the eastern side and maintain a good lookout. A destroyer would escort us on the passage. When we were clear of the anchorage he led us down the swept channel on the eastern side then sent a signal. PLEASE DO THE NAVIGATION WHILE I LOOK FOR SUBMARINES. We arrived off the entrance of the gulf at 7 a.m. When we got further in, a pilot boat was sighted lying off the breakwater, indicating the area to be clear of mines, so I proceeded at full speed. I had been asked at the conference to dress the ship with flags upon arriving in Kalamata, for publicity, so the code flags were strung up making a brave show as we entered port. The harbour was just an area enclosed by breakwaters. The short breakwater and the street were packed with crowds cheering and waving a welcome to the long-promised food ship. One of the officials, a Major Lawrence, was on the bridge when we entered the harbour.

'Captain,' he exclaimed, 'do you see what I see?'

'Yes major I do.' He was referring to a large flock of sheep which was being herded along the street. 'We have come to feed starving Greeks. Look at them, there are not starving.' When I got to my room the first person I met was the shipchandler.

'I can supply anything you require,' he said, 'except butcher meat and flour. Plenty of vegetables, fruit, chickens and eggs, also potatoes.' These were things we had not seen much of since leaving the US.

The question was how to get the cargo ashore as the ship could not get alongside the quays due to the harbour silting up. The two ration craft could carry the vehicles and land them as they had ramps, but to discharge all the cargo that way would take months. So a conference was held.

The lieutenant in charge of the Palestinian labourers came along to see me. 'I have,' he said, 'just had an interview with a delegate from the Dock Workers Union inquiring what wages I was paying for the dockers to discharge the cargo. I told him I had cargomen on board to do that. He said only members of the Union could load and discharge ships in this port. What are we going to do?'

S.A.M.Oland in the Gulf of Kalamata.

Major Lawrence was astounded. 'As the UNRA organisation is donating the food free I do not see where the question of payment arises, all we are doing is making the food available. I look on you, captain, as our nautical advisor, what do you suggest?'

'I would tell this delegate the cargo is not a commercial one and not subject to Union rules. When it is out of the ship they can make what arrangements they like for handling.' And that is how it went. The passenger UNRA officials vanished and were not seen again.

Now that local people were convinced the Germans were not coming back again, quite a change took place. The shops began to fill with goods that had been hidden away in the mountains when the Germans arrived. The menfolk appeared in German soldiers' summer uniforms, brand new. The German quartermaster's accounts must have been in a very confused state. No German could hold down these people, they were too cunning.

The knowledge had got round that vegetables and fruit could be obtained so a deputation waited on the steward to demand these items as they were sick of tinned food. He came to me with the suggestion that the army rations, left behind by the American soldiers, could be exchanged for fresh supplies. I agreed, but asked how he was going to do this. Later he came back with a scheme. He had worked out with the shipchandler the exchange value of bully beef in terms of vegetables, potatoes, fruit, eggs, chickens and milk. This was chalked up in Greek on a large board and they would hold a market each morning in the plaza. The chandler's van could be used as storage and to take the supplies to and from the ship. This turned out to be a complete success. We were getting the best of the barter but the local people were so eager to get meat that they didn't haggle. We managed to obtain sufficient supplies to carry us over the time we were there and on to Port Said. When we left there were 14 turkeys walking and roosting around the ship waiting for Christmas.

This was grape-growing country, so wine was one of the exports in peace time, along with dried fruit. The wine, during the war, could not be exported and they had no casks to store it in – the vats were full. Anyone from the ship, or UNRA personnel, could have all they wanted, for nothing, provided they brought something to take it away in. As a consequence wine was everywhere – in beer bottles, buckets and anything else that could be found. Two kinds of wine were made, both very good. If you stayed on one kind all the time you didn't get drunk just went around in a daze, but if you mixed the two you went out like a light and stank like a dead fish. There was no way of stopping the wine drinking. What saved the situation was that the Palestinians, being Moslems, did not drink and they ended up by having to do the routine work of the ship, including the cooking. The military people were having the same trouble. An officer could hardly bring a man up on a charge when he was doing the same himself. There was no one to see the ship off as we moved out of Kalamata harbour early one morning; we had been there one month.

We laid for a day in Port Said awaiting orders, then we were sent through the Canal to Port Tewfik, where we loaded a cargo similar to the one we took to Kalamata. We were there a week, then back to Port Said. I had heard we were to go to Volo in Greece. There must have been a problem concerning Volo because after a while we had to discharge all the cargo we had loaded. We laid there from 14th to 29th December, until it was finally decided to load Australian bagged wheat for Sicilian ports.

On Christmas Eve a buffet supper and dance was held in the Merchant Navy Club. All went well until the drink began to take effect. The party I was with stayed on beer, and remained sober, but in the large room where the dancing was in progress fighting was also well underway. When we went in to sort things out I saw my third mate in the middle of it all with the remains of a chair hanging round his neck. It was quite some time before things quietened down and it was by then well after midnight. We had a good Christmas dinner with enough turkeys to go round and plenty left for the New Year.

Finally on 30th December 1944 we left Port Said for Catania, Sicily. Also on board was a three-man commission whose job was to exchange the wheat for a cargo of lemons. We were the only ship in Catania harbour. The Germans, with their sense of humour, had pulled all the mooring bollards off the wharves and thrown them in the harbour. We laid alongside the pier with our anchor out and moorings made fast to anything that would hold. In some cases the cables passed around a house, or a pipe stuck in the ground. Fortunately the weather remained fine. There was no Naval Control or Sea Transport here, just a Ministry of Transport office. I asked about agents.

'I am the agent,' said the ministry manager, 'There is no government at present in Sicily, everything is in chaos – no one to collect harbour dues, no customs, nothing. When you leave I will give you a letter to the Sea Transport in Messina.'

Our stay in Catania was around four days. We were warned to keep everything locked up as stealing here was a way of life. I could not give the crew a sub as there was no money. I had replenished my stock of cigarettes in Port Said and, as cigarettes were now the customary currency in Sicily, an issue of cigarettes was all that was necessary.

We arrived in Palermo, via Messina, on 13th January. This must have been a beautiful city but had nearly been destroyed in what the Americans called a saturation raid. Several ships were there, both British and American. The orange and lemon shipping season was on and we discharged the remainder of the wheat and loaded half the cargo of lemons.

The pier where we laid was fenced off with barbed wire. One of the gates in the harbour wall opened into this area and it was under guard day and night. This was called the British compound. The Americans had a similar one at another pier. The ministry official explained to the crew that it was not advisable to go out of the compound at night, and in daytime only in groups of not less than half a dozen, or else the children would mob them. They would be surrounded by a mass of children screaming and yelling and before they realised what was happening their pockets would be emptied and, in some cases, all their clothes stripped off leaving them stark naked. Ships' crews being what they were didn't believe him until one night two of the crew did arrive back naked. Then the chief engineer and the second engineer decided one afternoon to go for a stroll and have a look around. Next thing they came racing back to the gate with a screaming horde of children at their heels. They just made it through in time. Poor old Mr Cook was terrified out of his wits and shaking like a leaf.

Then we went back to Messina for two or three days to load more lemons and completed loading in Catania. If I remember right we stowed, when full, 83,000 cases of lemons, and they had to be stowed so there was a free passage of air round each case. This was to allow the lemons to shrink to their usual size and change to their customary colour. In the process they gave off a gas and also shed a lot of water so the bilges had to be kept pumped out. Every alternate hatch cover had to be kept turned back and no tarpaulins were spread. We left Catania on the 3rd February bound for London and had 14 days to get there. If we were delayed longer than that the lemons would start to go bad.

We took a direct course for Gibraltar and were to proceed in convoy from there. There must have been a lot of oranges and lemons in that convoy as no time was lost, even though the weather was not ideal. The average speed must have been over 10 knots. Cold clear easterly weather up the Channel kept the fog away and we duly berthed in the old place in the South West India Dock, just inside 14 days.

Mr Watts came to have a look at the ship and I showed him all over. 'One could get lost in this rabbit warren,' was his comment. I could see he didn't think much of the *Oland*. 'You are coming out of this thing and back into one of my own ships,' was his verdict. After paying off the crew I went home on leave – my one and only voyage in an American ship.

Chapter 23

The Chiswick revisited

Come March I was on the Tyne, standing by the *Ocean Messenger*, a vessel Watts were managing for the Ministry of Transport. As these stand-by jobs sometimes developed into taking the ship for a voyage I took all my gear, and it was as well I did. The ship was lying at the buoys off North Shields waiting for dry-dock. May came with me.

There was no food left on the ship except the daily supply based on the rations. What the cook produced was uneatable, so May and I had our meals ashore. When the ship went into dry dock she had to be fumigated over the weekend so the Newcastle office arranged for May and I, and the chief engineer and his wife to stay at a hotel in Tynemouth. That hotel had taken a hammering. Part of it had been demolished, a number of windows were boarded up and the wind seemed to blow through holes and cracks everywhere. Only a few hundred feet away from the hotel was a battery of rocket launchers, luckily there were no air raids while we were there.

I discovered that a Captain Shields would soon arrive and after handing over I was to go to Birkenhead and the *Chiswick* again. May and I left Newcastle for Liverpool and booked into the Adelphi for the night.

The ship was over at the West Float in Birkenhead waiting for dry dock. Apparently she was just back from the Mediterranean and had taken part in all the landings. For a ship not yet two years old she was a sight. She had the appearance of a ship 10 years old, with dents and scores along both sides, and dirty faded paintwork. Everyone had left. When the crew were signed on, repairs finished, stored and coaled we had to proceed out into the river and anchor to await convoy and orders en route.

We left in convoy on a blustery day, and I was glad she was well ballasted. When clear of the north Irish coast we headed down towards 40°N latitude before hauling to the westward. Presumably the commodore considered the weather would be more favourable down there for the crossing. It was a good try but the latitude of the Azores was infamous in April. The weather was fine to start with, but when we turned westward it was gale after gale for over a week. The ships, well ballasted, stood up to the seas but the propellers were more often in the air than in the water. Rest or sleep was impossible with the racket of racing engines and the rolling and pitching of the ship. Lying on the settee in the dayroom, athwartships, I was sometimes standing on the side bulkhead. The convoy ploughed on making only a few miles each day. From the direction we were taking our destination could have been Halifax or St. Johns. One morning a number of ships were detached, ourselves among them, in charge of the vice-commodore to proceed to the St Lawrence river. I thought it was a little early as the ice in the Gulf would not have cleared – it was only 20th April. We were put on course for Cape Race and due to make landfall by daylight. There was a full moon in a cloudless sky, and the sea was like a sheet of glass with only the ocean swell. The temperature fell and kept on falling. I had experienced these weather conditions once before in this part of the world and knew what was coming. It grew colder and colder.

I remained on the bridge in the early hours. There was a light mist which might develop into fog at any time. If that happened we would have to alter to dead reckoning. The escorting corvette was ahead when daylight began to creep in. Then he flashed a signal by radar, CAPE RACE BEARING..., DISTANCE 10 MILES, that was right ahead. We were within five miles when we sighted the lighthouse, then the commodore altered course. The visibility was now very good with a north-westerly wind coming in. Some time later the signal CONVOY DISPERSE AND PROCEED INDEPENDENTLY TO FATHER POINT. I assumed the commodore considered a convoy would be difficult to handle if ice and fog was encountered in the Gulf, it was a wise decision. I was now on my old familiar ground. For the first time since I had known it there was no ice in the Gulf of St. Lawrence, or the river, at the latter end of April. We were ordered to Montreal to load bulk grain for Glasgow

We left for Sydney Cape Breton on 1st May for convoy. While there I went ashore and had a look around. The old wooden building that had housed the Dominion Coal pier staff had been demolished and in its place was a two storey brick building. Dominion Street seemed have disappeared and all the wooden houses had gone.

On 7th May news came through that the war had ended. The Naval Control insisted that the convoy proceed, so we did. They had the nerve to send their launch round all the ships for a supply of liquor for the celebrations that night. They didn't get anything from this ship. The convoy did not join up with the Halifax or New York contingents, but we did have a merchant ship aircraft carrier. No pretence was made of station keeping and the ships merely kept together, one might say, from habit. We had fine weather all the way and we eventually anchored off the Tail of the Bank to await a berth up river. It had been a long, long war.

Postscript

*T*his was not the end of William Donald's life at sea, but it is where his manuscript ended. He continued to sail around the world in a variety of ships, eventually settling in the *Wendover,* a ship I came to know well. In later years, as commodore, most of his time was spent between Canada and Europe. He did attain his half century in the Merchant Service, but chest pains suffered at the end of the war culminated in the loss of a lung. His remaining two years prior to retirement were spent as port relieving master, as he was no longer fit for sea.

To banish the boredom of retirement he began to write this manuscript. Day after day his old Corona typewriter could be heard clicking away, as he relived the life he had loved. To be a sailor had always been his goal in life, and he never regretted his decision. For 50 years he sailed the oceans and seas of the world a happy man. Not for him the big passenger liners, he was happier by far on the battered old tramps that served our country so well in times of war and peace. Having said that, the ships he commanded in later life were extremely comfortable.

Writing this book has brought back one vivid memory of the past. Once, when I was very young we spent a holiday on Dartmoor. I remember him carving small boats with paper sails for me to sail in the stream close to the farm. They must have brought back memories of his youthful attempts at boat building.